"Sir Maurice Bowra has given us in *The Greek Experience* the best book of its kind ... a simple, direct account and interpretation written by a great scholar, with clarity and understanding, for the layman who seriously wishes to know the meaning of ancient Greece. One puts the book down with the feeling that this is indeed what the Greeks did, that these were their essential and unique qualities."

—*Saturday Review*

# THE GREEK GENIUS

In this extraordinary study of Greek culture, Sir Maurice Bowra, the renowned classical scholar, probes the thought and mind of the Greeks—the essential principles and qualities which made their way of life a model for the ages.

He assesses their incredible achievements in art, poetry, drama and the natural sciences. He explores their attitudes and outlook on government, politics and religion. And he analyzes their unique capacity for genius, the impulses and restraints that set and kept them on a career of experiment and triumph which has never been surpassed in the history of man.

Sir Maurice has included forty-eight pages of photographs which form a valuable complement to the text and a representative anthology of Greek visual art.

## MENTOR Books of Plays

### Edited by Slyvan Barnet,
### Morton Berman, and William Burto

☐ **EIGHT GREAT TRAGEDIES.** The great dramatic literature of the ages. Eight memorable tragedies by Aeschylus, Euripides, Sophocles, Shakespeare, Ibsen, Strindberg, Yeats, and O'Neill. With essays on tragedy by Aristotle, Emerson and others.
(#ME1911—$2.50)

☐ **EIGHT GREAT COMEDIES.** Complete texts of eight masterpieces of comic drama by Aristophanes, Machiavelli, Shakespeare, Molière, John Gay, Wilde, Chekhov, and Shaw. Includes essays on comedy by four distinguished critics and scholars.
(#ME2008—$2.95)

☐ **THE GENIUS OF THE EARLY ENGLISH THEATRE.** Complete plays including three anonymous plays—"Abraham and Isaac," "The Second Shepherd's Play," and "Everyman," and Marlowe's "Doctor Faustus," Shakespeare's "Macbeth," Jonson's "Volpone," and Milton's "Samson Agonistes," with critical essays.
(#ME1889—$2.50)

# The Greek
# Experience

by C. M. BOWRA

*WARDEN OF WADHAM COLLEGE,*
*OXFORD*

A MENTOR BOOK
**NEW AMERICAN LIBRARY**
TIMES MIRROR

TO CYRIL CONNOLLY

DF
77
B731
1957

# CONTENTS

# LIST OF ILLUSTRATIONS

## ACKNOWLEDGMENTS

The photographs in this book are reproduced by courtesy of the following: 2, 4, 7, 8, 12, 13, 14, 19, 21, 22, 30, 31, 32, 36, 38, 39, 41, 42, 45, 46, 47, 48, 49, 50, 51, 74, Alinari, Rome; 28, Anderson, Rome; 35, 40, 73, Antikensammlungen, Munich; 34, 60, 66, 72, 81, Archives Photographiques, Paris; 43, 44, Bibliothèque Nationale, Paris; 59, 64b, 65 a-i, 68, 76, 77, 84, 86, British Museum, London; 9, 11, 18, 25, 26, 53, 55, 87, 90 a, b, Alison Frantz, Athens; 16, 17, 20, 23, 24, 37, 67, 83, German Archaeological Institute, Athens; 29, Giraudon, Paris; 3, N. Hadjistylianos, Athens; 62, Hermitage Museum, Leningrad; 71, 85, 88, Hirmer Verlag, Munich; 27, Mansell Collection, London; 52, 54, 56, 61, 63d, 89, Metropolitan Museum, New York; 70, Museo Nazionale, Taranto; 57, 63 a-c, 64a, c, d, 78, 82, Museum of Fine Arts, Boston; 10, Ny Carlsberg Glyptotek, Copenhagen; 58, 69, 75, Staatliches Museum, Berlin; 1, 5, 6, late Reverend J. P. Sumner; 15, H. Wagner, Athens; 79, 80, Wagnermuseum, Würzburg.

# PREFACE

THIS BOOK is in no sense an attempt to give a comprehensive account of the Greeks and their achievements. It aims at assessing what is most characteristic and most striking in them. As such it inevitably represents my own views and is to that degree subjective, and may not command general assent. Yet, if we are to try to form some general picture of what the Greeks were, we have to rely on our own judgment and hope that others will to some degree share it. That such a task is worth doing needs no defence. There is a danger that with the growth of specialization in classical scholarship we may lose our vision of the ancient world as a whole, and for this reason we must from time to time try to form general notions of it. I have set my limits roughly from the Homeric poems to the fall of Athens in 404 BC, not because I am uninterested in what happened after that date or unaware of its significance, but because I prefer to deal with a period which has a certain unity and allows a single treatment.

In such a work I owe an enormous debt to many friends, teachers, and colleagues, whose ideas I have absorbed in discussion or in reading, and whose thoughts have so become part of myself that I am not sure what is theirs and what is my own. I must content myself with expressing my gratitude to them in general terms and to ask them to forgive the omission of detailed references. My colleague, Mr T. C. W. Stinton, has done me a special service by reading several of my chapters and giving me the benefit of his acute and vigilant criticism. Miss Vanessa Jebb has shown untiring skill and patience in procuring the illustrations.

I am grateful to the following for permission to quote from copyright works; Mr R. E. Warner and Penguin Books for *Thucydides: the Peloponnesian War*; Professor George Thomson and the Cambridge University Press for *The Oresteia* of *Aeschylus*; Mr T. F. Higham and the Clarendon Press for *The Oxford Book of Greek Verse in Translation*; Mrs. Yeats, the executors of the late W. B. Yeats, Messrs Macmillan and Co. and the Macmillan Company for 'Colonus Praise' from his *Collected Poems*; the executors of the late E. R. Bevan and Messrs Edward Arnold for *The Seven Against Thebes of Aeschylus*; Professor H. T. Wade-Gery and the Cambridge University Press for the *Cambridge Ancient History*.

# CHAPTER I

# THE UNITY OF THE GREEKS

THE GREEKS, who gave to mankind its most imaginative myths, have themselves become almost mythical. In addition to their assured position in the development of European civilization they have another outside history, in an Olympian isolation fraught with mystery and splendour beyond the common lot of peoples. If their achievements are listed in the calendar of years, they have a second existence untouched and unsullied by time; if they themselves lived in their own Mediterranean world, it has been so glorified by soaring fancy and emulous desire that it seems to have no place on our workaday planet. Almost everything Hellenic has been so transfigured by centuries of admiring worship that it is difficult to see the Greeks with unclouded eyes or to know them as they really were. The process began when the Romans, conscious of their own boorish beginnings, patronized the Greeks as a race of artists and philosophers and failed to see that art and philosophy cannot be fully understood apart from the conditions which create them. If the Dark and Middle Ages paid scanty attention to the mirage which had obsessed Rome, the discovery of Rome at the Renaissance meant also the discovery of the Roman vision of Greece. Behind the power and the pomp of Rome men felt, not indeed very clearly or consciously at first but still with awe and questioning wonder, a driving, daemonic force, a sunlit ideal, a perfection of achievement, which was somehow not Roman, even if it accounted for everything that mattered most in Rome. To track this spirit to its home, to capture it and wrest from it its magical secrets, has been the inspiring ambition of many writers, artists, and thinkers since the fifteenth century. So potent has been the appeal of Greece, so passionate the devotion which it arouses, that there is almost no sphere of spiritual or intellectual activity which has not been touched by its living flame. The results have indeed been unreckonable in their

13

variety and their success, notable alike in philosophic or scientific endeavours to unravel the secrets of being and in the ardent hopes of artists in words or paint or stone to recover a lost youth of the world, a vision of a single, undivided universe, a sense of invisible forces at work in the familiar scene, of unreleased potentialities in the human mind and heart, of an ideal order lurking behind the manifold appearances of things. For some five centuries what the Greeks said or thought or made has affected living men and women and enabled them to discover new truths about themselves, their conditions, and their capacities.

This remarkable record is indeed a tribute to the inspiration of the Greek example. It shows how the achievement of a small and indigent people for a few centuries before the birth of Christ has exerted an incalculable influence on a posterity alien in its faith, its setting, its speech, its morality, its comforts, it machines. It proves that beliefs and philosophies, which seemed to have been swept away for ever by such a cataclysm as the triumph of the Christian Church could somehow survive it and humanize it and exert again in new territories some of their old dominion. We cannot but ask what qualities enabled the Greeks to exercise so wide and so liberating an influence, what was in the last resort responsible for their capacity to make men abandon inherited beliefs for what they believed to be an authentically Hellenic outlook and force their creative endeavours to conform to rules formed in distant ages under very different skies. To answer these questions, we must start again at the beginning and ask others which lead to them. What did the Greeks really do? What were their essential, their unique qualities? What were the central principles of their thought and the guiding spirits of their lives? What impulses and what restraints set and kept them on their career of experiment and triumph? What kind of men were they when they were alive?

To understand the Greeks we must try to recapture their experience, to ask what it did for them and what it cost. Such a search can never be wholly successful. To probe the past is always perilous, and no documents and no monuments can ever quite compensate for the loss of many things which enable us to see men as they really were. We cannot recover the casual remarks, the sights of every day in street and field and household, the immediate, effortless grasp of thought and sentiment which the living have with one another, the colours and noises of a community at its daily tasks, the ability to judge a society by its own standards and to understand it as it understood itself. Such limitations always hamper the historian, but with the Greeks the obstacles are even more formidable. Though we know their language as well as a dead language can ever be known, yet it remains a dead language, in which we cannot be sure of the management of the tonic accent or the pronunciation of certain sounds, still less of the rhythm and emphasis of actual speech. Greek music, which the Greeks themselves regarded as the most important of their arts and which was indissolubly connected with poetry, is almost completely lost. Of some fifteen more or less fragmentary scores, only one is earlier than 400 BC, and that consists of four very incomplete lines from the *Orestes* of Euripides. Even if Greek music had survived in a more generous quality, its number of differing scales, its unequal tones and semi-tones, and its lack of any harmonic structure would probably make it sound uncouth to our unaccustomed ears. Our main source of information, the written word, is woefully incomplete. We lack the main part of what was once a rich store of lyric poetry, of early philosophy and history, of early epic except Homer, of many tragedies and comedies. We have hardly a tithe of what the three great Attic tragedians actually wrote, and though the rubbish-heaps of Egypt have in recent years yielded precious fragments of lost works, they are only fragments, and make us all the more conscious that Greek literature must have been richer and more various than its surviving remains indicate. The relics of the visual arts are even more tantalizing. In the unequal battle against the depredations of time and the barbarity of man they have survived almost by accident. We have no full-size painting of the classical age; no statues in gold and ivory such as were once the glory of Phidias. Of the many temples which once existed only a few survive, and these are roofless and ruined, robbed long ago of their furniture and their treasures. Modern discovery has indeed added much to our knowledge and enlarged our vision, but we must at the start recognize that our evidence is certainly fragmentary and may be misleading. But even the fragments exert so powerful an attraction and have so abundant a vitality that they force us to ask what experience went to their making.

A people lives by its geography. What nature provides as a home and a background is the most enduring element in any national history. Physical type may be altered beyond recognition by new strains and cross-breeding; languages may disintegrate before the political pressure or social attractions of new tongues; habits, which seem to be indestructible,

collapse before unprecedented menaces or intoxicating nov-
elties. But nature remains in the end what it was in the beginning, a school which by its prizes and its penalties fashions
its children to a special pattern. In Greece the configuration
and the character of the landscape have been a primary
influence in shaping the destiny of its people ever since the
first Greek tribes moved down from the north into the lands
which still belong to their descendants. There have indeed
been a few changes. The mountains, which were once covered with forests, are now for the most part denuded, largely
because the omnivorous goat gobbles saplings before they
have time to grow, and wintry rains wash away the scanty
soil which has nothing to hold it, but the process is at least
as old as Plato, who complained that, in comparison with
earlier times, there remained 'only the bones of the wasted
body';[1] at a few places, as at Thermopylae, the sea has
receded before the silt of swollen torrents and changed
the coastline; wolves and boars, lions and bears, no longer
rove the mountains and wild places; here and there, as in
Boeotia, marshes have been drained to make fields and
orchards. But on the whole Greece is physically much the
same today as it was four thousand years ago: a land of
mountains, which are not huddled together in ungainly
lumps but flaunt their peaks in proud independence, and of
islands, which are themselves mountains with roots en-
gulfed in the sea. It presents dramatic contrasts between
barren marble or limestone masses and watered valleys, between rain and snow in winter and unbroken sunshine in
summer, between an unequalled magnificence of wild flowers and blossoming trees in March and April and parched,
crumbling earth from June to October. Though Greece begins
where the mountainous Balkan mass narrows and projects
into the midland sea, it is not Balkan, but emphatically itself
in its configuration, its climate, its eternal intimacy with the
sea.

Greece is a land of contrasts, but not of extremes. Even in
winter there is abundant sunshine; the heat is intense in
summer, but lacks the humidity which saps energy and
effort; districts, near enough to each other as the crow flies,
may be separated by almost impassable mountains, but often
have easy communications by sea; though most Greek rivers
become barren, stony gullies in summer, in winter they are
hurtling torrents, whose water is stored in pools and wells;
even the rudest shores may have safe harbours or sandy
reaches on which boats can be moored. Greece is indeed
a hard land, capable of maintaining only a small population,

but if this population faces its tasks with decision, it will reap its rewards. The country is still incapable of feeding flocks or herds on any large scale. Olive-oil takes the place of butter, preservatives, and cooking fats. Fruit and vegetables can be grown only in a few fertile plains or in terraces and holes carved in hill-sides and held by stone embankments; fish is not nearly so common or so various as in northern seas; meat is rare and more likely to be kid than beef or mutton. Yet the Greek larder has its compensations. Wine is abundant; in a land of many flowers honey yields an ample supply of sugar; the goat gives milk and cheese; the mountains have their hares and wild birds, the sea its mullets, lobsters, and squids. Scarcity of food has never prevented the Greeks from being healthy and vigorous; and the very difficulties which attend its supply have stimulated their efforts and their ingenuity.

Such a land demands that its inhabitants should be tough, active, enterprising, and intelligent. When the Greeks exposed unwanted children at birth, they showed how seriously they interpreted the exacting conditions of their existence, and followed the example of nature, which exerts its own selection and control by allowing only the strongest to survive. The physical capacity of the Greeks is clear enough from their many male statues, whose sturdy, muscular frames and limbs are combined with slim waists and competent hands. Men living in such circumstances needed more than the usual qualities of workers in fields, since much of their labour lay on mountain-slopes and in rocky hollows. They must be able to climb easily, to carry heavy loads up and down hill, to be handy with the shifting and shaping of stones, to travel long distances on foot, to drive ploughs through obstinate, stony soil, to tame horses and mules, to repel the onslaughts of wild animals, and to endure alike sun and storm. This physical equipment must be supplemented by unflagging industry, careful foresight, skill in essential handicrafts, and all the age-old virtues of the farmer who works on difficult land. As labour in the fields promotes endurance and strength of body, so the handling of ships demands quickness of eye and hand, agility and lightness of movement, unresting vigilance, and rapidity of decision. Geographical circumstances formed the Greek character by forcing it to make the most of its natural aptitudes in a hard struggle with the earth and the elements.

The peculiar position of Greece in the south-western corner of Europe has determined much in the course of its history. It is physically a blind alley, and once immigrants have moved in, they are not likely to move out except by sea. It is moreover not easy to enter by land. There is no royal road from the Balkan mass into northern Greece, and any penetration must be slow, over mountains where passes are not indeed uncommon but not often easy, and the sparse river-valleys usually lead in the wrong direction. Nature protects Greece from any swift, overwhelming conquest by land; it is difficult even for mechanized, modern armies to control the whole country effectively. On the other hand, Greece lends itself to gradual, piecemeal penetration. It offers many convenient refuges where bands of immigrants can consolidate before making their next move and collect their forces without interference or even notice. Though its first inhabitants were akin to the 'Mediterranean' figures whom we see on the frescoes of Minoan Crete, the Greeks who supplanted them came from the north, probably in intermittent waves. They brought with them their language, which revealed its northern and inland limitations by having to take from the indigenous speech words for sea, olive-tree, bean, fig, cypress, hyacinth, wine, tin, and bath. They absorbed the original inhabitants, of whom only vague memories survived on the mainland under the name of 'Pelasgian', which may have had the same kind of connotation as 'Welsh'. From them the Greeks took a number of place-names, religious rites, and even divinities. But these different elements were at an early date fused into a whole, except in some islands, notably Crete, where in the fifth century BC there was a corner where the old Aegean or 'Minoan' language was still spoken. The Greeks of historical times were physically a mixed people, and advocates of 'purity' of breed will find in them no support for their views. If their sculpture and painting present a recognizably standard type, that is probably because climatic conditions exert their own control and not only give preference in survival to a type which has long been adapted to them but make acclimatization slow and difficult. The Greeks were not the blond giants of Teutonic fancy. The majority of them seem to have been, as they are today, dark-haired and olive-skinned, but among them, then as now, there were a few whose fair hair marked them out for admiring comment, like Homer's Menelaus, who is called *xanthos* and looks as if he had brown hair. Since the same adjective is given not only to some other heroes but to goddesses like Demeter, we can hardly doubt that it was to mark their exceptional appearance. Zeus, who embodies the masculine spirit of the Greeks, is said to have eyebrows of dark blue,[2] and though we must make some allowance for poetical fancy, we recognize him at once as a type commonly to be seen in Greece today.

Though Greece is not easy to invade by land, it presents many promising openings to anyone who has control of the sea. From the sea it can be attacked at many points, and it is not difficult to establish beach-heads from which inland regions can be invaded and to some extent controlled. The possibilities of this situation were seen by Minos, king of Crete some two generations before the Trojan War. With his navy he ruled the Aegean and conquered the Cyclades, in which he put his sons to rule.[3] The absence of fortifications at his capital of Cnossus betrays his confidence that no sea-raiders could attack it, and six different places, all on the islands or the coast of the mainland, called Minoa, indicate where he established control-points. It is unlikely that he actually conquered the mainland, even though he exacted tribute from some places. But he had grasped an essential feature of Greek political geography, and soon after 1200 BC the first serious conquest of Greece, as opposed to gradual infiltration, came, from the north-west, with the arrival of a related Greek people known to posterity as the Dorians. We can hardly doubt that they came by sea, and it is significant that among the last documents to be written in the palace of Pylos before its destruction is one which records the movement of oarsmen to Pleuron at the mouth of the Gulf of Patras. The conquest that followed was indeed devastating. It gave a death-blow to the Mycenaean civilization, which may already have been enfeebled by over-exertion abroad and by intestine struggles at home, and it plunged Greece into a Dark Age, from which the Greece that we know emerged into history some four centuries later. A similar menace came with the two Persian invasions of 490 and 480 BC. In these a powerful army was sent overland by the eastern coastal route, but it was supported at almost every point by a fleet, manned largely by Phoenician sailors, which not only secured supplies but was also on occasion able to transport troops. The Greeks defeated the Persians first at sea and then on land, but the victory at Plataea in 479 would hardly have been final if the Persians had not been heavily handicapped by the previous destruction of their fleet and the reduction in supplies which this meant. Greece was indeed at the mercy of the sea, and in the fifth century it took steps to command it. The Greeks became a people because they lived in an enclosed space with marked natural frontiers, and so long as they were not attacked from

the sea, they were relatively free to develop on their own
lines without foreign interference.

The presence of the sea and a knowledge of seamanship
which goes back to early in the second millennium turned
the eyes and the appetites of the Greeks to what lay beyond
it. In the Mycenaean age they had already planted settle-
ments on the western and southern shores of Asia Minor,
in Cyprus, and even in Syria. The Dorian conquest drove
other colonists over the Aegean, where the regions known as
Aeolis and Ionia maintained the ancient traditions of the
great past and developed their own distinguished and in-
dubitably Hellenic civilization. From the eighth century onwards adventurous parties sailed farther afield, and Greek
cities were built and maintained so far west as Marseilles
and so far north as the Crimea. But the most favoured and
most promising field for exploitation was Sicily and South
Italy. Despite the hostility of the natives and the armed
menace of powerful competitors like the Etruscans and
the Carthaginians, the Greeks in 'Magna Graecia', or 'Great
Greece', took full advantage of territories broader and richer
than they had known at home to develop a varied and
brilliant life. Despite the barrier of the sea, they kept in
touch with the homeland, worshipped the same gods, took
part in the same festivals, maintained the same customs, and
spoke the same language. If they intermarried with the local
inhabitants, it did not interfere with their conviction that
they were full-blooded Greeks. Their law-givers were among
the first and the most famous. When the first strong tide of
Persian invasion drove Greeks from Ionia to seek new homes,
they found a ready welcome in the West, where philosophy
and mathematics took some of their most momentous forms.
The western Greeks insisted on their Hellenism, and were
right to do so, since they cherished it with unwavering devotion and knew from their acquaintance with more than
one kind of 'barbarian' how much it meant to be a Greek.
In remoter colonies, like the Crimea with its Scythian neighbours, the Greeks were probably in closer touch with native
populations. But they gave more than they got, and the remarkable gold-work found in Scythian graves testifies to the
power of their example. Indeed, Greek colonies did much
to spread the fame of Greek crafts by their exportation of
fine objects to distant places. A signal example is the great
bronze crater found at Vix in the middle of France, which
is Peloponnesian work of the sixth century BC (see Plate 66).
We do not know how or why it reached this destination, but
it shows the high esteem in which Greek handicrafts were

held and how the Greeks met local demands without making concessions to local methods or tastes. The Greek colonies were indeed outposts for trade, but through trade for civilization, and their way of life was all the more consciously Greek because they were on the limits of the known world. The sea, which might have broken the Greek system into scattered and separate fragments, held it together and gave it a special unity in which far-severed communities kept in touch with the homeland and felt that in every sense they still belonged to it.

In Greece itself geography shaped the pattern of political life. If, as is probable, the Greeks in the thirteenth century BC were united in a loose confederacy under the king of Mycenae, they were never again united until Alexander of Macedon led them against Persia. The most marked feature of Greek politics is the division of the country into a number of small states, each with its own independent government and its own local character. This was imposed by a landscape in which men lived in valleys divided from one another by mountains, or on uplands which presented few entrances to the outer world, or on islands which were largely self-sufficient and self-contained. Each district developed its own life and customs and local pride, because it was separate, complete, and difficult to control from without. Montainous barriers were not enough to prevent invasion, but they were enough to prevent one state from being merged into another. From time to time states might fall under the dominion of aggressive and powerful neighbours or be forced into union with one another, but they still maintained something of their political independence and many of their own institutions.

It is customary to speak of the units of Greek polity as city-states, and the phrase is apt enough if we recognize that such a state consisted of a good deal more than a city. If the city, usually walled, was the centre of government and justice and of many handicrafts and trades, other activities went on outside. If there were fertile plains, people would live in villages near their work. Beyond the plains was rising land, usually covered by scrub, hard to cultivate except in patches and pockets, and useful chiefly for pasturing goats. Beyond this, and still higher up, were the rough slopes of the mountains, perhaps here and there enclosing some isolated hamlet, but for the most part desolate, the haunt of hunters in summer and snow-covered in winter. Since many Greek cities lay close to the sea, there would be ports where ships could be built and harboured and a maritime population could have its home. In general, the inhabitants of a city-state would be formed of farmers, craftsmen, and sailors, and many would combine two or even three of the roles. Because all members of a city-state lived in close proximity within a more or less enclosed space, they had a strong sense of unity and kinship. This did not save them from internecine struggles or from class-war, but it meant that respect for local tradition made them look on the men of other cities as somehow different from themselves. Though the leading parts in Greek history were played by a few states, we can even today see from the remains of many almost forgotten places how distinctive their lives must have been. In obedience to their natural surroundings they found their own characteristics, developed their own individuality, and, without making much impression on the rest of Greece, conformed almost unconsciously to the general pattern of its habits.

By its very nature the city-state created its own special kind of social life. Governments might vary from the rule of the one to the rule of the many, but when conditions were fundamentally simple and homogeneous, differences in manners and outlook must have been more in degree than in kind, according to the size and powers of the wealthier classes. No city concealed divine monarchs in mysterious isolation or maintained privileged priests as a separate caste. Most men shared the same interests and the same pursuits. Even those who lived in cities and engaged in manufactures and handicrafts, or those who sought a livelihood on the sea, were brought up close to the soil and knew its ways. Such men tended to behave to each other as equals, because they had common concerns and backgrounds, and, despite differences of wealth, lived in much the same manner. Brought perpetually into contact with one another and knowing their neighbours' foibles and follies, they developed a remarkable forthrightness in their social relations. Even if they respected birth and breeding, there seem to have been few such formal restraints between men of different position as exist in more highly organized societies, where professional pursuits promote isolated groups of specialists. As in most Mediterranean countries, the centre of activity, at least for men, is the street or the public square, where all topics, and especially politics, are discussed with eloquence, frankness, and some degree of knowledge. If such circumstances foster a reasonable measure of decorum and courtesy, they also foster passionate quarrels, lewd banter, and scurrilous abuse. Hierarchical stiffness and commercial servility tend alike to be lacking. Such conditions encourage a lively curiosity about personal idiosyncrasies, with the result that a man cannot shelter behind any delusive disguise conferred by office or pedigree, and though good manners may be usual, they do not prevent men from saying frankly what they think of one another. Such a situation produces men who are fully aware of their surroundings, extrovert, and civically minded. The city-state did not by any means always promote democracy, but it fostered a freedom of intercourse, a sense of personality, and a social frame in which men were exposed to the full observation of their fellows but not prevented from being themselves.

No less powerful was the influence which the Greek scene had on the Greek eye and the Greek mind. The traveller who comes from the west or the north to Greece for the first time may feel a slight twinge of disappointment at the nakedness of its outline and its lack of exuberant colour, but he will soon see that he is faced by a commanding beauty which makes no ready concessions to his appreciation but forces itself slowly and unforgettably on him. What matters above all is the quality of the light. Not only in the cloudless days of summer but even in winter the light is unlike that of any other European country, brighter, cleaner, and stronger. It sharpens the edges of the mountains against the sky, as they rise from valleys or sea; it gives an ever-changing design to the folds and hollows as the shadows shift on or off them; it turns the sea to opal at dawn, to sapphire at midday, and in succession to gold, silver, and lead before nightfall; it outlines the dark green of the olive-trees in contrast to the rusty or ochre soil; it starts innumerable variations of colour and shape in unhewn rock and hewn stonework. The beauty of the Greek landscape depends primarily on the light, and this had a powerful influence on the Greek vision of the world. Just because by its very strength and sharpness the light forbids the shifting, melting, diaphanous effects which give so delicate a charm to the French or the Italian scene, it stimulates a vision which belongs to the sculptor more than to the painter, which depends not so much on an intricate combination or contrast of colours passing into each other as on a clearness of outline and a sense of mass, of bodies emphatically placed in space, of strength and solidity behind natural curves and protuberances. Such a landscape and such a light impose their secret discipline on the eye, and make it see things in contour and relief rather than in mysterious perspective or in flat spatial relations. They explain why the Greeks produced great sculptors and architects, and why even in their painting the foundation of any design is the exact and confident line.

Nor is it perhaps fanciful to think that the Greek light played a part in the formation of Greek thought. Just as the cloudy skies of northern Europe have nursed the huge, amorphous progeny of Norse mythology or German metaphysics, so the Greek light surely influenced the clear-cut conceptions of Greek philosophy. If the Greeks were the world's first true philosophers in that they formed a consistent and straightforward vocabulary for abstract ideas, it was largely because their minds, like their eyes, sought naturally what is lucid and well defined. Their senses were kept lively by the force of the light, and when the senses are keenly at work, the mind follows no less keenly and seeks to put in order what they give it. Just as Plato, in his search for transcendental principles behind the mass of phenomena, tended to see them as individual objects and compared his central principle to the sun which illuminates all things in the visible world and reveals their shapes and colours,[4] so no Greek philosophy is happy until it can pin down an idea with a limpid definition and make its outline firm and intelligible. That the Greeks were moved by some such consideration may be seen from their use of the words *eidos* and *idea* to mean 'notion' or 'idea'. Originally, they meant no more than 'form' and were applied to such obvious forms as the human body. The transference of the word from concrete to abstract, from visible to invisible, shows how the Greek mind worked when it moved from the gifts of the senses to the principles behind them.

If the light is the first element in the Greek scene, the second is the sea. Its 'watery ways', as Homer calls them, bind most districts in Greece, whether mainland or islands, to one another. It plays a larger part there than in any other European country because for most places it is the best, and for many the only, means of communication. There are few districts from which it is not somewhere visible. Often in isolated solitudes among the mountains a man will feel that he has lost sight of it, only to see it again round the next corner. Mastery of it was indispensable to survival, and once mastery was gained, new vistas inspired to adventure. The Greeks were sailors from the dawn of their history, and, because they were bred to ships, they were saved from sinking into the narrow, parochial round which would otherwise have been the lot of dwellers in small city-states. The sea drew alike those who wanted profit and those who wanted excitement, and was the chief means by which the Greeks expanded their knowledge of men and manners. But it was more than this. Its special enchantment, 'the multitudinous laughter of the sea-waves', of which Aeschylus speaks,⁵ took hold of the Greek consciousness and helped to shape some of its most characteristic convictions. At times no sea can be more alluring than the Aegean with its rippling waves or its halcyon calm, and then indeed it presents an image of that celestial radiance which the Greeks regarded as the most desirable state of man. But even when it seems to be most welcoming, it suddenly changes its temper and menaces with ruin on hidden reefs from merciless winds and mounting waves. By its unpredictable moods and its violent vagaries it provides a lesson on the precarious state of human life, which in the very moment when all seems to be lapped in golden calm is overwhelmed in unforeseen disaster. It is not surprising that when Sophocles sang of the unique achievements of man, he put seafaring first in his list:

> He makes the winter wind carry him
> Across the grey sea
> Through the trough of towering waves.⁶

Command of the sea was indeed something of which to be proud, and it left an indelible mark on the Greek character.

The people shaped by this physical setting was divided politically, but was none the less proud that all its members were Greeks and as such different from the rest of mankind. This conviction was founded on sound sense, as we can see from the words which Herodotus gives to the Athenians when they reject the proposal of the king of Macedon that they should desert the Greek cause against Persia: 'It is not well that the Athenians should be traitors to the Greek nation, which is of like blood and like speech, and has common buildings to the gods and common sacrifices, and manners of the same kind.'⁷ Herodotus, who divined the main principles of anthropology, assumes four criteria for being a Greek—common descent, language, religion, and culture. Of all these the Greeks were conscious, and to all they appealed when they wished to stress their essential unity and their difference from foreigners. Their common descent was known from legends of a heroic age, whose famous figures gave a start to many genealogies and were celebrated throughout Greece in song and stone. Their common language was an indisputable fact. Though Greek falls into four main dialects and though each has many branches, they are all parts of a single, highly individual language, and were mutually intelligible despite considerable differences of vocabulary and pronunciation. In comparison with it the Greeks thought foreign languages to be like the twittering of swallows.[8] Their common religion was revealed not only in the names and characteristics of the Olympian gods, but in the existence of shrines, like those of Zeus at Olympia and Apollo at Delphi, where Greeks from all parts joined in sacrifices and games and forgot local differences in a consciousness of Hellenic unity. Common culture calls for no comment in a people who matured so strong a national life, but what mattered most to them in it was liberty. They insisted on being free alike from foreign domination and from the whims of irresponsible autocrats, and this, more than anything else, persuaded them that they were unlike other peoples.

The Greeks called a foreigner *barbaros*, and from it our own word 'barbarian' is derived. But in its early days the Greek word was not necessarily contemptuous or hostile, and meant little more than 'foreign'. The Greek attitude towards foreigners varied, as we might expect, from age to age and from person to person. Though Homer tells of a long and violent war between Greeks and Trojans, he makes the Trojans the equals of the Greeks in all the manly virtues and never hints that they are inferior because they are alien. In the seventh and sixth centuries the Greeks of Asia Minor were not in the least ashamed to learn new refinements of living from their Lydian neighbours. Herodotus, who travelled widely, saw much to admire in the Persians, and Xenophon fought for them as a friend. But such admiration was often tempered by an amused contempt for outlandish ways. Even Herodotus enjoys a sly smile when he records such items of foreign diet as lice, monkeys, and elderly relatives;[9] and if we want a vivid picture of what the average Greek felt about Egyptians, we have only to look at the vase by the Pan Painter on which Heracles deals decisively with Busiris and his snub-nosed attendants (see Plate 83). After the Persian Wars had revealed what hideous destruction could be wrought by barbarian invaders, the Greek attitude hardened, and the word *barbaros* began to assume some of its modern associations.

It was felt that foreigners, being without liberty, had at the best the morality of slaves and might all too easily indulge in acts of violence fit only for brutes.[10] Just as freedom was what the Greeks valued most highly in their own traditions, so what they most deplored in alien peoples was their tendency to behave below the level of free and responsible men. In their conception of 'barbarians' the Greeks paid a tribute to their own ideal of a rational and self-controlled humanity.

When Herodotus observes that the Greeks were united by their language, he touches on something of the first importance. It is indeed central to any consideration of them, because its structure and its scope throw a vivid light on Greek thought, its methods, its capacities, and its means of expression. From it we can understand more fully some qualities of which the Greeks themselves were hardly conscious, but which are relevant to any clear view of their achievement. It was indeed one of their most precious assets. If they brought it from the north when they first came to Greece, they never ceased to develop and enrich it, until it became a most masterly instrument, capable of dealing with any form of expression, from the richest poetry to the most practical prose. Despite its air of simplicity, it is highly advanced and far removed from any connexion with primitive language, which is notable for its complexity, its inability to advance from particular perceptions to general notions, and its concern with impressions rather than with ideas. The very discipline of Greek is evidence for its maturity. The system of its syntax, which may seem unnecessarily formidable to those who are bred on a loose analytic language, was none the less a triumph of the organizing mind over the obstinate material of consciousness.

The advantages of Greek can be seen if we compare it with familiar modern tongues. Its most striking quality is its clarity. However complex its rules may be, it has not been fuddled by overwork or impoverished by sloth. Its ability to say what it means is largely due to its syntax, which has indeed abandoned some of the original Indo-European cases, like the ablative, the locative, and the instrumental, but has kept the old wide range of moods and tenses for verbs because they are necessary to make a point plain. This is true even in some respects which we might think unduly finicky, like the retention of both the subjunctive and the optative moods. Both deal with notional possibilities, and the distinction adds a clarification to language. No doubt the same result could have been obtained by auxiliary verbs, but it might not then be so clear or so neat. The Greeks were not shy of complexity if it served a real need, and their loyalty to an elaborate syntax is a testimony to their desire to say things shortly and directly without circumlocution or ambiguity. If the system of conjugations and declensions makes for clarity, this is reinforced by the nature of the Greek vocabulary, in which each word has normally a central, well-defined meaning and, even when this is extended to new purposes, is seldom unclear, and there is a marked shortage of words which assume their meaning from their context, and are in consequence neither precise nor expressive. This is not to say that every Greek word can be translated by a single equivalent word in English. On the contrary, one of the main difficulties in translating Greek is that there are often no single English equivalents for words which are perfectly clear in Greek. For instance, the words which we conventionally translate by 'good', 'beautiful', 'just', and 'virtue' all have meanings which do not coincide with their English versions. But once we know how they work, there is no great difficulty in translating them, even if we have to render them differently in different places. The clarity of Greek both in structure and in vocabulary may owe something to the spoken word. Since even the most exalted literature was meant not to be read but to be heard, every sentence had to be forceful, carry its full load of meaning, and leave no doubt of its purpose.

Another notable characteristic of Greek is its flexibility. There seems to be no topic and no occasion to which it cannot rise with effortless ease and appropriate dignity. As Greek civilization developed and explored new territories of thought, so the language developed, adapted itself to new demands, and found its suitable instruments for them. Just as from a remote past Greek poetry enriched its vocabulary by the formation of compound adjectives and the admission of many synonyms and alternative forms, so Greek prose, faced by the formidable problem of shaping a language for philosophy and other branches of abstract thought, was no less resourceful and successful. If it was fortunate in being able to form abstract nouns from adjectival stems, it used this and other means with confident skill and seems never to have failed to make its theoretical statements simple and lucid. The Greeks displayed an extraordinary capacity for making words assume new duties without losing their freshness or their force. This is all the more remarkable since it meant a complete break with their old mythical and pictorial way of thinking, and it is likely that they reinforced their vocabulary from common actions, habits, and handicrafts by extending the implication of familiar words to unprecedented duties. The early Greek thinkers succeeded in making quite new ideas readily intelligible. This was a decisive stroke of the intellect and reflects a remarkable capacity for rising to opportunities revealed by new perspectives in speculation. Such a language expands because men feel an urgent need to meet certain intellectual requirements, and force their speech to act for them. It reveals an energetic, enterprising intelligence, which is impelled by the expansion of experience and the birth of ideas to find words for them; which likes fine distinctions and insists upon making them; which appreciates the nuance of the spoken word and employs effective means to get it right; which forces its way beyond habitual concepts to others more rarefied and more abstract and does not in the process lose its nerve or loosen its grip.

The intellectual capacity of Greek is matched by its aesthetic virtuosity. It exerts to a singular degree the attractions of the living word. Though it is impossible to list these systematically, some of them spring to the mind if only because they are less ample in our own language. Just because Greek is inflected, it has a formal elegance which is too often lacking in analytic languages like English; the mere grammar imparts discipline and harmony to almost any sentence, allows a wide variety of word-order, and is all the neater because it has no subsidiary aids. Through the firm significance of its words, Greek has a freshness which fixes the attention on the dominating idea without reference to vague or irrelevant associations. Though it is less marmoreal than Latin, it has none the less a majesty which is the more impressive because it has no air of being calculated, but rises naturally from the demands of a mood or a situation. In the full gamut of its sounds, its rich array of vowels, whether pure or diphthongs, and its control of all the chief consonants, it has a far richer tonal variety than English, in which the vowels tend to deteriorate to a dead uniformity and consonants are too often slurred or neglected. Even within the formal frames imposed by tradition on the different kinds of literature, writers could display to a high degree their own individual taste in words and give full play through them to their temperaments. There is no danger of Greek becoming muscle-bound, as Latin sometimes does, or

being confined to a limited and standardized vocabulary, like
French classical poetry. With all its strength and majesty, it
remains supple and sinuous and easy to manage. Through its
rich store of words and its innate resourcefulness, it is able
to go straight to the point, to say with clarity and assurance
just what has to be said, and to leave us wondering that so
much can be said so briefly. This might seem to imply an
unsophisticated and untutored simplicity. But this is far from
being the case. The simplicity is founded on strength, and just
because the expression is so direct, it reflects all the more
powerfully the feelings that inspire it.

The unity of the Greeks contained a great diversity of
local variations. If Athens and the cities of Ionia were the
most adventurous and enterprising, Sparta and its kindred
island of Crete clung most tenaciously to the traditions of
the past. But Athens did not take any less interest in its own
legends and ceremonies, or Sparta, in the seventh and sixth
centuries, fail to develop a gay and charming art in metal,
ivory, and pottery. In the middle of the sixth century the
island of Samos was in the van of mathematics, engineer-
ing, poetry, and sculpture, but lost its supremacy when it was
conquered by the Persians. The merchant-princes of Aegina
and Corinth were generous patrons of the arts, and even in
sluggish Boeotia there was a time-honoured tradition of local
song. Even isolated or insignificant places have yielded evidence that sculpture and architecture were living arts in them
and developed their own local individuality. Systems of government varied from place to place, and comprised hereditary
monarchies, landed aristocracies, mercantile oligarchies,
and aggressive democracies. These diversities represented
differences of local temperament, and it was common form
to look on the Spartans as unduly apprehensive of change
and on the Athenians as too prone to it. In remote districts,
such as Arcadia and Thesprotia, rites might survive which
had passed out of use elsewhere, and there must have been
many places which were little touched by the more revolutionary movements in thought. But Greece is a small country,
and inevitably even the poorest places responded to current
fashions. A new-style in painting or sculpture found ready
markets and inspired local craftsmen to imitate it, and quite
small cities would take a pride in seeing that their coins
rivalled those of richer rivals in design and finish. Poetry,
which might have been handicapped by differences of dialect,
transcended them by devising a special poetical language
which was based on that of the epic and, like it, could be
understood in any part of Greece. Poets, philosophers, and

doctors toured the country and were welcomed alike by kings, tryants, nobles, and democracies. The variety of life was indeed remarkable, but it was built on a solid foundation, the traditions and the customs which were the common heritage of the Greek people.

The beginnings of Greek history are lost in an irrecoverable past, and though the first decipherable records come from about 1400 BC, yet the story, as far as we can reconstruct it from the Greeks' own thoughts, begins with the Homeric poems in the last part of the eighth century. Here indeed through the eyes of genius we see how men and women lived and died, and here we see the beginning of almost everything that is authentically Hellenic. For some three hundred years the Greeks advanced and matured and became more and more like themselves and less and less like other peoples. This is their great, their classical age. After the fall of Athens to Sparta in 404 BC something was extinguished for ever, not merely a zest for life and a boldness of enterprise and experiment, but certain assumptions which had never been seriously questioned but now lost their authority and their hold. Greek civilization in its heyday depended on a fine balance of forces, an equilibrium between tradition and innovation. When this was broken, the old strength and completeness began to decay, and though the fourth century has indeed its high achievements, it lacks the old assurance. None the less it maintained much that was important and characteristic, until Alexander carried his Greek army across Asia to the Hindu-kush and created so many opportunities for Greeks that the homeland was improverished and enfeebled by the lure of new empires and ever-receding horizons. But between Homer and the fall of Athens the Greeks displayed a remarkable unity in the variety and the scale of their undertakings. They might maintain different systems of government, or conduct bloodthirsty wars with one another, or make deals with barbarians for private ends, but the main pattern of their achievement is clear enough. In the countless complexities of local history we see a people forging new instruments of civilization and advancing from outlook to outlook and from style to style. In this rapid succession of changes we may discern the permanent elements, the beliefs and the assumptions, the enduring human temperament, the political passions and convictions, the vision of the gods, and the searching curiosity about man and his place in the universe.

# CHAPTER II

# THE HEROIC OUTLOOK

THOUGH THE NEW GREEK WORLD which emerged from the Dark Age was different indeed from that of the Mycenaean kings, it cherished legends of that resplendent past, and, with the longing admiration which men feel for a greatness which they cannot recover or rival, the Greeks saw in this lost society something heroic and superhuman, which embodied an ideal of what men should be and do and suffer. Their imaginations, inflamed by ancient stories of vast undertakings and incomparable heroes, of gods walking on the earth as the friends of men, of a noble splendour in external circumstances and in courtly manners, formed a vision of a heroic world which they cherished as one of their most precious possessions. From it they derived the notion that a man should live for honour and renown and play his part with style and proper pride among men as notable as himself. They knew of all this through a long tradition of poetry which derived its stories and its characters, no less than much of its technique and its language, from Mycenaean times and was passed from generation to generation by an oral tradition on the lips of men. For us this tradition survives in the Homeric poems, which came indeed towards its end but kept its authentic spirit in their generous outlook and strong sense of human worth. Since they were from an early time the staple of Greek education, they encouraged a conception of manhood in which personal worth held pride of place, and strengthened an ideal favoured already by other circumstances. The smallness and self-sufficiency of city-states promoted a degree of independence which was impossible in the centralized theocracies of Egypt and Asia. A nation of seafarers had opportunities for enterprise which would have been denied to mere workers on the land. The individualism, which conditions imposed on Greek life, suited its inherited cult of heroic manhood and endured in historical times as one of the most striking elements in its beliefs and its behaviour.

The essence of the heroic outlook is the pursuit of honour through action. The great man is he who, being endowed with superior qualities of body and mind, uses them to the utmost and wins the applause of his fellows because he spares no effort and shirks no risk in his desire to make the most of the gifts and to surpass other men in his exercise of them. His honour is the centre of his being, and any affront to it calls for immediate amends. He courts danger gladly because it gives him the best opportunity of showing of what stuff he is made. Such a conviction and its system of behaviour are built on a man's conception of himself and of what he owes to it, and if it has any further sanctions, they are to be found in what other men like himself think of him. By prowess and renown he gains an enlarged sense of personality and well-being; through them he has a second existence on the lips of men, which assures him that he has not failed in what matters most. Fame is the reward of honour, and the hero seeks it before everything else. This outlook runs through Greek history from Homer's Achilles to the historical Alexander. It is countered and modified and altered, but it persists and even extends its field from an individual to a national outlook. It is a creed suited to men of action, and through it the Greeks justified their passionate desire to vary the pattern of their lives by resourceful and unflagging enterprise. Though in its early stages, as we see it in Homer, it has much in common with similar ideals in other heroic societies, it is more resilient in Greece than elsewhere and endures with unexpected vitality when the city-state is established with all its demands and obligations on its members, and when the new conception of the citizen might seem to exclude an ideal which sets so high a value on the single man and his notion of what is due to him.

The strength of this heroic ideal may be judged by the spirit in which the Greek philosophers treat it. With their love of the contemplative life and of knowledge for its own sake, they could hardly be expected to favour a system which gave such pre-eminence to action. Yet, though they did not think it the highest kind of life, they still paid their tributes to it. Pythagoras divided men into three classes: the seekers of knowledge, the seekers of honour, and the seekers of gain, and in comparing life to the Olympic Games, matched the first class with the onlookers, the second with the competing athletes, and the third with the hucksters.[1] In this he intended no great compliment to the seekers of honour, but the Greeks would not have found his parallel derisory, and would appreciate that he thought honour at least more reputable than gain. So too Heraclitus, in deploring the general lack of wisdom among men, evidently thinks better of those who 'choose one thing above all others, immortal glory among mortals' than of the majority who 'are glutted like beasts'.[2] Even in the fourth century, when the disasters of the Peloponnesian War had dealt an irreparable blow to the self-confidence of Athens, the pursuit of honour still kept a respectable place in philosophy. In the psychology which Plato built on the tripartite nature of the soul, the self-asserting principle, which seeks honour through action, has an essential function and is said to be more likely to side with reason than against it,[3] while Aristotle conforms to a more traditional outlook when he approves of the pursuit of honour because 'it is the prize appointed for the noblest deeds' and 'the greatest of external goods' and is, after all, what we pay to the gods.[4] Whatever the philosophers thought of the pursuit of honour, they could not dismiss it. It was an inalienable part of Greek life and meant much more to the average man than any philosophical theory of conduct.

The heroic outlook, which is based on honour, has much in common with other systems of behaviour. Those who follow it regard themselves as bound by obligations which they must fulfil and as forbidden to perform certain actions which are shameful. There is no more appeal against it than against the most rigorous categorical imperative. Nor do many of its injunctions differ from those of ordinary moral codes. The murder of Agamemnon by his wife and her lover is as strongly condemned by the system of honour as by any system of morality. But honour and morality differ on important points of principle. First, honour is more positive than negative; its obligations are more to the fore than its prohibitions. It expects a man to exert himself all the time and to make the most of his opportunities, often indeed to create them. In this no doubt it reflects its origin in a society whose first interest is war; for in war initiative and enterprise are of primary importance. But the Greeks applied the lesson to peace. Many of them felt that it was somehow disgraceful to remain contented with their lot, that they must try to better it, to make more of themselves and their conditions. Pericles even applies this to the making of money: 'As for poverty, no one need be ashamed to admit it; the real shame is in not taking practical measures to escape from it.'[5] Honour thus becomes what morality not always is: an incentive to vigorous action in many fields. Secondly, the ultimate test of honour is human dignity. Anything that lowers this is dishonourable; anything that enhances it, honourable. This is both a subjective and an exacting system, subjective because the concept of dignity is not precise and may well vary from man to man, and exacting because the passage of time is more likely to widen than to narrow it. Honour, no doubt, forms its own case-law, but it tends to be more demanding and more critical as precedents are formed and accepted. Thirdly, in the last resort the only court of appeal is a man's own feelings. Against these it is useless to invoke the anger of the gods or the disapproval of men; for the hero is so sure of himself that he will not allow his final decisions to be dictated by anything but thought or his own honour. Thus, when Achilles, moved to anger by an affront to his honour, refuses to fight for his fellows at Troy, it is futile for them to plead with him. Their needs are a far less cogent argument than his own sense of injury, and their plight merely hardens him in his conviction that he is right. Such a system of behaviour is not easily calculable and leads to many an unforeseen crisis as well as to conflicts between men of similar outlook when their personal dignity is at stake. In the tangled controversies of Greek politics honour was always a force to be reckoned with, and often confused issues which might otherwise have been clear.

The heroic outlook of the Greeks confirmed them in their taste for war, and was itself confirmed by it. It was in this that the famous heroes of the past had proved their superiority, and their descendants wished to rival them. Greek states went to war with each other almost as part of political routine, and it is significant that neither Plato nor Aristotle thought it unusual or undesirable or suggested any means to avoid it. No doubt mixed motives were at work: lust for loot, territory, or markets; desire for excitement, fear of domination from without, envy of prestige or wealth or influence. The Greeks fought each other for the same reasons that other men do, and their attitude towards war was no less ambivalent. Just as Homer calls it 'hateful', 'tearful', 'baleful', and the like, but also speaks of 'battle which brings glory to men' and 'the joy of the fight', so other Greeks both deplore and praise war. They complain that it takes the best men and leaves the worst, that it creates unprecedented situations, that it promotes violence, that it lowers the level of decency and morals, that it destroys the grace of life and brings disease and starvation, that it robs the defeated of their liberty and their happiness. If we wish to see how well they understood the horrors of defeat, we have only to look

at the *Trojan Women* of Euripides, which was produced in
415 BC, when, in a reckless passion for conquest, Athens was
embarking on the fatal expedition to Sicily, and shows how
even at such a time the frenzy for war was countered by a
horror of its insensate brutality. In the Peloponnesian War,
Aristophanes, whom nobody could call a crank, spoke out
boldly for peace and poked satirical gibes at generals and
politicians who did well out of war. The Greeks were well
acquainted with its horrors but none the less felt that it had
its recompenses and its consolations. They enjoyed its appalling thrills; they regarded victory as the greatest of all
possible glories and honourable defeat as only less glorious.
In it they were able to display to an unexampled degree that
harmonious collaboration of mind and body in which they
delighted and to escape from the deadening routine of
daily effort into something more exciting, more varied, and
in some ways more rewarding. In their attitude towards war
the Greeks maintained the old heroic spirit, which frets at
the limitations set on human effort and strives to break
through them by some prodigious exertion and achievement.

Though the heroic ideal set a high value on war, it was not
for this reason narrow in its choice of qualities to be sought
and honoured. The greatest of the heroes who goes to
Troy, Achilles, is not only the strongest and swiftest of warriors but the most beautiful man, who completes his other
excellences by eloquence, courtesy, generosity, and counsel.
His aim is to carry out his father's command 'ever to be the
best and to surpass others',[6] but he interprets this in a wide
sense, and is by any standards the authentic hero. So too the
Greeks sought to live up to the heroic ideal in other spheres
than war, to find, if not a moral equivalent to it, at least
activities which needed and encouraged the same qualities.
From early times they discussed the true excellence, or
*aretê*, of man, and even in the seventh century in Sparta,
Tyrtaeus, who comes to the conclusion that it is to stand
against the foe in battle, gives serious consideration to the
rival claims of athletic prowess, physical beauty, and royal
power.[7] The Greeks would at least admit that the whole
matter was one for frank discussion and that other qualities
than the purely warlike had good claims to respect. Though
war was never far from the Greek consciousness, and though
prowess in it was always prized, this was not an exclusive
or intolerant ideal. It kept a place for gifts mental, moral,
and physical, which might indeed be useful in war but
found plenty of scope outside it.

In its beginnings the heroic ideal was confined to a chosen

few. In Homer the great heroes dominate the scene, and the common soldiers are hardly mentioned. The few people of humbler birth who make an appearance, like Thersites and Dolon, are soon dismissed with contempt. To absorb such an ideal into a city-state called for considerable elasticity. In aristocracies, which claimed descent from the heroes of old and believed that the blood of the gods had not yet failed in them, a man might behave like a Homeric warrior and seek personal glory, and be all the more highly regarded for it by his fellows, who felt that he brought honour alike to his city, his class, and his family. So an epitaph of c. 600 bc from Corcyra shows how a man who has fallen in battle is seen like a hero of old: 'This is the tomb of Arniadas. Flashing-eyed Ares slew him as he fought by the ships on the streams of Aratthus and was by far the best man in the lamentable din of battle.'[8] Nor were such tributes necessarily paid only by friends or kinsmen. A couplet, attributed to Archilochus and possibly the seventh century, suggests that their country is pleased to honour its noble sons: 'Two lofty pillars of Naxos, Megatimus and Aristophon, o mighty earth, thou holdest beneath.'[9] In aristocracies, with their cult of personal distinction, there was place for a man to win renown by his achievements, but we might expect that democracies would be less tolerant and insist upon some diminution of the old emphasis on individual honour. But in Athens, which is the only democracy on which we are well informed, equality of renown was achieved by assuming that the whole people was capable of behaving in a heroic manner and deserved gratitude and praise when it took advantage of its challenges and showed its superiority. So when Pericles speaks about Athenians who have died in battle, he refers not to a favoured few but to the nameless fallen, and pays his tribute to all alike: 'In the fighting they thought it more honourable to stand their ground and suffer death than to give in and save their lives. So they fled from the reproaches of men, abiding with life and limb the brunt of battle; and in a small moment of time, the climax of their lives, a culmination of glory, not of fear, were swept away from us.'[10] This is language suited to a democracy, and worthy of it, but it is founded on the old idea that a man who dies bravely in battle has done all that can be asked of him.

One of the reasons why the heroic ideal survived in Greece was that it was attached to the service of a city. In the true heroic age Achilles fights not for his city, nor even for his fellow Achaeans, but for his own glory. The

hero is an isolated, self-centred figure, who lives and dies
for a private satisfaction. But just as against Achilles Homer
sets the antithetical figure of Hector, who fights for Troy
and with whose life that of Troy is inextricably bound up,
so in Greek history the heroic ideal takes a new meaning
when it is placed at the disposal of a city. War again provides test-cases. A city may honour an individual, as Abdera
honours Agathon: 'For mighty Agathon, who died for Abdera, this whole city mourned at his pyre.'[11] More often a
city commemorates a whole company of dead, because they
are its worthy representatives and champions and in their
united efforts show what it lives for. So no details are given
of the Corinthians who died on Salamis: 'Stranger, once we
dwelt in the well-watered city of Corinth, but now Salamis,
island of Ajax, holds us,'[12] or of the Spartans who fell at
Thermopylae: 'Stranger, bring news to the Lacedaemonians
that we lie here in obedience to their words.'[13] So too Pericles, with a larger sense of what such deaths mean to a democracy, has an equal appreciation that heroic excellence
may be displayed in devotion to Athens: 'To me it seems
that the consummation which has overtaken these men
shows us the meaning of manliness in its first revelation and
in its final proof.'[14] It was no more difficult for the Greeks
to attach the heroic ideal of manhood to a city than it was
for the men of the Middle Ages to attach it to Christen-
dom. If a man has a cause which inspires him, he will exert
himself to the utmost, and if the heroic ideal begins by being the privilege of a gifted and chosen few, it can be extended to a whole people and permeate their lives by making them give to the city what they might have kept for
themselves.

A society which cherishes, in no matter how reformed a
shape, a heroic ideal is not always easy or happy in its
treatment of women. A fiercely heroic world, like that of
Iceland, may honour women who behave for many purposes
like men and delight in danger and bloodshed. The Homeric
Greeks were not like this. Their women move freely and
easily among men, but take no part in war or public affairs,
and are excluded from rule and government. On the whole
this seems to have persisted in Greece and to have been the
normal pattern in historical times. Greek women and girls
took a lively part in local ceremonies and made their contribution to songs and dances, but they do not seem to have
been allowed any power. An exception is Artemisia, queen
of Halicarnassus, who contributed five ships to the navy of
Xerxes in the Persian War and is credited by Herodotus with

much sage counsel. But we may suspect that Herodotus, who was a native of Halicarnassus, was moved by local patriotism to exaggerate her importance. Otherwise Greek women seem to have had a considerable share of liberty provided they avoided tasks reserved for men. Athens, it must be admitted, has a bad name for the seclusion and subjection of women. It is true that some statements, usually of a proverbial character, stress that the right place for a woman is the home and that her noblest part is silence.[15] But such statements need not be taken too literally, since they plainly contain an element of wishful thinking, and it is hard to imagine any Greek woman being silent for long. Not only does Attic tragedy show women taking grave decisions and assuming heavy responsibilities, and in doing so it can hardly have flown altogether in the face of actual experience, but even comedy, which is far more realistic, makes great play with them. In Aristophanes' *Lysistrata* the leading character is a woman who displays a copious eloquence and a notable lack of inhibitions. No doubt women worked while men talked, and in humbler households did much that would be done elsewhere by slaves, but that need not have prevented them from speaking their minds freely or taking command in their own sphere. Attic gravestones and funeral vases show that the Athenians were just as capable of deep affection for their wives as other men, but what was lacking was not only a conscious or artificial cult of womanhood, such as existed in the Middle Ages, but any public or proclaimed demonstration of affection. Women had their own sphere, and men had theirs. They kept their relations with women in the background, as an essential element in their daily life, but separate from politics and public affairs and the call to action. Even in poetry, love of women plays a much smaller part than we might expect, and no conception of Greek society should shirk its essentially masculine character. It was an inevitable feature of an outlook which regarded action as the main end of life and attached it to an ideal which demanded that a man must make the utmost of his body and his mind.

Because of this outlook much of the sentiment which in most countries exists between men and women existed in Greece between men and men. The Greeks gave to friendship the attachment and the loyalty which elsewhere accompany the love of women. Of this Homer presents a classic example, when he makes the friendship of Achilles and Patroclus a pivot in his story and tells how grief and anger at Patroclus' death send Achilles back to battle that he may

take his vengeance on Hector. The essence of such a relation was for a friend to share another's fortunes, both good
and bad, to support him with complete truth and faithful-
ness in his loves and his enmities, his pleasures and his sorrows, to be scrupulously candid, and to fail in no call made
upon him. This is the burden of much literature from convivial songs of the sixth century to Aristotle's schematic
analysis of friendship in the *Nicomachean Ethics.* Attic
tragedy presented it dramatically through devoted couples
like Ajax and Teucer, or Orestes and Pylades; Xenophon reports as a commonplace that 'a clear and good friend is the
best of all possessions'.[16] Friendship of this kind was easy
in a society where men partook of common interests and re-
laxed in each other's company. It has its noble and impressive side, but it also means that in the Greeks we miss the
gentleness and tenderness which soften the asperities of
masculine life when women share the activities of men and
bring their own point of view to them. Friendships between
men may have their own reserves of emotion, but these are
not easily brought to the surface and tend to be masked by
restraint and decorum. Moreover, when men share so much
together, there is a suspicion of self-interest in their relations. We feel this in Aristotle, whose analysis of friendship
speaks too much of mutual advantage for our taste. Yet this
is probably misleading and due to a natural reticence, since
he touches the springs of Greek sentiment when he says that
friendship lies in loving rather than in being loved and
that a man wishes well to his friend not as a means to his
own happiness but for his friend's sake.[17] We cannot doubt
that in friendship the Greeks found an ideal which did much
to satisfy their need for affection, even if to us it seems a
little severe and one-sided and too much concerned with
purely male interests.

The affection which Greek men felt for one another had
its physical side. Of this there is no trace in Homer, who implicitly denies it for Achilles and Patroclus.[18] But from the
eighth century onwards it plays a marked part in Greek life.
If tradition ascribed its introduction to the Dorians,[19] it
seems to have been prevalent and accepted in most parts of
Greece, and usually to have taken the form of an older
man's love for a younger. Its origins may be variously explained, by the relative seclusion or scarcity of women, by
the isolation and emotional tensions of military life, by the
cult of the naked body in games, by the natural tendency of
the sexual impulse to assert itself where the affections are
engaged. That it had its crude side we cannot doubt. Ar-

chaic inscriptions of the seventh century from the Dorian island of Thera suggest a forcible rite of initiation,[20] and many vases depict a courtship which is quite unconcealed.[21] But where so strong an instinct was at work, it was easy for other elements to enter and take control. Love-songs by Ibycus and Anacreon express feelings which might in different circumstances have been given to girls, and even the grave Pindar goes out of his way to invent a story that Posidon falls in love with the boy Pelops.[22] In Athens, Harmodius and Aristogiton, who were renowned in history and song for the assassination of the tyrant Hipparchus, were not the less honoured because their motives were based on love for each other.[23] Above all, the practice found an outlet in many fields of active life, where younger boys were disciplined in skills and hardship such as the chase and the use of arms. In Sparta and Crete it was a regular feature in the training of the young;[24] in Thebes the Sacred Regiment of 300 men was trained on it.[25] Plato, who understood the matter from the inside, was uneasy about it and hardened his views as he grew older. In the *Symposium* he builds an ascending scale of relations, which starts with physical attraction and moves through asceticism and intellectual effort to something close to mystical contemplation; in the *Republic* he tries to control it because it is coarse and ill-bred;[26] in the *Laws* he condemns any manifestation of it.[27] Aristotle hardly commits himself on the subject beyond regarding it as a morbid state resulting from habit and comparable to the plucking of hair and the biting of nails.[28] Some people indeed condemned the whole thing, but they seem to have been a not very influential minority, and there is no doubt that in Greek life it had an established place. It was a result of the predominantly male character of Greek civilization and its cult of the more specifically masculine qualities.

The comparative absence of the gentler and softer affections from Greek life was to some degree compensated by the strength of its loyalties, especially to the family. The family was an older unit than the city and kept its prestige and even some of its powers in the fifth century. At the back of their minds the Greeks felt that the bond of blood was stronger than any tie of citizenship and in the last resort imposed obligations which could not be shirked. Sophocles shows what this means when he makes Antigone bury her brother, when she has been forbidden to do so, and defy the state at the cost of her own life. The law might reinforce family obligations, like that to look after parents in their old age, or even take them on itself, as in Athens requital for murder was transferred from the family to a public law-court. But loyalty to the family remained stronger than that to the state and was likely to win if there was a conflict be-tween them. The harsh temper which often marks Greek politics is due in no small measure to the quarrels and jeal-ousies between families and the loyalty of the members of each to his home rather than to any ideal of national unity. This is characteristic of the heroic outlook, which makes a man proud of his kith and kin because they belong to him, and in exerting himself for them he obeys something very deep in his nature. Achilles is unwavering in his affection for his old father, and Hector feels that he is fighting for his wife and child as much as for his city. Greek family-life might at times present fierce conflicts which could be de-cided only by the shedding of blood among the closest rel-atives, as when Meleager's mother destroys her son because he has killed her brothers or Orestes kills his mother for murdering his father. Such conflicts belong to the heroic system. If men sought to be superior to others, one of their most inspiring impulses came from the conviction that they must live up to the standard of their ancestors and be wor-thy of the stock from which they were bred.

Yet this respect for intimate ties and loyalties had its dark and destructive side. If a man expected a friend, or a family its members, to share alike all interests and to be un-flinchingly faithful in all circumstances, it almost made ha-tred a virtue and vengeance a duty. The Greeks insisted that a friend must share hatreds as well as affections, and, if he failed to do so, he was regarded as a coward or a traitor. They saw nothing wrong in hatred provided that there was a reason for it, and the reason was usually in-sulted or injured pride. Once a man felt it and was con-vinced that he was right, the only solution was a bloody vengeance. The few exceptions only emphasize the strength of the usual rule, as when the Pythagoreans said: 'A man should never willingly start an enmity with those who are not completely evil, but if he has started it, he should con-tinue nobly in the fight to the finish, unless the character of his opponent changes and is replaced by good will.'[29] That perhaps is something, but it is not much. More striking at first sight is the remark which Pittacus, tyrant of Myti-lene, is said to have made to his inveterate opponent, Alca-eus: 'Forgiveness is better than vengeance',[30] but this was probably due more to political prescience than to any feel-ing that vengeance is in itself undesirable. And these are exceptional cases. The Greeks never thought it possible or desirable to love their enemies, and forgiveness is a rare word in their vocabulary except for trivial or involuntary offences. More often they found a positive pleasure in hating their enemies and enjoyed the prospect of revenge. They would see nothing wrong in a couplet attributed to Theognis: 'Think of my hatred and my violence, and know in your heart that for your offence I shall avenge myself as I can.'[31] This outlook began with the family and was the source of savage feuds with other families, but it spread to class-war and to war between one city and another. A man might have enemies in his own class or in another or in other cities, and in each case he felt that he should treat them as harshly as he could. He believed that, if he failed to harm them, as he assumed that they wished to harm him, he failed in honour. The relation was reciprocal and insoluble. Every act of vengeance called for another, and whether the feud was between individuals, or between cities, it was used to justify a merciless treatment of the enemy. Since many wars were thought to begin with some injury inflicted by one side on the other, it meant that they were seldom conducted in what we should call a chivalrous spirit, and if the defeated had earned the condemnation of the victors, they might have their male citizens killed and their women and children sold into slavery. The notion of honour, applied in this way, was a source not only of brutality but of insecurity and fear. It emphasized the harshness of the heroic system when its pride was wounded, and the violence to which the love of action will turn in a crisis when its claims are at stake.

The heroic outlook gave an unexpectedly prominent place to intelligence. If the *Iliad* portrays in Achilles the most authentically heroic of heroes, the *Odyssey* presents in Odysseus a man who is indeed brave to the point of recklessness but is renowned pre-eminently for counsel and resource. The Greeks liked and admired intelligence, whether practical or theoretical, and no doubt felt that they surpassed other peoples in their possession of it, but they had qualms about its uninhibited exercise and felt that it must be balanced by other qualities of character and self-control. If a man relied sorely or chiefly on it, he was thought likely to frustrate even his own ends by being too clever and even to fail to understand much that was obvious to an ordinary man. In the city-state, with its predilection for intestine and foreign controversies, and especially in democracies, with their public debates and their susceptibility to rhetoric and showmanship, the skilful politician was at a great advantage and often had more influence than his purely political qualifications deserved. This became more dangerous in the Peloponnesian War, when leaders of the Athenian democracy, like Cleon and Hyperbolus, were astute manipulators of popular passions but lacked a clear-sighted vision of events. Deceived by their own sophistries, they deceived others also, and graver spirits condemned them for their ultimate frivolity and lack of judgment. Just as Thucydides presents Cleon as a debased perversion of Pericles, so both Sophocles and Euripides are concerned to show that mere cleverness in argument or policy may be disreputable and pernicious. By a strange irony of literary history, the character whom they used to display what this meant was Odysseus, whom Euripides in his *Hecuba* (*c.* 425 BC) and Sophocles in his *Philoctetes* (409 BC) made the essential type of unscrupulous and cold-blooded schemer who uses specious arguments to justify ignoble ends. Their presentation of him is the more remarkable because, though he is without decency or compassion or honesty, he is in his own way a patriot. The safety or at least the success of his country really means something to him and provides him with excuses for his unsavoury actions. Sophocles and Euripides were patriots too, but not in this way or with this damage to the balance and integrity of the heroic ideal. In their view a man's city did indeed make many calls on him, but not that he should surrender his decency to it. They stood for an older conception in which a man served the state best by being himself in the full range of his nobility and not by sacrificing it to some abstract notion of political power or expediency. The cult of cleverness might appeal to something deep in the Greek character, but to some independent observers it seemed to reject what they most valued and to exalt one side of human nature at the expense of others, which were no less important and without which it lost its usefulness and its dignity.

These were not the only discords which might arise when the heroic ideal was absorbed by the city-state. There are other occasions when the man who lives for honour finds his own notion of it at war with what might be regarded as his duty to his fellows or his people. The heroic age presents a pre-eminent case of this in Achilles, who, because he has been insulted by Agamemnon, withdraws from battle and causes humiliating losses to his own side. Nor does he ever apologize for what he has done. When he returns to battle, it is to avenge the death of Patroclus, and he accepts without hesitation, as his rightful due, the handsome amends offered by Agamemnon. For Achilles honor is more important than anything else and is indeed the spring of his whole being, but in later times we might expect such behaviour to be rare in a people so patriotic as the Greeks, and yet there were spectacular cases of it. In the Persian Wars the exiled king of Sparta, Demaratus, and the dispossessed tyrant of Athens, Hippias, joined the Persian side in the hope of being restored to power. Soon afterwards Themistocles, the victor of Salamis, after being exiled by the Athenians and condemned to death in absence, joined the Persians and took office under them. In 415 BC Alcibiades, already acting as an Athenian general in Sicily, was condemned in absence to death for impiety, but made his escape and joined the Spartans, to the irreparable harm of Athens. These men were driven by injured honour to help their country's enemies and to act against its interests. What the Greeks felt may be seen from Herodotus' account of Demaratus and the Persian king, Xerxes. Demaratus makes no pretense of his grievances against Sparta, but says frankly: 'You know very well what little affection I have now towards them, who took from me the honour and the rights of my fathers, and have made me a man of no city and an exile.'[32] None the less he goes on to praise his countrymen and to forecast that they will not be defeated. Herodotus saw no contradiction in a man who almost in the same breath wishes his country to be humiliated and thinks it better than all others. Such a paradox was perfectly explicable by heroic standards, and even in the fifth century these were still sufficiently strong to create serious trouble. More remarkable still are the words which Alcibiades speaks at Sparta when he explains his treachery to his own country: 'The Athens I love is not the one which is wronging me now, but that one in which I used to have secure enjoyment of my rights as a citizen. The country that I am attacking does not seem to me mine any longer; it is rather that I am trying to recover a country that has ceased to be mine.'[33] There is a touch of sophistry in this, but the average Greek would probably think that Alcibiades had something to be said for him, because he had been unjustly treated. Though the pursuit of honour was a potent influence in making men serve their city, it could at times turn sour and create situations for which there was no outlet but treachery.

The conflict between honour and loyalty is part of a wider conflict which runs through Greek history. With their

stormy, self-assertive vitality and their desire to do all that
men can, they took great risks, both personally and nation-
ally. Just as legendary heroes like Achilles or Heracles tax
themselves to the uttermost and do far more than other
men, so Greek cities would essay tasks of prodigious danger and difficulty and either succeed beyond all probability,
as the united Greeks succeeded against Persia, or fail catastrophically, as Athens failed in Egypt in 454 BC and
in Sicily in 413 BC. Just as the hero differs from the common run of men in the unusual degree of his *dynamis,* or
innate power, so a city displays its vitality by exerting the
same force over other cities. The desire to excel feeds on the
humiliation of others, and Greek individuals and cities alike
slaked their ambitions in this way. It was this which gave
so ruthless a character to Greek party politics, in which the
losers were often exiled or executed, and to international
relations, in which a strong power like Athens or Sparta
enforced its will on feebler neighbours. The self-assertive
principle in the soul should, as Plato said, be on the side
of reason, but often enough it drove its victims to a desire
for power and domination.

The Greeks were conscious of this and uttered grave
warnings against it. Poets and philosophers dwelt on the
merits of the Mean, of the middle state between obscurity
and excessive power, and claimed that only if a man follows this is he likely to be happy. While poets expressed the
idea by saying that a man must not climb the sky, or try
to marry Aphrodite, or sail beyond the Pillars of Heracles,[34]
the philosophers took the conception of the Mean and
built moral systems on it. But when Aristotle seeks to explain the several virtues as Means between opposite extremes,
he fails to convince us either in logic or in experience. Such
a doctrine as the Mean works well enough if we are already
persuaded that a quiet life is best, but it is no final deterrent
to those who believe in action for its own sake and feel
that the greater the risk, the greater the glory. The attention
which the Greeks paid to the Mean suggests not so much
that they observed it as that, in the fullness of their blood,
they felt that they needed some curb for their more violent
ambitions amd more reckless undertakings. The Mean might
at least have the virtue that it gave some consolation for
defeat by explaining that too much had been attempted,
but as a guide in the practical government of life it was
as much neglected as observed. Rich oligarchies, like Corinth
and Aegina, might claim that they followed it while their
neighbour Athens did not, and it is perhaps true that they

lacked the impetus which drove Athens to her wilder adventures. But the ambiguous attitude of the Greeks towards the Mean is not to be explained by differences of class or government. It lay deeper and rose from a real contradiction in the Greek view of action and honour.

The conflict may be regarded as one between the morality of common sense, which deplores dangerous ventures and regards happiness as the best of possible ends, and the vaulting ambitions of the heroic mentality, which appeals to instincts and desires beyond morality and regards happiness as an unworthy or irrelevant aim. The moralists worked out a scheme in which men became infatuated through pride, incur the hatred of their neighbours, and, by attempting too much, are ruined. This could be applied to local politics, as Solon applied it to the rich of unreformed Athens,[35] or to international politics, as Herodotus applied it to the imperial designs of Persia. It has its own truth and its own appeal to the conscience, and it won eloquent advocates in influential circles. What it meant for some men can be seen from words which Pindar wrote for an Aeginetan in 446 BC, when there seemed to be a hope that Aegina might free herself from Athenian domination. He implicitly condemns Athens, when he appeals to 'Kind-hearted Quiet, daughter of Right':

> You too, if any
> Drives home into his heart
> Unsweet anger, will harden your face
> Against the might of your enemies, and clap
> The upstart in the bilge.
> —Porphyrion did not know this
> When he aroused her too far;
> (The gain I like best
> Comes from a willing giver,
>
> But Force trips up
> At last even the loud boaster.)
> —Cilician Typhos, with a hundred heads,
> Did not escape her,
> No, nor the Giants' King;
> They went down before
> The thunderbolt and the arrows of Artemis.[36]

So Pindar, in his allusive way, foresees the doom of Athens because she has offended against the Mean. Against this we may set in contrast the Athenians' own view of themselves. When Pericles tried to hearten his people after the ravages of the plague, he offered an alternative to the Mean:

'All who have taken it upon themselves to rule over others have incurred hatred and unpopularity for a time; but if one has a great aim to pursue, this burden of envy must be accepted, and it is wise to accept it. Hatred does not last for long, but the brilliance of the present is the glory of the future, stored up for ever in the memory of men. It is for you to safeguard that future glory, and to do nothing now that is dishonourable.'[37]

In this the heroic outlook is revealed without reservations, and it is a complete denial of the Mean. No doubt the two could often be brought together in theory and in practice, but there was between them an ultimate discord which the Greeks never completely solved.

How serious the problem was, and how gravely it could be treated, can be seen from Sophocles, the friend of Pericles, who built more than one tragedy on it. His most forbidding heroes, Ajax and Heracles, present the heroic type as the Athenians saw it in the fifth century. Both are in some sense remote from ordinary men not only in their strength and endurance, but in their pride and inaccessibility; both come to fearful and even humiliating ends through their disregard for ordinary human qualms, Ajax through his contempt for the gods, Heracles through his utter disregard for his tender, all-too-human wife; both are condemned not only by the advocates of the Mean but by all who admire the warmer and gentler instincts of humanity; and both in the end are justified, Ajax for his noble services in war, Heracles for the labours which he has heroically undertaken for the good of mankind. Sophocles presents the heroic type in its forbidding inhumanity and its incredible fortitude. He does not spare us even its least attractive qualities, the failure of Ajax to be moved by the entreaties of his concubine or the stony refusal of Heracles to forgive his wife, who has unwittingly and unwillingly caused his death. Against this he sets the unrelenting courage of Ajax in his decision to die because he has lost his honour, and the supreme self-command with which Heracles endures his last hideous tortures as his superb body is devoured by a burning poison. Sophocles presents in dramatic form what the heroic ideal meant in Athens. He saw its faults and its limitations and took care to show them in their formidable reality, but he suggests that they are justified by the nobility which accompanies them and redeems them from the taint of common clay. In these plays we see what heroism meant to the age of

Pericles, and why the Athenians placed so high a value on it.

The hero fulfils himself in death. Just as the advocates of the Mean and happiness say that no man must be counted happy till he is dead, because there is no knowing what disasters may befall him in life, so the exponents of the heroic ideal regard death as the climax and completion of life, the last and most searching ordeal to which a man is subjected and the true test of his worth. It is then that he makes the greatest sacrifice of which he is capable, the life which has meant more to him than to most men and is at last thrown away in some splendid gesture of defiance. For those who believe that action is an end in itself, any career must be crammed with it, and what counts is the pressure which a man brings to it, the zest with which he devotes himself to it. To fill his life with brave doings is indeed to make the most of the gifts which the gods have bestowed on him at birth. Such a life cannot be allowed to decline with fading strength and failing powers; it needs for its appropriate end some dramatic finale, in which the hero exerts himself for the last time in the finest and fittest way. Then indeed he reveals himself in his full magnificence and ends his crowded existence with a last call to the glory which is his right. Just as the grand figures of legend, like Ajax and Heracles, die violent and fearful deaths, so other men were glad to die in battle because this set a crown on their lives and proved that in the ultimate test they shrank from nothing to prove their worth. To die in ease and comfort would be a concession to a happiness which they had never sought and to debase their search for honour. The Greeks lived close to death, and so far from being afraid of it, they often sought it as the culmination of what they most valued, the self-realization which a man finds when he sacrifices everything that he has, and exercises a privilege which belongs to him alone.

The nobility of this outlook lies in the place which it gives to sacrifice. Whether a man gives his life for his family or his friends or his city, he gives the utmost that can be asked of him, and his action means that, however boldly he may assert his own worth or however ardently he may desire glory, he himself will not reap the fruit of them. The Greeks were as well aware as anyone of what such a sacrifice means and costs in its inexorable finality. In an uncharacteristic moment of indecision, when he questions whether war is worth all the efforts that he gives to it, Achilles says:

> Cattle and good fat sheep are things to be had for the
>     looting,
> Tripods and tawny heads of horses are there for the
>     taking,
> But man's life will come not again, nor will it be
>     captured,
> Once it has passed through his teeth, nor can any
>     power restore it.[38]

No Greek would dispute that there is truth in this, but they
would for the most part disagree with the lesson that
Achilles draws from it. It is just because the sacrifice is
irrevocable that it is worth making. Against the doubts of
Achilles we can set the mood in which Hector faces him.
Hector knows that he is certain to be killed by Achilles,
who is swifter and stronger than he is, but he goes out to
fight him because he feels that this is what he must do for
his city, his wife, and his small son. This sense that a man
owes a supreme sacrifice to his own people was deeply ingrained in the Greek character, and is a triumphant example
of its adaptation of heroic ideals to a civic frame. Because
he lives among other men and is bound to them by ties
which he cannot explain or assess, his first concern is their
protection and their safety. In this sense, and to this degree, the city was more important than the individual. If, as
every Greek thought, it made life possible and agreeable for
him, it was a fair return that he should spare no effort to
secure the same advantages for others. This was a duty
owed not to the gods but to his fellow-men, part of his un-
breakable association with them, a recognition that, despite
all his personal claims, he was part of a unity greater and
more lasting than himself. It was one of the more remarkable
achievements of the Greeks that they were able to combine
a generous view of the rights of the individual with a strong
sense of what he owed to his city. It was this balance between the two views that not only made it possible for the
old notion of heroic worth to have a new meaning in the
city-state, but gave it a place more honourable than when a
man lived and died simply for his own glory. In the last
resort kinship and the bond of blood were the most powerful tie known to the Greeks, and when it asserted its claims,
they were glad and proud to give all that they could for it.

    This sense of fulfilment was emphasized by the Greek ap-
proach to what happens after death. On this they had,
naturally enough, no single view. Some indeed believed that
in the afterworld men are punished or rewarded for what

they have done in life; others tempered this to a belief that a few chosen heroes are conveyed after death to an island of eternal spring in the western sea. But the absence of creeds and dogma meant that such beliefs were vague and uncertain. More common and more powerful was the general notion that, if a man survives at all, his afterworld is but shadowy and bears little resemblance to the solid earth which he has left. Many men would accept in some degree the heroic conception found in Homer, who tells how all the dead alike go to a grey world, where even the greatest are but shadows almost without understanding and recover consciousness only when they drink blood. Their plight is told to Odysseus by the ghost of his mother:

This is the law of mortals: whenever anyone dieth,
Then no longer are bones and flesh held together by sinews,
But by the might of the blazing fire they are conquered
    and wasted.
From that moment when first the breath departs from the
    white bones,
Flutters the spirit away, and like to a dream it goes drifting.[39]

The dead are like bats fluttering and screeching in a cavern,[40] and it is no surprise when the ghost of Achilles says that he would rather be the serf of a poor man on earth than rule over all the dead.[41] The Greeks never quite forgot this notion. At the worst they might think that there is no life at all in the grave and that at the end man puts on a garment of clay; at the best they might hope that the virtuous or the initiated might enjoy an Elysian beatitude. But before the oppressive majesty of death most of them maintained an awe-struck uncertainty.

This accords with their belief in the value of life and the need to fill it with noble deeds. Because death annihilates all that matters, life is all the more valuable and must be turned to the utmost account. Achilles complains not that he is fated to die young, but that too much of his life is spoiled by misfortunes which hinder his pursuit of glory. In the thought of glory most Greeks found a consolation for the shadowy doom which awaited them in the grave. Without asking very closely what it means to the dead, they found in the reality of remembrance or renown something which counteracts the obliteration brought by death. They followed their heroic tradition when they applied this idea to the dead in battle, like those who fell during the advance of the Persians through Thessaly and were commemorated by Aeschylus:

'These men, also, steadfast among spears, dark Fate destroyed, as they defended their native land rich in sheep;
though they are dead, their glory is alive, who endured and
clothed their limbs in Ossa's dust.' [42] So too Pericles applies
the same idea to the Athenian dead, but gives it a more
sweeping and more confident range: 'For famous men have
the whole earth as their memorial; it is not only the inscriptions on their graves in their own country that mark
them out; no, in foreign lands also, not in any visible form
but in people's hearts, their memory abides and grows.' [43]
Whatever such remembrance might mean to the dead, the
Greeks believed that it was well deserved and would at least
be an inspiration to unborn generations.

If those who died gloriously were held in common remembrance, they had their modest companions in many otherwise unconsidered dead, in whose epitaphs, gravestones, and
lêkythoi, or painted vases placed in their graves, we see a
constant attempt to catch the essential nature of a dead man
as he was when alive. This too was a tribute to what he
made of his earthly career, to his personality and his achievements. The epitaphs are usually brief, and often give no more
than a name and a place and perhaps a profession, but sometimes they say more and make a man more vivid, as on a
gravestone from Athens: 'His father Cleobulus set up this
monument to dead Xenophantus, because of his courage and
his modesty.'[44] So, more splendidly, lines ascribed to Simonides commemorate the daughter of Hippias, once tyrant of
Athens: 'This dust hides Archedice, daughter of Hippias, fore-
most man once among those of Hellas in his time. Though
she had princes for father, husband, brothers, and children,
she did not lift up her mind to pride.'[45] The essential point
is made quickly and quietly, and the dead woman lives in
the brief summary of her character. So too tombstones present the dead in characteristic and revealing poses. The warrior Aristion stands, tall and lithe, holding his spear; a
young brother stands with his small sister; an old man
holds out a cicada to a dog; a girl nurses pigeons; a woman
sits while her servant brings her a box (see Plates 51-55).
What counts is the suggestion of life as it really is, what the
dead have found in it and got out of it. On the lêkythoi
the contrast between life and death is often stressed by some
symbol of death set among living forms. A woman brings
offerings to a tomb, while a tall young man with a spear,
perhaps her husband, stands by it in the full strength of manhood; a little boy with his toy cart stands on the bank of a
river and waves his hand to his mother, while Charon, the

ferryman of the dead, waits for him in a boat; a young man sits on a tomb, while a friend speaks to him and a woman holds his armour in readiness (see Plates 87, 89, 90). The collocation of emblems of death with living figures shows how the Greeks saw the world of light against a background of darkness but did not for that reason lose any of their love of it. Against the mystery and the uncertainty they set the positive achievements of the living, and knew that they should be honoured for their own sake.

In such ways the heroic outlook, which the Greeks inherited from a distant past, shaped much of their thinking and their action. They fitted it into the frame of the city-state and its demands, and, when occasion called, into the larger pattern of Hellenism, of which they were never quite oblivious. When they claimed that they were superior to barbarians because they pursued a higher type of virtue, they were not wrong. In comparison with the herded multitudes of Egypt and Asia, or with the more primitive peoples on their own frontiers, the Greeks had found a principle which gave meaning to life and inspired them to astonishing achievements. Because they felt that they were different from other men, that they must always excel and surpass them, that a man wins his manhood through unflagging effort and unflinching risk, they broke away from the static patterns of society which elsewhere dominated their age, and inaugurated a way of life in which the prizes went to the eager and the bold, and action in all its forms was sought and honoured as the natural end of man.

# CHAPTER III

# THE GODS

A PEOPLE gets the gods which it deserves. The wayward and inscrutable demons who pester primitive man are born of nameless terrors and inhibiting ignorance; the grinning, gloating ogres of the Aztecs mirrored a race brutalized by incessant war and fearful of unknown privations; before the Romans were moved by Greek influences to abandon their stubborn rusticity, their gods were prosaic, functional, and sanitary; the passion of the Jews for legalistic discipline in all departments of life and their provincial, exclusive nationalism found an appropriate champion in Jehovah. So too the Greek gods reflect with illuminating clarity some salient features in the Greek character and are so closely connected with it that we can hardly think of the Greeks without them. At the start Greek religion is unusual in its very lack of system, of any organization such as we find in the dominating religions of the modern world. It begins at no fixed point and has roots which stretch indeterminately into an unchronicled past. It has no eminent prophet or law-giver who expounded the nature of the gods, no sacred books whose authority is final on doctrine or morals, no central organization for its hierarchy, no revealed cosmology, no conception of a dedicated religious life, no insistence on orthodoxy, no agreed eschatology, no accepted scheme of redemption. Greek religion shows its essentially Greek character by not conforming to any plan and by its generous freedom and inclusive tolerance. Any approach to the Greek gods must be made not through dogmas and creeds, but through the actual views and practice of their worshippers. Our concern is not so much to study a religion as to recover a religious experience, to see what the gods meant to those who believed in them, what appeal they had to the heart and the imagination, how they fitted into a scheme of life which was already full to overflowing with the appetites and the ambitions of men.

In the study of what their religion meant to the Greeks, it

is not necessary to inquire into its origins. What matters is its character in historical times, and on this we are abundantly, if not always very satisfactorily, informed. At first sight the Greek divinities seem to present an ordered system, living on Olympus with Zeus at their head, and each concerned with a more or less recognized sphere of activity. This air of organization, which Herodotus attributed to Homer and Hesiod,[1] may well owe something to traditions canonized by eminent poets, but it masks a bewildering variety of practice and belief. It is true that the names of the chief gods were constant throughout Greece; that many of them had the same functions wherever they might be worshipped; that others might differ in character from place to place but still maintain a certain identity; that legends of the gods were common property everywhere. But against this appearance of substantial uniformity we must set less tractable elements, which do not fall into the general scheme because fundamentally they have nothing to do with the Olympians, but come from some older, less rationalized world—age-old cults of the dead, exorcism of evil spirits, ritualists to raise crops, ceremonial cleansings from impurity, taboos on sexual intercourse and certain classes of food, sacrifices not at all like those offered to the Olympians, gods and goddesses conceived not quite in human shape, like a four-armed Apollo and a horse-headed Demeter. All such things existed and had a place in Greek religion, because they were consecrated by immemorial practice and connected with daily or seasonal tasks or with critical occasions like marriage and death. There were also cults, which, if they did not actually conflict with those of Olympus, had in their very peculiarity a special place. Dionysus, the god of wine and frenzy, was worshipped in Crete as far back as Mycenaean times, but remained something of an outsider among the Olympians, and when his adherents retired to the mountains and tore live animals to pieces, they demonstrated the survival of an ancient cult in which the life-blood of animals was needed to renew that of men. A whole set of beliefs, conveniently but incorrectly labelled Orphic, was based on initiation in jealously guarded mysteries and offered prospects after death more substantial and more enjoyable than those in common currency. Medicine-men, like Epimenides, and mystical mathematicians and scientists, like Pythagoras and Empedocles, made their own amendments to current ideas and revived obscure superstitions in new forms. Rationalists tried to impart order and decency to systems which shocked their reason or their sense of propriety. The Greek mind had more than one way of approaching the gods, and if it was often inconsistent in its assumptions, that is common enough in religious experience, which is usually less interested in assumptions than in their results. But behind the variety and the contradictions, certain constant or predominant features emerge at all periods of Greek history and in most parts of Greece on which we have any information.

The Greeks, like other peoples, needed gods to explain what is otherwise inexplicable. To the pre-scientific consciousness, nature, both human and physical, is encompassed with mysteries which cry to be penetrated and mastered. The Greeks solved the matter to their own satisfaction by believing in gods who not only rule the visible world but are at work in the fortunes and the hearts of men. Just as it was natural to explain by divine agency thunder or storms or earthquakes or the growth of crops, so it was equally natural to attribute to gods the inspiring thoughts or qualms of conscience or onslaughts of passion which assail human beings. Both classes of phenomena were outside control or prediction. If it was reasonable to assume that rain was sent by Zeus, it was no less reasonable to assume that a happy thought came from Athene. Even today the workings of the human mind are at least as obscure as the workings of nature, and the Greeks can hardly be criticized for believing that both were in the control of the gods. They were indeed proud of their own powers, but they recognized that much lay beyond their own summons and that all this belonged to the gods. It was therefore important to form relations with them and to solicit the utmost help from them, not merely because otherwise the order of physical nature might be reversed and the earth cease to yield her fruits, but because the very springs of human action depend on unpredictable moments of inspired thought or accesses of energy which man cannot evoke by his own will.

The Greeks saw their gods in human shape, and as such depicted them in sculpture and painting. In the remote past they were probably conceived as animals or birds, and faint echoes of this survive in Homer's use of such adjectives as 'owl-faced' for Athene and 'cow-faced' for Hera, though he himself must have given a different meaning to the words; in the worship of Zeus Meilichios as a snake; in legends in which he took the shape of a bull; in the connexion of Apollo with wolves and mice, of Posidon with horses, of Artemis with bears. But though such beliefs were implied in many local rituals, they were not treated literally in the classical age. If a god had once been an animal, he was now revealed in human shape with the animal as his companion or symbol. This transformation of the gods into the likeness of men was a prodigious stroke of emancipating thought. It means that the Greeks were so impressed by the range and possibilities of human gifts that they could not conceive of the gods in any other shape. They believed that nature was governed by powers similar to their own, vastly stronger, indeed, and active in many spheres beyond human scope, but ultimately of the same kind. Instead of acquiescing in the depressed conclusion that the gods are beyond comprehension and therefore suitably displayed in the uncouth lineaments of beasts or monsters, they tried to impose some order on the whole scheme of things by assuming that it conformed, if not exactly to reason, at least to human nature in an advanced and extended degree.

If the Greeks thought of their gods as possessing human shape and a nature like that of men, they recognized that between gods and men there are enormous differences. The first is that the gods suffer from neither old age nor death. They are able to live as men would like to live if they were not continually dogged by care for the morrow and the consciousness that at any moment they may pass into nothingness. In their undecaying strength and beauty the gods have something denied to men, which makes them objects of awe and wonder. The Greek sense of the holy was based much less on a feeling of the goodness of the gods than on a devout respect for their incorruptible beauty and unfailing strength. If this was a price which the Greeks paid for seeing the gods in human shape, it had vast compensations; for it both made the gods more real than many religions can and gave to men an increased self-respect because they resembled them. It presented an ideal which was indeed not possible to rival but which by its fascinating challenge made men feel that it was good to possess, even in the humblest degree, qualities shared with the gods, and when they saw an unusual manifestation of these in their fellows, it was a matter for delight and pride.

The difference between men and gods goes deeper than this. Pindar, who understood the Greek religious temperament from the inside, states the position:

Single is the race, single
Of men and of gods;
From a single mother we both draw breath.
But a difference of power in everything

Keeps us apart;
For the one is as nothing, but the brazen sky
Stays a fixt habitation for ever.
Yet we can in greatness of mind
Or of body be like the Immortals,
Though we know not to what goal
By day or in the nights
Fate has written that we shall run.[2]

Gods and men are both children of Earth, and fashioned,
as it were, in the same mould, but between them lies an im-
measurable difference of power. The distinguishing quality
of the gods is, above everything, power. They can do on an
enormous scale what man can do only faintly and fitfully,
and much that he cannot do at all; they are assured of unfailing success and satisfaction, but he knows that he is all
too likely to fail. Their power is manifest everywhere, and before it he can only be humble and hope for its help. He
can pray that by some god-given fortune he may for a time
come near to them in the possession of gifts like their own.
He is not severed from them by an absolute difference of
nature; he resembles them in his essential being, which is indeed hampered by grave handicaps but can none the less
at times realize astonishing possibilities of mind and of body.

With such beliefs the Greeks made their images of the
gods in the likeness of men at their most impressive and
most beautiful, so that Artistotle comments: 'Doubtless if
men differed from one another in the mere forms of their
bodies as much as the statues of the gods do from men, all
would acknowledge that the inferior class should be slaves
of the superior.'[3] Though the most famous statues of the
gods have perished, and we have nothing but cheap and inferior copies of such masterpieces as the Zeus and Athene
of Phidias or the Hera of Polyclitus, yet enough survive to
show what visions held the artists' minds. These majestic
figures are indeed beautiful, but with the uncommon beauty
of superhuman power and self-sufficiency. A bronze figure
of Zeus, fished up from the sea off Artemision, suggests
prodigious reserves of strength in the muscular, lightly poised
body and the right arm lifted to throw a thunderbolt (see
Plate 18). Apollo at Olympia has all the grace of young
manhood in his features and his form, but what counts most
is his calm domination of a tumultuous conflict as he directs
it with a kingly gesture of command (see Plate 38). Coins of
Posidonia show a stalwart, menacing Posidon wielding his
trident with a determination well fitted to his title of Earth-

shaker (see Plate 65). The beauty which the Greeks imagined in the gods has no facile or obvious appeal; it is the beauty of divine strength and capacity, of powers in full reserve and emotions in full control. When, on an Olympian metope, Athene helps Heracles to support the firmament, she takes her task easily and shows no sign of strain or effort (see Plate 33). Even when the gods go into relentless action and show their unforgiving spirit towards those who have offended them, they have no emotion in their faces or their gestures, but stand unmoved, like Artemis directing the death of Actaeon on a metope from Temple E at Selinus (see Plate 36) or aiming an arrow at him on a vase by the Pan Painter (see Plate 82). The gods were beautiful in a way that appealed to more than the eye, in their inexhaustible power, their self-reliance, their perfect adjustment of mind and body. When in the fourth century artists aimed less at this ideal of divine strength than at a purely physical appeal, it was a sign that the gods had begun to mean less than in a more exuberant and more full-blooded age.

If the gods resembled men, it was natural to try to bring them into contact with human society, and this affected the Greek conduct of sacrifice and prayer. Once indeed in the far past sacrifices had been made to placate anger and inscrutable gods, and in times of guilty fear even human beings might be offered to them. So Iphigenia was said to have been sacrificed by her father, Agamemnon, to appease Artemis and get favouring winds to enable his fleet to sail to Troy; and here and there in historical times traces of the old practice could be seen in the sacrifice of a doll or of an animal disguised as a man. But sacrifice had by then become literally a feast, at which oxen were slaughtered, and, after a portion had been set aside for the gods, the votaries ate the rest. It was assumed that the gods were present and took their places among the worshippers. Such rites could be cheerful and convivial without lacking reverence. The transformation of sacrifice from an act of expiation to an act of hospitality is typical of the Greek approach to the gods and underlines their notion that the gods ultimately enjoyed the same pleasures as men and appreciated the same courtesies.

A similar directness can be seen in the conduct of prayer. A prayer normally falls into three parts. First comes the Invocation, in which the god is invoked through his titles and shrines, as if this were the respectful way to address him; next comes the Sanction, in which the votary appeals to services which he has himself rendered in the past and which establish his credentials and assert a claim on the god's attention; finally comes the Entreaty in which the god is asked to do something in an urgent need. So when the priest Chryses, whose daughter had been carried off by the Achaeans, prays to Apollo for vengeance, he follows the correct form:

> Hearken, o lord of the silver bow, protector of Chryse,
> Who in Cilla the holy and Tenedos mightily rulest,
> Mouse-god, if ever I roofed for thee a beautiful temple,
> Or if I ever have sacrificed the well-covered thigh-bones
> Either of oxen or goats, accomplish what now I beseech
>    thee:
> Now may the Danaans pay recompense for my tears
>    with thy arrows.[4]

There is no confession of shortcomings, no promise of amendment, but simply an appeal for practical help. Such an appeal is valid only between friends, between men who have proved their devotion and gods who recognize and welcome it. If a man wishes to be helped by the gods, he must pay due attention to them, and then he may reap his reward.

It is one thing to ask the gods for their help, and another to ask for counsel or some revelation of their purposes. The Greeks had their own apparatus for probing the future, though they did not attach equal importance to all its forms. Necromancy was regarded with some disapproval, forbidden in some states, and practised by men of bad character in remote districts. Self-proclaimed sibyls and prophets might have their day of glory, but they too tended to awake distrust, especially when they claimed too much for their powers. The flight of birds was studied with wondering attention, notably before battles, but Socrates probably reflected good military opinion when he said: 'The augur should be under the authority of the general, and not the general under the authority of the augur.'[5] Dreams were more seriously regarded, and were said to come from Zeus, but Homer knew that not all dreams could be trusted, and that it was not easy to say which could and which could not.[6] Such means of prying into the future were treated with different degrees of scepticism, and it is the more remarkable that the Greeks paid great respect to the oracular utterances of gods given by their priests and priestesses, and especially to those given at Apollo's shrine at Delphi. The very setting was enough to inspire an awe-struck sense of the god's overpowering presence. On a ledge under two sheer crags, by the stream of Castalia, where the eye looks down on the plain below, dark-green with olive-trees and flecked with the shadows of eagles, and over it to the sea and to the mountains of the Peloponnese beyond, here among the statues and the treasure-houses was the shrine where Apollo's priestess, the Pythia, fell into a trance and uttered words which were put into order by interpreters and given in answer to the questions of pilgrims. The trust and respect in which the Delphic Oracle was held were a tribute to its wisdom. Whoever controlled it was well informed on public affairs and knew that most private troubles are easily settled by common sense. The prestige of the Oracle survived even such grave miscalculations as its support of the Persians in 480 BC, and was based on its excellent information and its understanding of human nature. Its whole procedure and success illustrate the Greek talent for keeping age-old rites and making sense of them. Men believed that through it they were brought into contact with Apollo, and went away comforted and strengthened.

The gods might live on Olympus or retire to the seclusion of their favourite shrines, but they also moved among men and took part in human affairs. Homer indeed not only makes them fight in the Trojan War but brings them into close contact with his heroes, as when Athene, seen by Achilles alone, takes him from behind by his hair and tells him not to draw his sword on Agamemnon,[7] or on many occasions comes to the help of Odysseus and treats him with a humorous, admiring familiarity. This was a glorious time when the gods walked visibly on the earth, but the vision of them was not quite unknown to later generations. There was more than one kind of occasion when the gods were believed to be present, in feasts, in ceremonial songs and dances, in marriages and funerals. In the world of action their place was often taken by heroes or demi-gods, who would come to the assistance of their own cities, as Theseus and the Aeacids did at Marathon and Salamis.[8] Nor was a private vision of the gods lacking. Pindar must have known what it meant when he told how Iamus prays to Posidon 'at night under the sky' and hears the god's voice in answer.[9] More strikingly, Sappho builds her hymn to Aphrodite on a past occasion when the goddess appeared in immortal, smiling beauty, asked what troubled her, and promised that all would be well.[10] Such experiences were no doubt exceptional, but they show that to the Greeks the gods were real persons, with whom they could enter into a special intimacy. Yet in these relations there is no self-abasement or conscious humility. The glorious splendour of the gods is indeed recognized and respected, but their human companions are not afraid of speaking freely and frankly to them. Even at this level the rules of Greek friendship are at work, and insuperable differences of station do not affect the need for complete sincerity and candour.

This happy conception of the gods was marred at times by their apparent failure to carry out their obligations to men. If men failed like this in their dealings with one another, they would be guilty of disloyalty, but such a charge could hardly be made against the gods, and other explanations had to be found. The simplest was that it was really a man's own fault. If he failed in honour to the gods, he could hardly hope to be treated well and must expect things to go wrong. Nor could the gods in their wisdom take the same view of men and their needs as men took themselves. In the last resort it was a divine privilege to refuse gifts without giving any explanation. But there were other occasions more troubling, when the gods might seem to have deceived or betrayed their friends. The problem arose in an acute form with oracles which often seemed to have foretold the opposite of what actually happened. The impartial and scientific Thucydides notes that this was common in the Peloponnesian War, but does not think it worthy of serious notice.[11] But the belief in oracles was surprisingly prevalent in the fifth century, and their apparent failures provided not only Herodotus with some excellent stories but Sophocles with main themes in his *Women of Trachis* and *King Oedipus*. Both writers believed and did their best to demonstrate that, if an oracle went wrong, it was because it had been misinterpreted. A lesson to this effect was publicly drawn in 447 BC, when an Athenian army in Boeotia, after receiving an oracle which seemed to promise victory, was routed at Coronea. The explanation was that the god had really foretold the victory of the other side, but the Athenians had failed to see it. So when the official memorial to the dead was erected at Athens, the inscription closed by saying:

> To the whole of mankind for the future
> Well did he prove that no oracle will ever fail.

This is a large conclusion to draw from a single case, but it shows how seriously some Greeks treated the matter, and how, rather than admit that the god had deceived them, they decided that it was their own fault. That an oracle should speak ambiguously was to be expected; for gods need not speak with the clarity of men. If men wish to know the divine will, they must give great care to their inquiries, and if something goes wrong, they have only themselves to blame.

Yet, though the Greeks believed that men could form something like friendship with the gods, they knew that it was not a friendship between equals, and that if men presumed too much on it, they would have to pay the penalty. Legends contained many horrifying examples of divine vengeance on men who had gone too far. When Niobe boasted that her children were as beautiful as Leto's, they were destroyed by Apollo and Artemis. When Actaeon accidentally saw Artemis naked, she had him devoured by his own hounds. When Pentheus mocked and imprisoned Dionysus, he was torn to pieces by the Bacchants who worshipped the god. When Marsyas was defeated by Apollo in a competition on the flute, he was flayed alive. Greek gods, like Greek heroes, were moved by considerations of personal honour, and anything which might be construed as an affront to it, excited their anger and called for violent vengeance. Forgiveness was not in their nature, and once a man had offended them, he had no excuse and could expect no mercy.

In their jealousy for their own honour, the gods may also humble men who are too prosperous and enjoy more happiness than is fit for mortals. In the heroic world there is no hint of this. The gods may treat Achilles or Hector with what looks like wilful indifference, but they are not envious of them. But as the Greeks tried to elucidate the divine treatment of men, they evolved the notion that all happiness and success are insecure because the gods dislike them. Such a doctrine was useful in explaining why men in high position fell from it, and appealed, for instance, to Herodotus, who in his account of momentous political changes was able to demonstrate his view that 'deity is envious and interfering'[12] and does not scruple to overthrow even those, like Croesus, king of Lydia, who have served it with exemplary devotion. This belief was certainly not based on any trust in the ultimate justice of the gods, but it appealed to advocates of the Mean, who could argue that, if men listened to them, they would avoid disaster. So Euripides, disturbed by the decline of moral standards, claims that the lack of belief in divine envy can only undermine morality:

> What can the face of Modesty
> Or of Virtue avail,
> When what is unholy has power,
> And henceforward Virtue
> Is neglected by men,

> And Lawlessness rules the laws,
> And men do not strive together
> That the gods' envy may not come?[13]

This was indeed a denial of the old heroic system and opened the door to the view that the envy of the gods might be turned not only against the successful and the great but against all who follow freely their own inclinations.

Once this was admitted, it was perhaps idle to attempt to explain why the gods send suffering and catastrophes. None the less, men could hardly shirk the issue and must take up some position towards it. The more scientifically and less religiously minded might find the answer easy enough, as when Democritus argued: 'The gods, both of old and now, give men all good things. But all things that are bad and harmful and useless, neither of old nor now are they the gifts of the gods, but men themselves come to them through their own blindness and folly.'[14] This was perhaps too simple and left too much unexplained. At least it did not win much support, and other men sought some more transcendental explanation, like that of Heraclitus: 'For God all things are beautiful and good and just, but men think some things unjust and others just.'[15] This assumes that in the end the gods are right, but even that is not really necessary. It was possible, and even reasonable, to argue that these matters are beyond human understanding, that the gods are not to be judged by human standards, but act as they do because they will. So Sophocles tells how Heracles, after a life devoted to self-denying labours, comes to a hideous end. For this no consolation or explanation is offered, but, when it is all over, Heracles' son, Hyllus, says:

> We have seen great deaths and strange,
> And many a sorrow of unknown shape,
> And nothing of these that is not Zeus.[16]

The problem remained unsolved, perhaps because it was insoluble. For most men it would suffice that in the last analysis the decisions of the gods are inexplicable and must simply be accepted, as was to be expected in beings who, despite their likeness to men, could follow without hindrance their own whims and desires and passions.

This uncertainty about the gods made the Greeks slow to accept them as models or judges of human behaviour. Though Homer hints in the *Iliad* that the sorrows of Troy are due to the lechery of Paris,[17] and in the *Odyssey* makes the gods

1. Temple, so-called 'Basilica', at Paestum (Posidonia) in Lucania, southern Italy. 6th century B C.

2. Pediment of the Siphnian Treasury at Delphi, showing the struggle of Apollo and Heracles for the tripod. Middle of the 6th century B C. *Delphi Museum.*

3. Temple of Posidon at Sunium, Attica. Late 5th century B C.

4. The Acropolis, Athens, seen from the west.

5. The Parthenon, Athens, seen from the north-west. 447-432 B C.

6. The Propylaea, Athens. Built in about 435 B C by the archi-tect Mnesicles.

7. Porch of the Erechtheum on the
Acropolis, Athens. 421-407 B C.

8. Delphi with, in the foreground, the temple of Apollo, rebuilt
between 370 and 330 B C on the site of the earlier temple which
was built after 548 B C and completed by 505 B C by the Alcmaeonid
family from Athens.

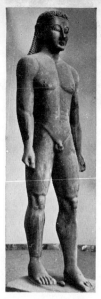

9. Marble *kouros* from Sunium.
Early 6th century B C. Larger than
life size. *National Museum, Athens.*

10. Reclining lion, in limestone, from Perachora near Corinth.
The eye-teeth are restored. Middle of the 6th century B C. Life size.
*Ny Carlsberg Glyptotek, Copenhagen.*

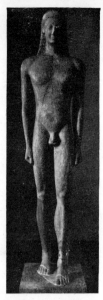

11. Marble *kouros* from Melos. Second quarter of the 6th century B C. Larger than life size. *National Museum, Athens.*

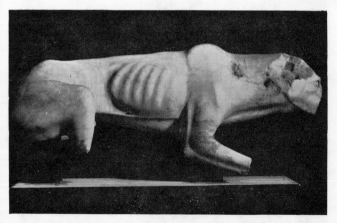

12. Crouching dog, of island marble. Second half of the 6th century B C. Life size. *Acropolis Museum, Athens.*

13. Marble sphinx on top of a column, Naxian work. About 575–560 B C. *Delphi Museum.*

14. Marble man carrying a calf, 'Moscophoros', dedicated by (Rh)onbos on the Acropolis. Mid-6th century B C. Life size. *Acropolis Museum, Athens.*

15. Marble female figure, 'Acropolis 679', with traces of colouring on the hair and dress. Third quarter of the 6th century B C. Life size. *Acropolis Museum, Athens.*

16. Marble female figure, 'Acropolis 686'. Early 5th century B C. Life size. *Acropolis Museum, Athens.*

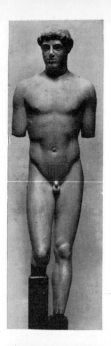

18. Bronze statue of Zeus (or Posidon) from the sea off Artemision. The eyes and the thunderbolt in the right hand are missing. About 470–460 B C. Larger than life size. *National Museum, Athens.*

17. LEFT: Marble statue, 'the Critian boy'. Early 5th century B C. Life size. *Acropolis Museum, Athens.*

19. Limestone three-bodied god, 'Tricorpor', from the right-hand part of the pediment of the temple on the Acropolis. Middle of the 6th century B C. Larger than life. *Acropolis Museum, Athens.*

20. Limestone lioness. About 570–540 B C. Life size. *Royal Palace, Corfu.*

21. Marble head of Gorgon. Early 6th century B C. *Acropolis Museum, Athens.*

22. RIGHT: Bronze charioteer, part of a chariot-group made for the royal Syracusan house of Deinomenes. About 470 B C. Life size. *Delphi Museum.*

23. Limestone lioness. Detail.

24. Marble head, 'the blond boy'. About 480 B C. *Acropolis Museum, Athens.*

25. Marble relief, on a statue-base, of young men with a cat and dog. About 510–500 B C. *National Museum, Athens.*

26. Young men playing at ball, on another side of the same statue-base.

27. Marble relief, on a statue-base, of young men playing at hockey. About 510–500 B C. *National Museum, Athens.*

28. Goddess rising from, or being dipped into, the sea, from the marble back of the 'Ludovisi Throne'. Sicilian or south Italian About 470 B C. *Museo Nazionale, Rome.*

29. Blue-veined marble relief of a lion attacking a bull. About 460–450 B C. *Louvre, Paris.*

30. Marble relief of Orpheus, Eurydice and Hermes. A late copy of a work of the late 5th century B C. *Museo Nazionale, Naples.*

31. Limestone metope of Perseus cutting off the head of Medusa, from Temple C at Selinus. About 550–540 B C. *Palermo Museum.*

32. Limestone metope of Heracles and the Cercopes, from Temple C at Selinus. About 550–540 B C. *Palermo Museum*

33. Marble metope from the temple of Zeus at Olympia. Heracles supports the sky while Athene helps him and Atlas brings him the golden apples. About 460 B C. *Olympia Museum.*

34. Marble metope of Heracles subduing the Cretan Bull, from the temple of Zeus at Olympia. About 460 B C. *Louvre, Paris.*

35. Bronze relief, on a tripod, of Bellerophon on Pegasus. Third quarter of the 6th century. *James Loeb Collection in the Glyptothek, Munich.*

36. Limestone metope of Artemis killing Actaeon, from Temple E at Selinus. Second quarter of the 5th century B C. *Palermo Museum.*

37. Marble Gorgon from the pediment of the temple of Artemis in Corfu (Corcyra). Larger than life size. Early 6th century B C.

approve and aid the punishment of the Suitors by Odysseus, yet on the whole his picture of the gods suggests that they are very little concerned with good or evil either in themselves or in men. They do what they please, and their society is what human society would be if men could follow their desires without risk of failure. That is why they sometimes provide a sort of comic relief. In their divine security they lack something of the dignity which man gains from the short time at his disposal, and if their existence, given largely to pleasure, provides occasions for laughter at one another, there is no reason why men should not join in it. This laughter is in no sense sceptical; it is not even irreverent. It is based on affection for the gods, and even on envy and admiration for their happy state. But it implies a notion of them as almost indifferent to right and wrong, because in their own existence the distinction has little meaning. Nor is their treatment of men based on any clear principle. Their attitude is explained by Achilles to Priam in a parable of two jars at the door of Zeus, one of which contains good things and the other evil. Zeus gives a mixture to some men, to others only evil, and such are driven by hunger over the earth, respected neither by mortals nor by immortals.[18] The gods interfere often enough with men, but they do not, according to Achilles, base their interference on the rightness or wrongness of men's actions. This is the old, heroic outlook, and the Greeks never quite escaped from it.

The notion that the gods are concerned with the doings of men was a natural development in a society which was rapidly becoming more conscious of its domestic and civic obligations. If men felt the need to punish evil-doers, it was only logical to assume that the gods whom they honoured felt the same. The impulse towards such a belief was hardly rational, since evidence for it must always have been dubious, but at least it rose from something deep in the human heart and was not inconsistent with certain elements in the code of honour. If honour bound a man to look after his family and his city, it was natural to assume that the gods supported him in it. Their aid could be invoked for any breach of these obligations, and their curse called down on those who neglected or defied them. Their own lives might indeed display most of these failings, but it was not too impossible a kind of 'double thought' to believe that they punished men for them. Above all, they were the guardians of civic and domestic sanctities. A parent might invoke their wrath on a disobedient son, as the old Oedipus does on the treacherous and neglectful Polynices,[19] and many would agree with

Plato that such a curse would infallibly be heard by the gods.[20] As the guardians of loyalty, they exacted punishment for any violation of domestic rules, such as treachery, murder, neglect of parents, breaking of oaths, and double dealing. From such assumptions it was easy to move to the belief that the gods watched over the doings of men and in the end punished the wicked. We find this belief growing in strength from the sixth to the fourth century, when Plato makes an essential part of his whole scheme a system of rewards and punishments after death which would redress the injustices of this world.[21] He was not the first to put forward such a scheme, nor the last, and his ideas were in due course to make their contribution to the Christian notion of Hell. But even if he won a wide acceptance for his ideas, which is doubtful, they were not impressed very violently on the Greek mind, and there is no sign that any Greek felt the nagging fear of torment after death which haunted the Roman Lucretius or takes such sinister forms in the paintings of Etruscan tombs.

Even this left much unexplained. The Greeks saw that suffering is not always the result of misdoing, and that the wicked have a regrettable talent for avoiding it. They might try to explain the sorrows of the innocent by playing with theories of hereditary guilt, in which the sins of the fathers are visited on the children. So Solon, in the conviction that the wrath of Zeus may be slow but is none the less sure, foretells his vengeance:

> So Zeus avenges. And, unlike a mortal,
>     He is not swift to wrath at each thing done.
> Never does one with sinning heart escape him:
>     But in the end he's utterly made plain.
> One may pay now, another later. Vengeance
>     Will come to those who flee the wrath of God
> Full surely after. Innocent are punished,
>     Both children and their children after them.[22]

Yet though this looks like a theological theory, it is in fact more social and political. Solon is concerned with a social class, with the rich who abuse their position and their privileges, and we cannot dispute that from this point of view what he says has a measure of truth; for if a class treats its responsibilities too frivolously, there is a real probability that it will have to pay for it. Another version of this theory was that certain families had something like a hereditary curse, an inborn inclination to violence which appeared in successive generations and brought disaster to each. This could be applied alike to Oedipus, whose father, Laius, defies the oracles of the gods, and whose sons, Eteocles and Poly-nices, die in war against each other, and to the House of Atreus, in which crime leads to crime until the gods inter-vene to stop the hideous sequence of bloodshed. In these stories the Greeks shaped their notions of heredity, of qual-ities in a family which seem to be inextricably bound to it, and which lead to destruction. This too had something to be said for it, but neither it nor the social theory of Solon cov-ered the whole problem or dealt with all cases of suffering. Indeed, the Greeks seem to have shrunk from any such comprehensive theory, perhaps because it was at variance with their common belief that a man makes his own destiny. He was indeed to some degree the plaything of the gods, but he was not a mere puppet, and it was of some importance to morality whether he acted of his own choice or not.

If the Greeks were no more successful in finding answers to these questions than later generations have been, it does not mean that they were not deeply concerned with moral issues. If divine sanctions played some part in their ethics, it was because they felt strongly that right and wrong ought to be a concern of the gods because they were emphatically a concern of men. In so far as they did what they thought to be right not for hope of ultimate reward but simply be-cause their own natures impelled them to it, it is a tribute to the strength of their human instincts and the satisfactory nature of their main assumptions and beliefs. When Aristotle speaks about things which are 'good in themselves', he re-peats what had long been a feature of Greek thought, and though it could be applied to much which we should regard as lying outside the sphere of morality, it had none the less a real relevance to conduct. Indeed, one of the most notable of Greek contributions to ethical thought was precisely the idea that the goodness of an action lies in the action itself, and that a man may be judged by the degree of choice and decision which he gives to it. This was perhaps a develop-ment of the system of honour. A man felt that he owed cer-tain obligations to himself, to his own idea of what he ought to be, and if he carried these out, he was satisfied and asked for no further reward. Even if he believed that the gods watched his actions and approved of them, he still acted from his own inner promptings and found in the gods the kind of approval which he thought to be natural in such a case. Because they believed in their own human nature and liked to see it harmoniously at work, the Greeks developed a morality which was founded on human values and able to operate freely and confidently without worrying too much what the gods thought about it.

In such matters the gods were treated as a whole, as the embodiments of a single divine principle which worked equally in all of them and displayed the divine as such in its relations with men. But the gods had none the less their own spheres of action and their own personalities. Whatever their origins may have been—and it is quite possible that these were indeed various, that Zeus was the Sky-god of the Indo-European peoples and Aphrodite the fertility-goddess of the Aegean—yet when we see them at work, the gods are not only formed into a divine family but each combines control of some part of physical nature with a special function in regard to men. The first office may be older and more fundamental than the second, but it is easy to see how one could pass into the other. Zeus, the lord of the sky and 'cloud-gatherer', is also the father of gods and men, who as *paterfamilias* on Olympus is as unpredictable in his wrath as he is in his storms on earth. Apollo is the god of light, and therefore of inspiration, which does for the soul what light does for the world. Swift and fierce as the light, he is the master of song and prophecy, who raises men above their common level by the sudden accesses of power which he gives to them. Aphrodite is born of the sea, and though she is indeed the goddess of physical desire, which is equally strong in gods, men, and beasts, yet she is more than this. Like the sea, she sheds an alluring enchantment which may too easily lure her victims to destruction, and, like it, she is unaccountable in her distribution of delight and suffering. In contrast to her stands Artemis, who presides over wild nature, over untamed animals and the whole world of creatures outside the haunts of men. She dwells on the hills, and her virginity is appropriate to her character as one who loves solitude. To her young women make their last offerings before marriage and, by an understandable paradox, call for help in childbirth. Hermes is the master of flocks of herds, who embodies the mischief and the cunning of primitive creatures and patronizes craft and guile. Posidon is the lord of the sea, and therefore of storms and earthquakes, and he is held in honour by cities, like Athens, which live from the sea and owe their wealth and power to it. Athene, whose first task may have been to protect the olive-trees without which no Greek population can survive, is a civic Artemis, who stands for the national spirit in its intelligence, its virginal independence, and its love of fine things. Hera, the queen of the gods, pales before her husband, but has her maternal place as the protectress of children. Dionysus is the god of the grape and therefore of ecstasy and intoxicated excitement. It looks as if these gods and goddesses began their careers as powers of nature but were given other fuctions and attributes by worshippers who wanted more from them than the control of the elements and equated their powers with other powers in the human mind and heart.

Below the Olympians there were other divinities, who did not equal them in honour but had their own place in local cults and belief and might be asked for help in matters for which the Olympians were too august or remote. The powers of animal nature fostered a belief in nymphs, whose existence was bound to the trees or the waters which they haunted; in satyrs, with human forms and the tails of horses or goats, who stood for primitive bodily instincts and became a symbol for revel and riot as the companions of Dionysus; and in Pan, the goat-god, who has much in common with them, but, after appearing to the runner Philippides during the Persian invasion of 490 BC, won so special a place in Athens that he was thought to have a place on Olympus. Such minor figures had their own shrines and cults and were believed to give help to men who watched over crops and herds. In their physical ebullience they looked after the breeding of animals, and it was appropriate that they should have something in common with them. Quite different, but at a similar secondary level of importance, were the heroes, great men of the past, who may have had divine blood in them, but who were exalted after death to honour because of what they had done, for the special degree of power and vitality in them. They belonged to public life, and were thought to be present at feasts or with armies on the march or in battle. They had their cults, where offerings were made, and songs might be sung to them. They helped to fill the world with divine guardians and to see that all needs for divine support were met.

Greek religion, which began with the individual and the family, passed easily into the domain of the city-state, which had some characteristics of the family and cherished the individual. Every city was protected by its own special deity, who had his or her own temple and festivals. At these festivals, which were still feasts and combined the worship of gods with the gaiety of men, a whole people might feel that it was protected by watchful presences and united in its admiration for them and its sense of belonging to them. Such was the Panathenaea at Athens, which is depicted on the

frieze of the Parthenon. Here are young men riding bare-
back on horses, priests driving oxen to sacrifice, men carrying
pitchers with offerings, women standing and talking in grave
dignity, all in the calm and friendly presence of the gods
(see Plates 47, 48, 49). It is a happy, decorous holiday, with a
high pomp but without pomposity, easy and natural and not
self-conscious. What binds the people together is their reverence for the goddess who has made them great and to whom
they have erected the most splendid shrine in Greece. Its
spirit may be seen in the words which Aeschylus wrote to be
sung indeed by guardian divinities, but which reflect with
happy fidelity the feelings of Athenian men and women:

> Joy to you, joy of your justly appointed riches,
> Joy to all the people, blest
> With the Virgin's love, who sits
> Next beside her father's throne.
> Wisdom ye have learned at last;
> Folded under Pallas' wing,
> Yours at last the grace of Zeus.[23]

The goddess who presided over the destinies of a city was
responsible not only for its existence and its safety, but for its
civic harmony and its grace of life, and it was right that she
should be honoured by all who enjoyed them.

By stressing and sanctifying local loyalty, the cult of national deities emphasized the divisions between Greek states.
It is true that in times of universal peril, like the Persian
invasions, the Greeks united and could honestly say that they
were fighting for common gods. It is also true that some
great shrines, like Olympia and Delphi, were genuinely Hellenic, and access to them was guaranteed by international
pacts. But the more a god was honoured in his own city, the
more he was expected to give help against others. In theory
this should have led to theological complications, in which
a god, who was worshipped in more than one place, fought
against himself. But this did not trouble the Greeks any
more than it has troubled Christian peoples in more recent
times. What matters is that by stressing national differences
these cults were yet another obstacle to Greek unity. Trust
and pride in the gods made men feel that they were better
than others and more likely to succeed in war. If they were
in a patently inferior position, they might invoke the gods
of Hellas against aggressors and appeal to them above national divisions. So the Melians did, when they made their
pathetic attempt to frustrate the sinister designs of Athens

in 415 BC: 'Nevertheless we trust that the gods will give us fortune as good as yours because we stand for what is right against what is wrong.'[24] But such an appeal was ineffective because national feeling over-rode its assumptions. If the Greek gods were part of a common inheritance, they were also a potent influence in keeping that inheritance divided.

Greek religion was based on a belief in power in a wide sense, and especially in power to make the most of capacities and opportunities; and the gods, who embodied this belief, helped men by strengthening their capacities in many kinds of activity. Religion stressed the dignity of action and gave an inspiring impetus to it. But in this it neglected something which we associate with religion, and indeed demand from it. It was not till their civilization began to collapse that the Greeks formed their first glimmerings of the brotherhood of men, and even then it was more an abstract ideal than a purposeful conviction. What we miss in Greek religion is love. The gods may have their favourites among men, but in moments of crisis they desert them, as Apollo deserts Hector, when he is faced at last by Achilles, or Artemis deserts Hippolytus, when Aphrodite destroys him. Men may respect the gods and make friends of them, but there is nothing that can strictly be called a love of God, and, though Aristotle was dimly conscious of such a possibility,[25] one of his school says: 'It would be eccentric for anyone to claim that he loved Zeus.'[26] If such a relation was missing between gods and men, it lacked divine encouragement between men themselves. The Greeks had their deep affections for family and friends, but these had little support in religion. Zeus was certainly the god of the hearth, of friendship, and of hospitality, but he asked more for loyalty than for love. Indeed, just because the gods personified power, and because this was so strong in local and national allegiances, they could hardly accept so uniting a principle as love. Though the Greeks admired order and sought it everywhere in the scheme of things, they did not see that its most enduring basis is to be found in the affections. So their religion, with its cult of power, fostered forces which inevitably conflicted with one another, and failed to discover a single, unifying principle embodied in the gods and worthy of universal imitation by men.

If the survival of Greek religion was assured by its cults, it was also helped by its ability to absorb new ideas without spoiling its essential qualities. Just because it had no creeds or scriptures, it permitted a wide variety of speculation on the nature and the functions of the gods, and was normally

tolerant provided that its fundamental assumptions were not
challenged. It was none the less bound to be attacked by
critics, and from at least the latter part of the sixth century
this attack came from more than one quarter. One movement was intellectual and claimed that current beliefs in the
gods were not tenable by intelligent men. An obvious target
was the anthropomorphic conception of them, and Xenophanes put his finger on a vital spot: 'Yes, and if oxen and
horses and lions had hands, and could paint with their
hands, and produce works of art, as men do, horses would
paint the forms of the gods like horses, and oxen like oxen,
and make their bodies in the image of the several kinds.'[27]
In the place of the familiar gods he offered: 'One god, the
greatest among gods and men, like unto mortals neither in
form nor in thought.'[28] So sweeping a proposal was perhaps
more than most men could accept, because it would remove
the whole conception of divinity by setting it beyond comprehension. If a god is not like mortals even in thought, they
can enter into almost no relations with him, and the religious
instinct is starved for lack of communion with the divine.
These criticisms, and the real difficulties behind them, were
understood by a few bold thinkers. Heraclitus indeed rejected the anthropomorphic conception of God, but held that,
in some vastly superior way, he still resembles man: 'The
wisest man is an ape compared with God, just as the most
beautiful ape is ugly compared with man.'[29] In the fourth
century this line of thought was taken up with consummate
power by Plato and Aristotle, both of whom concluded that
God is not shaped like man but has some affinity with him,
whether, as in Plato, in his deep concern about right and
wrong,[30] or as in Aristotle, as pure mind and the prime
mover of all being.[31] Such ideas cannot have filtered very
deep among ordinary men, but they were the final criticisms
of some inadequacies in the traditional theology.

At the same time, as men moved away from the belief that
gods resemble men, they sought to find a single principle behind the various gods and even to define it as what is essentially divine. Just as the Greeks often speak of 'god' without
specifying what particular god they mean and imply that all
gods have something in common, so imperceptibly they felt
their way to the notion of a single divine power which may
indeed be embodied in separate gods, but is none the less real
and central in the scheme of things. So even Pindar, who
was well aware of the different personalities and functions
of the Olympians, seems to go behind them in his search for
something which transcends them:

God reaches, as soon as thought, his ends:
God, who can catch the wingled eagle
And overtakes the dolphin in the sea.[32]

Once this general idea of divinity had been suggested, it led to speculations which were indeed reverent, but had in them some touch of agnosticism, as when Simonides, on being asked by Hieron about the nature and the attributes of the gods, kept on putting off his answer, until, when pressed for it, he said that the longer he thought about the question the darker it became.[33] From this position some indeed advanced to an idea of divine omnipotence, like the Pythagoreans, who believed: 'It is not the case that for the gods some things are possible and some impossible, as rationalists think, but all things are possible',[34] and were to this extent the precursors of Plato. On the other hand, there were those who sought not to make godhead the ultimate power, but to find something else behind the gods which was more powerful than they. They might call this Necessity, as Simonides does when he says that even the gods do not fight against it,[35] or Fate, which, according to Herodotus, a god cannot escape,[36] or combine both in an ingenious scheme, as Aeschylus does when he makes Prometheus say that Zeus cannot alter what is ordained, which is itself the work of the Fates and the Furies in obedience to Necessity.[37] In either case we can see men feeling their way towards a notion of an ultimate order to which even the gods have to conform and which removes any imputation of irresponsibility or personal whim from the governance of the universe. It was part of the Greek desire to discern an underlying discipline in even the most intangible events and to bring the gods under a rule comparable to that which they exercised over men. Such ideas at first did not seriously interfere with the belief in the familiar gods, but added mystery and majesty to them. But they opened the way to vast speculations and new systems, and in due course they made their influence felt.

A second attack was made on moral grounds, and again Xenophanes was in the van: 'Homer and Hesiod have ascribed to the gods all things that are a shame and a disgrace among men, thefts and adulteries and deceptions of one another.'[38] Once the gods were regarded as overseers of right and wrong, such an attack was fully justified, nor was it repugnant even to the orthodox. It is true that when Euripides made play with the savagery or the lechery of the gods, his attacks were viewed with anxious suspicion by Greeks who felt that he was undermining the old faith. But against him we may set Pindar, who was unquestionably pious, and often corrects in a quiet way stories to the discredit of the gods, as when Demeter was said to have eaten the shoulder of Pelops, or Heracles to have fought in Pylos against Apollo, Posidon, and Hades.[39] In the next century Plato took up the cause and exonerated the gods of all the faults and crimes attributed to them. This was the logical conclusion of the movement, but the movement itself was inevitable as soon as the gods were thought to be concerned with good and evil and expected to practise what they preached.

Parallel with these movements came something more sinister and more destructive, when divine power was quoted by men as a precedent for their own behaviour. If Zeus in the *Prometheus Bound* of Aeschylus behaves like a young tyrant and asserts the rights of superior strength, there is no reason why men should not model themselves on him. This happened on at least one ugly occasion. When the Melians invoked the gods of Hellas against the unjust oppression of the Athenians, the Athenians answered:

'So far as the favour of the gods is concerned, we think we have as much right to that as you have. Our aims and our actions are perfectly consistent with the beliefs men hold about the gods and with the principles which govern their own conduct. Our opinion of the gods and our knowledge of men lead us to conclude that it is a general and necessary law of nature to rule wherever we can.'[40]

Such an attitude certainly owed something to the general corruption of standards in the Peloponnesian War, but it shows that, if one side of Greek religion could move towards monotheism and morality, another side, derived exclusively from the notion of divine power, might be turned to this disastrous end. If the gods stood for narrow national interests, the Athenians made a legitimate deduction about their character and the example which they set to men. This situation arose at a time when religion had been much shaken by political and intellectual convulsions, and was no doubt abnormal in the sense that in better conditions it would not have arisen. But its emergence shows a real weakness in the Greek religious outlook. Its ability to absorb new ideas was determined by its conception of the gods as embodiments of power. So long as this was satisfied, the religious conscience could make no real complaint. But the trouble was that the best ideas of the time were not concerned with this, and not only failed to be absorbed, but were in some cases rejected with contumely and hostility. The faith which had been an inspiring source of strength when Greece was young and healthy, was in danger of becoming a menace when the social structure which held it was shaken by the corruption of war.

Greek religion embodies an impressive paradox. Though it gives a first place to divine power and insists that the gods bestow this in different ways on men, we are often surprised to find the Greeks not rejoicing in their achievements but coming to the melancholy conclusion that life is a shadow of smoke and man a dream. So Sophocles, whose life was coterminous with the greatest days of Athens, gives voice to a common sentiment:

Never to have lived is best, ancient writers say;
Never to have drawn the breath of life, never to have looked
    into the eye of day;
The second best's a gay goodnight, and quickly turn away.[41]

This is hardly what we should expect from a poet who moved as an equal among the great men of the Periclean age. Nor is it enough to say that it is not a personal confession but a dramatic utterance. What matters is that the Greeks often said this kind of thing, and there is no doubt that their zest for life was countered by a sense that nothing is worth doing and that it is best not to be born.[42] It is as if, after their prodigious exertions, they asked what they had gained by them, and the answer was 'Nothing'. Such a mood was perhaps inevitable in an outlook which called insistently for vigorous action and expected a man to live all the time at the top of his powers. It was only natural that at moments his spirits should flag and that he should feel that the effort demanded of him was too much. If nothing but darkness lay ahead, there was indeed little reason to make any effort, and it might well be comforting to lament the futility of everything.

The Greeks were aware of this and did not deny that there was truth in it. They accepted the melancholy fact that much of life is indeed frail and unsubstantial and that even the greatest endeavours might fail, but they believed that it could suddenly be enhanced and illuminated and made full and wonderful. This could happen only if they exerted their powers to the utmost and set them harmoniously to work. At such times a man realizes his full nature and, if the gods are willing, enjoys an exalted happiness, which is indeed like their own in its celestial completeness. It is not for him to command this or to do more than hope that unaccountably it may be granted to him. It may last for only a short time; at the best it cannot come often. But when it comes, it is beyond price. Pindar speaks of it in calm and comprehensive words:

> Man's life is a day. What is he?
> What is he not? A shadow in a dream
> Is man, but when God sheds a brightness,
> Shining light is on earth,
> And life is sweet as honey.[43]

Though the Greeks knew that they must not and could not usurp the rights of the gods, and that hard efforts often brought no reward but a sense of emptiness, they knew also that at times they were given something which brought them close to divine felicity. This belief lay at the centre of their lives and sustained them in all their misgivings that the generations of men wither like the leaves and that impartial death waits at the end for all alike.

# CHAPTER IV

# CITY AND INDIVIDUAL

THE GREEKS thought that the city-state was the natural and right unit for human society. They knew that it did not exist among other peoples, but that was just another sign of the inferiority of barbarians, and if any argument was needed for it in Greece, they had only to make comparisons with the past, when men lived precariously in villages and were able to satisfy little more than their barest needs. They felt that the city-state was a natural development first of the family and then of the village, and that it had the advantages of both without their limitations. Nor did they look beyond it to some more embracing unity. Even in the fourth century, not long before Alexander was to unite all Greece and a large part of Asia under his single suzerainty, Plato and Aristotle still regarded the city-state as the logical end of social development and framed their conceptions of ideal societies on it. Though the future lay with the vast dominions of the Hellenistic monarchies and of Rome, the Greeks did not foresee it or desire it; so deeply committed were they to their own system and its multifarious attractions. It did not occur to them that it might be desirable in the interests of peace and security to transform the cultural unity of Greece into a political unity. The city-state remained the focus of their loyalties and their thinking. Even when Athens and Sparta built empires in the fifth century, these were largely coalitions, in which the members maintained a considerable degree of local autonomy, and there was little sense of corporate identity. If the predominance of the city-state was enhanced by powerful local traditions, it kept its hold by the solid advantages which it offered to its citizens and by its guarantee of an ordered framework for their lives.

The strength of the city-state is expressed by Aristotle when he says that 'It comes into existence for the sake of mere life, but exists for the sake of the good life'.[1] It was

77

this good life that the Greeks valued and were willing to defend at any cost. If we ask wherein lay its particular excellence and what advantages it had over other ways of life, the answer in the first place is the rule of law. The Greeks believed that, whereas barbarians were at the mercy of an irresponsible monarch, they themselves had laws which protected their lives and property and enabled them to shape their careers as they wished. Though the Babylonian and Hittite law-codes show that Asiatic monarchies had evolved complex systems of law many centuries before the first Greek law-givers, the Greeks were either ignorant of them or dismissed them, as they dismissed the laws of the Medes and Persians, because they implied a different conception of law allowing the final fount of authority to be the whim of a single man. In Greece, whatever type of government might exist, the law was still regarded as the foundation of society. Just as the democrat Pericles claims for the Athenians: 'In public affairs deep respect for the laws prevents us from breaking them',[2] so his opponent, King Archidamus of Sparta, claims that his people are 'to rigorously trained in self-control to be able to disobey their laws'.[3] Respect for the law was deeply ingrained in the Greek character and strengthened alike by poets like Aeschylus, who was much concerned with its functions and its sanctions, and by philosophers like Heraclitus, who spoke for most Greeks when he said: 'The people must fight for a law as for a rampart'.[4] They felt that because they were ruled by law, they had an inestimable advantage over the slavish millions of Asia, who were driven by fear of an autocrat and lacked the discipline which they themselves accepted willingly and proudly. So Herodotus makes the exiled Spartan king, Demaratus, say to Xerxes about the Spartans: 'Being free, they are not free in all things, but the law is over them for master, which they fear in their hearts much more than your people fear you.'[5] The Greeks attached a paramount importance to the rule of law and had good reasons for doing so.

Laws were believed to embody ancient traditions and to give a precise form to what had for centuries been canonized by custom. In Homer the kings are the repositories of traditions or 'dooms', which they guard as their inherited right and interpret either themselves or through their judges.[6] The danger of such a system is that the knowledge of the traditions is confined to the king and his agents, and that his subjects cannot tell how they stand with regard to them, and are therefore easy victims of injustice. Hesiod knew of this system and complained of it:

Tumult arises when Justice is dragged away, and whenever
Eaters of bribes seize her and give dooms by crooked
   decisions.[7]

The only safeguard was to have codes of law which were
known to everyone, and from the seventh century famous
law-givers codified tradition and custom in many parts of
Greece and provided a proper legal structure for civic life.
Once laws were codified and made public, sometimes by
being carved on stone in a public place, there was no doubt
of their contents, and a festering grievance was removed.
Such codes could cover both constitutional and private law
and lay down both how a city should be governed and what
penalties should be paid for crimes against the person. They
also dealt in detail with property, inheritance, the owner-
ship of slaves, and kindred matters. The Greeks did not in
principle set any limits to the fields of conduct covered by
law, and though some systems came in for severe criticism,
it was more for their constitutional prescriptions or the se-
verity of their penalties than for any breach of what we
might consider the rights of man. It was thought so much
better to have laws than to be dependent on the personal
whims of kings and their agents that laws were allowed to
invade spheres which, in our view, should lie outside their
control. In their love of liberty the Greeks saw that the
rule of law, no matter how invasive, was essential to their
well-being. Nor in fact did the structure of Greek society
allow laws to be too irksome or to interfere unduly with
individual enterprise. If they had tried to do too much, they
could not have been carried out. What they did was to
provide a firm basis on which men could pursue orderly
lives.

   Since laws were derived from ancient custom, it was only
natural to assume that they had a divine sanction and represented in some sense the will of the gods. This was the
Greek equivalent to the notion of natural law, and it was
held by Heraclitus, who said, 'All human laws are fed by
the one divine law'.[8] Historically this may mean no more
than that the state took over responsibility for offences
which had once been the concern of the family, but it also
meant that the laws were revered because ultimately they
were sanctified by the will of the gods. When in a simile
Homer tells how the gods are angry at unjust judgments
and send storms and floods to punish the city which toler-

ates them,[9] he reflects at an early stage the notion which
the Greeks continued to cherish, that the laws are under the
protection of the gods because they embody the divine will
and can be transgressed only at the risk of divine wrath.

Though the Greeks did not believe in progress with the
happy optimism of the nineteenth century, they saw that
men had risen from humble and even brutish origins, and
attributed a decisive part in this to the power of law. So
Protagoras described man's conquest of physical nature as
a divinely ordered process and told how Zeus sent Hermes
to earth with the instructions: 'Give a law from me, to kill
as a disease in the city the man who cannot partake of
decency and justice.'[10] The root of this theory is that men
are educated and improved by law and that civilization
rests on it because it inculcates moral and social virtues.
Sophocles expresses a very similar idea in a famous song,
where the wonderful achievements of man are praised and
the conclusion is reached that of all these law is perhaps the
most fundamental:

> With cunning beyond belief,
> In subtle inventions of art,
> He goes his way now to evil, now to good.
> When he keeps the laws of the land
> And the gods' rule which he has sworn to hold,
> High is his city. No city has he
> Who in rash effrontery
> Makes wrong-doing his fellow.[11]

The Greeks believed that law is an essential element in
prosperity because it expresses the will of the gods who
watch over it and support it. Fortunately the Greek conception of the likeness between men and gods meant that law
was not, as in oriental countries, largely concerned with religious rites, but gave its main attention to the behaviour of
men with each other.

If the laws reflect the will of the gods, it must be wrong to
disobey them, and Socrates would not have seemed so para-
doxical as usual when he said that they should never be
disobeyed, because disobedience to them at one point undermines their whole authority, and because they protect a
man's country, which is even more holy than his family.[12]
It is therefore at first sight remarkable that one of the
most renowned of Greek tragedies, Sophocles' *Antigone*, presents as its heroine a young woman who defies the order of
Creon, king of Thebes, that her brother shall not receive

burial because he is a traitor, and dies for it. That Sophocles'
sympathies are with Antigone against Creon, there is no
doubt, and yet we may be surprised by her defence:

> It was not Zeus, I think, gave this decree,
> Nor Justice, dweller with the gods below,
> Who made appointment of such laws to men.
> Nor did I think your edicts were so strong
> That any mortal man could override
> The gods' unwritten and undying laws.
> Their life is not today and yesterday
> But always, and none knows from where they came.
> I would not pay the price before the gods
> Of breaking these for fear of any man.[13]

This suggests that there may be a conflict between the laws
of men and the unwritten laws of the gods, and that when
such a conflict arises, the laws of the gods must be obeyed.
The mere assumption that such a conflict is possible might
seem to indicate that the divine basis of law is not always
taken for granted, and if this is so, Sophocles might be
thought to attack one of the most precious beliefs of the
Periclean age. But the conflict in the *Antigone* is not to be
explained in this way. The command which Antigone defies is
not a law in the true sense, but the irresponsible edict of a
tyrant. In forbidding burial to a dead man, Creon defies the
laws of the gods, and his edict has no validity or claim to
respect. His action is but another example of the importance of having laws codified and not leaving them to the
private whim of political authority.

None the less we may ask whether the Greeks regarded all
laws alike as just and thought it wrong to change them. That
this was a real problem is clear from Aristotle's discussion of
it and his inability to come to a clear decision; for while he
admits that since laws are based on ancient customs, some of
which may well be barbarous, 'even when laws have been
written down, they ought not always to remain unaltered',
yet he is frightened of too many changes because 'a readiness
to change from old to new laws enfeebles the power of the
law'.[14] But though the difficulty is real enough in theory, in
practice it could be solved on the simple principle that,
though human laws should embody the will of the gods, it
was obviously not easy to do this correctly and therefore
changes were permissible. So though Pericles might seem to
go far indeed when he said that 'laws are all the rules approved and enacted by the majority in assembly, whereby

they declare what ought and what ought not to be done',[15] this
is logically tenable if we associate it with his other statements
that the Athenians obey the unwritten laws of the gods[16] and
that those who offend against them should be punished.[17] His
doctrine is that the Athenian people is the only authority
which can rightly determine how the laws of the gods should
be applied to men. It is a bold proposition, but it is not inconsistent with traditional Greek views, even though it displays
more confidence in the sovereign people than many Greeks
would allow. At the same time it shows that the conception of
law as custom sanctified by the gods was not so rigid or so
intractable as we might expect.

Greek laws were concerned with the character of political
constitutions, and the changes which came with the decay of
monarchy. By the end of the eighth century hereditary king-
ship had almost ceased to count in Greece. It had either been
restricted to a formal post, as at Athens, where one of nine
magistrates was called 'king', or severely circumscribed, as at
Sparta, where there were two kings, who had indeed considerable powers when they commanded in the field, but
very little in peace or over domestic affairs. It is true that in
Thessaly minor princes still held office, and that in other
places, notably Cyrene, hereditary kings kept some of their
old state. But on the whole from about 700 BC monarchy in
the old sense hardly existed and was replaced by written constitutions, which gave power to a fixed class or number of
persons, whether small or large. The Greeks divided these
classes into oligarchies and democracies, in the first of which
power belonged to a few, in the second to the people as a
whole. If originally the rule of the few meant the rule of
nobles who had shared among themselves the old rights of the
kings, with the passing of time it came to mean the rule of
the rich, whether their wealth came from land or from trade,
and its foundation was often a property qualification. A democracy, on the other hand, claimed that its government was
in the hands of the whole free male adult population. This
was a later growth than oligarchy and was always less
common. Democratic institutions may have existed in Chios
in the middle of the sixth century, but it was Athens which,
after the reforms of Cleisthenes in 507 BC and of Ephialtes in
461 BC, took the lead in democratic practice and gave confidence and courage to other states which wished to imitate
her. The whirligig of politics might vary the pattern, but on
the whole oligarchies prevailed in the Peloponnesian states,
which were allied with Sparta, and democracies in the Ionian,
which had traditional ties with Athens. The difference be-

tween government by the few and by the many was a formidable factor in Greek politics. Each form developed its own sentiment and its own characteristics, and each had a profound distrust of the other.

Greek oligarchies were based on the familiar aristocratic notion that their members were superior to other men in birth and blood. They speak unaffectedly of themselves as 'good' or 'noble' or 'just' and of their political opponents as 'base' and 'bad'. Their acquaintance with animals taught them the virtues of breeding, and they believed that their own descent was a guarantee of excellence and gave them a title to rule on the principle that 'it is natural that the best counsel should come from the best men'.[18] Though they might fear, distrust, and dislike those who were not of their own class, within it they showed a high degree of tolerance and of appreciation for the varieties and vagaries of human personality. The aristocratic age presents us with formidable figures like Archilochus, who spoke his mind with unrestrained candour on anything that touched him, and Alcaeus, who varied the thrills of political agitation and civil war with a keen sense of enjoyment and a fine eye for natural things. Perhaps only such a society could have allowed enough liberty for a woman like Sappho to develop her genius without hindrance and to follow her own vision in contrast to the robust, male activities around her:

> On the black earth, say some, the thing most lovely
> Is a host of horsemen, or some, foot-soldiers,
> Others say of ships but I—whatsoever
>    Anyone loveth.[19]

If men like Archilochus and Alcaeus strike us by their uncontrolled reactions and their readiness to give full vent to the first impulses that assail them, this is treated with a confident style and an engaging forthrightness. Such men were fully themselves and encouraged by their fellows to be so. They took pleasure in their clothes, their weapons, their ornaments, their hair. They enjoyed wine and feasting, and would welcome any excuse for them, from bad weather to the death of a political enemy. Even on campaign they would find occasions for conviviality, whether on board ship or 'standing to' before battle. They believed in themselves, their position, and their privileges, and made them the basis of a gallant and generous existence.

The strength of this life was that it was founded on the land. Greek oligarchs were in the first place landed proprie-

tors, and what this meant to them was made clear when, like
Theognis, they were expropriated by social revolution:

> Cyrnus, I have heard the voice of the crane crying shrilly,
> It comes to me with its message that it is time
> To plough. It sets my black heart beating
> That other men have my fields with all their flowers.[20]

Living on the land meant also that its owners knew about
horses and dogs and bred them for their points, that they
enjoyed hunting the hare, which can be so exciting that 'it
makes even a lover forget his heart's desire',[21] or looking at
a prancing mare which is 'so admirable that it holds the eyes
of all who see it, both young and old'.[22] The land too had its
immemorial cults, which fostered the songs and dances in
which young people delighted and which provided an education in rhythm and balance and style. It was not without
reason that a nameless poet praises Earth, Mother of All, as
the source of these graces and festal dignities:

> The ploughland's heavy with wheat of life, in the pasture
> Cattle abound, good substance fills the house,
> Fair women are in their city, and with just laws
> They rule, in wealth and great prosperity.
> The boys go proudly in fresh-blossomed gladness,
> The girls with flowery dances and gay heart
> Gambol and frolic in the turf's soft flowers
> If thou giv'st grace, great Queen, Goddess of Beauty.[23]

Nor was this aristocratic life narrow, at least in the sixth century, when landowners took to trade and foreign adventures.
Alcaeus' brother, Antimenidas, fought with the king of
Babylon and may have taken part in Nebuchadnezzar's campaign against Jerusalem. On the legs of a colossal statue before
the great temple of Abu-simbel are carved the names of
Greek mercenaries who fought for Psammethichus II, king
of Egypt (594–589 BC). Sappho's brother, Charaxus, was
entangled by a famous courtesan in Egypt and was severely
rated by his sister for it. Pindar says of one of his patrons:

> He would cross to the Phasis in summer seasons,
> And in winter sail to the shore of the Nile.[24]

and though he speaks metaphorically, his metaphor is
founded on fact. The aristocratic world was indeed solidly
based in its home, but from this it extended its horizon with
travel and trade and war.

The Greek oligarchies came to power by getting rid of the old monarchies, and they based their position on the rule of law. The chief catch-word of their politics was *eunomiâ*, or lawfulness, by which they meant not that the laws were good but that they were kept, that their regime at least guaranteed order. Pindar expresses their ideal when he says of Corinth:

> There Lawfulness dwells, and her sisters,
> Safe foundation of cities,
> Justice and Peace, who was bred with her,
> Dispensers of wealth to men,
> Golden daughters of wise-counselling Right.[25]

If law protected them on the one side from the claims of irresponsible monarchs, it protected them on the other from the claims of the unprivileged populace. Their position was often threatened, and they developed a class-consciousness which might mean that they looked more to the past than to the future, and were more concerned to keep what they had than to develop new opportunities. But though the aristocratic life was confined to a few, it solidified Greek civilization and gave a special pattern to it. Those who enjoyed its liberties were expected to shoulder the responsibility for maintaining them, and their respect for individuality was guaranteed by the social frame which held it. The combination of law and liberty, of active life and an instinctive respect for the arts and even for the sciences, the transposition of the old sense of honour from a heroic to a social significance, the ideal of the full man who makes the most of himself and his chances, the happy union of natural exuberance with a sense of style which does not impede it but gives it a direction and a distinction—all these were strong in Greek life, and all were the results of the oligarchic system. This had indeed its own *douceur de vivre,* but it was built on firm convictions of a man's worth and possibilities.

Democracy, which reached its most advanced and most active form in Athens, arose from a series of extensions of power to a bigger and bigger class, until in the end this included all free male citizens. It soon developed a marked character which distinguishes it from modern democracies in more than one way. It had, at least in its early days, an undeniably aristocratic tone. A tradition of taste and elegance was maintained by noble families like the Alcmaeonids, who, despite their wealth and lineage, welcomed the new system and took a leading part in establishing it. From them a sense of style spread to a wider circle and was en-

riched with a new strength and scope. Artists and writers,
conscious that their public was no longer a few select families
but a whole people, gave a new meaning to traditional forms
and spared no effort to be worthy of their wider horizons.
So too in civil and domestic life, as we see it painted on
vases, there is nothing vulgar or mean. Style and taste are
always dominant and have an aristocratic distinction, as if
they belonged to men who knew instinctively how to infuse
any occasion with charm and dignity.

This aristocratic quality was made possible by the existence
of slavery. By it the common people of Athens had a degree
of leisure which is almost unknown in a modern proletariat.
It is easy to condemn this system, but its defects were not
perhaps so grave as we might think. Athens differed from
many slave-owning societies in its large proportion of free
men to slaves, which has been calculated as about two to one.
This is nothing like the scale of slavery in imperial Rome or
any oriental empire or even classical Sparta, and the reason
was partly that Athens was too poor to buy or maintain
slaves in large numbers. Slaves were usually employed not on
the land but in mines and quarries and ships, and slave-
women were often nurses in well-to-do homes. They were
seldom Greek by origin, since sentiment resisted such an
exploitation of Greeks by their countrymen. Of course, as
everywhere, slaves in Athens were at the mercy of their
masters and might suffer from their whims and vices, though
no doubt good tempers and common prudence assured that
they were quite often well treated. We cannot doubt that the
distinction of the Athenian democracy owed much to slavery,
since it provided the free citizen with leisure to spend his
time on other matters than finding his livelihood. The majority of citizens must still work hard, but at least they had
times when they could leave their work and attend to public
affairs or the graces of leisure. However much we may deplore slavery in any form, we must remember that in Athens
the variety of origin in slaves and their relatively small numbers prevented the development of anything like a 'colonial'
economy. The citizens composed the greater part of the
population and almost the whole indigenous part of it. And
this was indeed democratic in the extent of its powers and
its responsibilities.

A second feature of the Athenian democracy was its ebullient vitality. Once the people found themselves in control of
their own destiny, their powers were released in many new
directions. In poetry, in which hitherto Athens had not been
very distinguished, the songs and elegiacs of the aristocratic

age yielded to the magnificent form of tragedy, which was itself a development of improvised rustic songs and impersonations connected with the worship of Dionysus, but was now raised to an extraordinary power and dignity. The Parthenon and the Propylaea (see Plate 516) still show in their ruins how the new democratic architecture surpassed that of previous generations in scale and richness, and the sculptures on the former depict in mythical form the new spirit at work. The east pediment shows the birth of Athene on Olympus: a celestial world of dreaming calm is awakened by the sudden appearance of a fully grown goddess in its midst, and stirs with awe and amazement at the sight. The west pediment shows the struggle of Athene and Posidon for the possession of Attica: two great divinities are in conflict, with a fearful sense of power and effort (see Plates 43, 44). Each pediment presents a different aspect of the national myth. If the eastern shows what the emergence of Athene, the divine power of intelligence, means even on Olympus, the western shows what such a goddess must be, that even the god of the sea quails before her. Both are concerned with power, either emerging or fully in action, and both present to the eye the unexampled force which the Athenians felt in themselves and believed to be inspired by the gods.

This formidable, irrepressible spirit was not content to stay at home and win its victories solely in domestic affairs. Like the triumphant champions of the French Revolution, the Athenians felt an irresistible urge to burst beyond their frontiers and to impose the blessings of their system on other Greeks. Their more conservative neighbours were naturally alarmed, but did not deceive themselves about the facts, as we can see from the words of a Corinthian at Sparta in the negotiations before the outbreak of the Peloponnesian War in 432–431 BC: 'Their view of a holiday is to do what needs doing; they prefer hardship and activity to peace and quiet. In a word, they are by nature incapable of either living a quiet life or of allowing anyone else to do so.'[26] This meant that in the fifth century the Athenians gradually transformed the alliance which had been formed to fight against Persia into an empire whose members paid tribute to Athens. The allies remained independent in their own affairs, and the recompense for their tribute was not only that the Athenian fleet protected them against Persia, but that Athenian armies were ready to fight for them against the no less imperial designs of Sparta. But more important than this was that Athens liked its allies to have democratic governments. Though this was a source of deadly hatred in dispossessed oligarchs, it meant that the allies were commonly content with their condition, even though it was one of inferior partners and allowed their money to be used not only for ships but for buildings which glorified Athens. With such resources Athens was a potential menace to all Greek cities who did not share her views and to foreign countries, like Egypt, which promised fields for conquest. Pericles spoke with justice of the far-flung scale of Athenian enterprise: 'For our adventurous spirit has forced an entry into every sea and into every land; and everywhere we have left behind us everlasting memorials of good done to our friends or suffering inflicted on our enemies.'[27] Athens provides a signal refutation of the optimistic delusion that democracies are not bellicose or avid of empire. The confidence of the Athenian people could not be held within local bounds and sought fresh fields of adventure at the expense of others.

A third characteristic of Athenian democracy was freedom of speech. This was regarded as fundamental and interpreted in a generous manner. The Athenians had almost no laws of libel or slander, and their political debates were as candid and vituperative as their private and forensic quarrels. They seem to have welcomed a remarkable degree of outspokenness, and to have felt that it was part of the game to vilify one's opponents. In politics, of course, this had its dangers, when demagogues like Cleon and Hyperbolus carried the assembly of citizens with them by the crude violence of their words, and we can understand why they provoked answers in a like spirit, as when Andocides says of Hyperbolus: 'I am ashamed to mention the name of Hyperbolus; his father is a branded slave, who up to the present day works in the public mint; he himself is a foreigner, a barbarian, and a lampmaker.'[28] More surprising is the unlimited licence allowed to comedy, which stuck at nothing in deriding public characters. Aristophanes makes unbridled fun of philosophers like Socrates, generals like Lamachus, politicians like Cleon, and poets like Euripides. This fun is reckless, scurrilous, and often ill-natured. His Socrates is a verminous charlatan, his Lamachus a preposterous fire-eater, his Cleon a violent and revengeful crook, his Euripides a conceited and touchy exhibitionist. In these caricatures there must be an element of truth, since otherwise they would fail to make their full effect. Aristophanes was not frightened by any influence or reputation and knew exactly where to plant a wound. No modern society, however democratic, would allow such licence, and it is a notable tribute to the self-assurance of the Athenians, that even in anxious times of war they were able to tolerate and enjoy it. It had of course the virtue that it was a safety-value for emotions which might otherwise have taken more violent forms than mere words. Athenian democracy may sometimes have suffered from it, but the assumption that it was indispensable to a civilized community was in the main a source of strength. A people which can laugh at itself is well armed against many catastrophes.

Though hereditary monarchy disappeared early from the Greek scene, autocracy was by no means unknown in the form of 'tyranny'. The word comes from the Greek *tyrannos*, which is said to have been of Lydian origin, and may have meant no more at first than 'king'. Tyrannies arose in several ways and from different causes. Tyrants might be the champions of a less privileged class against established aristocrats, or of national claims against foreign encroachment, or of the populace against corrupt government, or of one section of aristocrats against another. They usually appeased Greek sentiment by some concession to legality, whether in the mode of their appointment, or the limits imposed on it, or their respect for existing laws, but they often kept themselves in power through their own armed supporters. At times they might pass their rule to their sons in imitation of hereditary kings, but usually it came to an end with their own lives. Tyranny was a product of the struggle for power between different sections of the population and reflected discords so sharp that some sort of autocracy was thought to be the only remedy for them. It was most prominent in the sixth century, when the social struggle was exacerbated by the emergence of a new trading class with the development of handicrafts, the invention of coinage, the opening of new foreign markets, and the hunger for land which pressed hard when the population increased to any noticeable degree. In the fifth century it was most likely to succeed in outlying places, like Sicily, where Greek populations were exposed to the menace of Carthaginian conquest, and a good general might call for special powers to defend his city. In later years the Greeks condemned tyranny almost without reservation, but at the first they were not averse from it, and it is noteworthy that even in Attic tragedy the word *tyrannos* is often used, with no unfavourable associations, in the sense of 'king'. Modern views of it are coloured by the discussions of Plato and Aristotle, both of whom condemned it as the worst possible form of government. By their time it had outlived its original usefulness and developed vices which were as familiar as they were ineradicable.

In the sixth century Greek tyrants exercised on an en-

hanced scale the cultivated tastes of the aristocracy and used
their superior financial resources and political influence to
make themselves notable patrons of arts and science. Poly-
crates of Samos not only maintained poets summoned from
abroad, like Ibycus and Anacreon, but employed the famous
goldsmith, Theodorus, the greatest doctor of the age, Demo-
cedes, and the engineers who built his mole and his under-
ground aqueduct, which may still be seen at Tigani. When
Pisistratus and his son ruled in Athens for a large part of the
century, they gave a new splendour to the city by building
the Hekatompedon on the Acropolis and encouraged sculpture in its portrayal of lions, horses, and dogs as well as of
men and women. In the fifth century powerful Sicilian
tyrants, like Theron of Acragas and Hieron of Syracuse, not
only sponsored some of the most beautiful of Greek coins
(see Plate 65), but were generous hosts of such poets as
Simonides, Bacchylides, Pindar, and Aeschylus, and the
temples of Acragas still bear witness to the pride of life that
planned them. The tyrants were able to patronize the arts on
a lavish scale because they were wealthier than the old nobles,
and of course such patronage was an important means for
getting themselves known and admired. In an age of refined
splendour they knew how to give to it a special impres-
siveness.

A revealing light on tyrants is shed by the poems which
Pindar wrote for them. He himself was a Theban aristo-
crat, and in so far as he had any defined political views, he
supported the rule of the landed nobles and made his best
friends among the aristocrats of Aegina. But in Sicily he was
undeniably impressed. Here indeed were wealth and display
such as were not to be found in Greece proper, and here too
was an air of royal majesty which touched him very deeply.
For him Hieron and Theron were not upstarts who had
fought their way to power, but kings with all the glamour of
the heroic past, whose lot was indeed admirable and enviable:

> One man is great in this way, another in that,
> But at the peak of all
> Are kings. Look no farther than this.
> I pray you may walk exalted
> All these days of your life.[29]

Pindar felt that kings could exercise, as almost no other men
could, the time-honoured virtues of generosity and hospitality, and were thus equipped in a special degree for the
good life. But he felt also that their high state not only

imposed special obligations on them but exposed them to special dangers. Just as in one place he draws for Hieron a distinction between the bad king, Tantalus, and the good king, Pelops, so elsewhere he points a lesson from more recent times, and his words contain almost a warning:

> The excellent kind heart of Croesus does not perish,
> But the pitiless soul
> That roasted men in his bull of brass,
> Phalaris, in every land
> His evil name overwhelms him.[30]

After his first excitement, Pindar came to see that there was something wrong with tyranny and that he himself was not happy in its company. He found the atmosphere of its courts oppressive, and disliked the intrigues and flatteries which flourished in them. He felt that his own, more quiet way of life was better, and that it was perilous to pass beyond the Mean.

Pindar's final rejection of tyranny shows how a serious and sensitive man judged it from his own experience. In the generation or two before him Ibycus, Anacreon, and even Simonides seem to have felt few qualms about it, but it seems always to have excited the distrust and dislike of land-owning aristocrats. Theognis sees nothing wrong in overthrowing a tyrant 'who devours the people'.[31] Alcaeus mocks Pittacus as a vulgar upstart and derides him for his splay feet, his boastful bearing, his big belly, his personal filth, and his drunken habits.[32] Such dislike, based on social differences and strengthened by class-war, had no difficulty in justifying itself, and a whole set of propositions was advanced to show how a tyrant was corrupted by power. It was claimed that he is moved by arrogance and envy, and, since there is no one to control him, 'he meddles with ancient customs, violates women, and kills men without trial.'[33] In other words he offends against the deepest Greek proprieties by acting above the law. Of course this was not equally true of all tyrants, and it was admitted on behalf of the Athenian Hipparchus that on the whole he observed the laws,[34] but in the end the temptations of power were too strong to resist, and tyrants sought above all the satisfaction of their own whims and appetites. By the fourth century no abuse was too bad for them. Plato depicts a tyrant as one who is so dominated by fear and lawless appetites that he creates around him a havoc as great as that in his own soul,[35] and Aristotle tells how tyrants become the tools of

flatterers, destroy the confidence of their subjects by sending
spies among them, are given to self-indulgence and sensu-
ality, prefer bad men to good, and are indeed the incarna-
tion of injustice.[36] Such were the men who might seize
power if either oligarchies or democracies ceased to be vigilant in looking after themselves.

Though both the few and the many feared tyrants, this
was no bond between them and did not abate their hatred
for each other. Indeed, much of Greek history in the sixth
and fifth centuries was determined by this conflict. The
class-war turned mainly on the possession of land in a
country where it was never abundant and a growing population cried for a full use of every acre. Feuds between the
landed and the landless were not only long and bitter, but
fortified by passionate arguments on both sides. Outbursts of
hatred and contempt show how violently the threatened or
the dispossessed reacted against their opponents. When Alcaeus hears that his adversary Myrsilus is dead, he cries out
that he must get drunk to celebrate the good news;[37] another poet, who had lost everything, prays that he may live
to drink the blood of his enemies;[38] in some cities the
governing oligarchs took an oath: 'I will be an enemy to the
people and will devise all the harm against them that I
can'.[39] Such sentiments found their bloodthirsty counterpart
in action. In Corcyra in 427 BC the democrats slew everyone
whom they suspected of being an enemy; in Athens in 404
BC the government of the Thirty put to death the democrats
who opposed them. In these conditions the old notion that
a man should injure his enemies became the first article
of a political creed. In the heroic world it was applied mainly
to those who had insulted a man's honour; it was now applied
to all political adversaries and had behind it the embattled
solidarity of a social class.

Not all men took part in these bitter struggles, and there
must have been many who sought to keep their cities free
from it. How seriously some could treat it can be seen from
two passages of high poetry, which deal with it from opposite sides and yet show a considerable similarity in their
approach. The first may have been written by Simonides,
though we do not know when or for whom. What survives
is the beginning of a Hymn to the Fates in some place where
they are held in high honour:

Listen, Fates, who sit nearest of gods to the throne of Zeus
And weave with shuttles of adamant

Inescapable devices for counsels of every kind beyond
 counting,
Aisa, Clotho, and Lachesis,
Fine-armed daughters of Night,
Hearken to our prayers, all-terrible goddesses
Of sky and of earth;
Send us rose-bosomed Lawfulness
And her sisters on glittering thrones,
Right and crowned Peace, and make this city
Forget the misfortunes which lie heavily on her heart.[40]

The Fates are summoned as the highest authorities next to
Zeus and asked to send to the troubled city the Hours, who
in the traditional manner are named as the three great civic
virtues. This comes from the aristocratic side, which boasted
of the possession of them, but it shows how deeply the
poet feels in a time of trouble and in what a solemn mood
he invokes the gods to restore peace and happiness. Against
it we may set some lines of Aeschylus, which are not directly
inspired by a similar crisis, but show how fear of it weighed
even on this stalwart champion of democratic Athens, when
he prays that his city may be kept free from intestine
strife:

Ne'er, I pray, ne'er may that
Root of evil, civil strife,
Rage within her boundaries;
Ne'er may the earth's dust drink of the blood of her children,
And wroth thereat thirst greedily after revenge,
Blood in requital of blood;
Rather in friendly communion
Gladness be rendered for gladness,
All at one in love and hate.
Therein lies a cure for human ills.[41]

Both poets have the same desire that the city should not
be divided and rent by internal warfare; both appeal to a
love of peace and order as indispensable to the enjoyment
of the good life. But though many Greeks would echo these
sentiments, it did not save them from vicious quarrels and
bloodthirsty struggles for power and position. Just because
such struggles took place within a single city, they were
all the more violent, since political differences were sharpened by personal injuries and resentments, and hatred throve
on an intimate knowledge of what other men did and wished
to do.

The savagery of the class-war reached unprecedented proportions when Athens fought Sparta in the Peloponnesian War, and each side had friends in the other camp who fostered its cause. Athens set up and supported democracies, Sparta oligarchies. This meant that the horrors of civil war were sometimes added to those of international war, and what this produced can be seen from Thucydides' account of events in Corcyra and the spirit which was, as he says, typical of many Greek cities:

> 'Fanatical enthusiasm was the mark of a real man, and to plot against an enemy behind his back was perfectly legitimate self-defence. Anyone who held violent opinions could always be trusted, and anyone who objected to them became a suspect. . . . Family relations were a weaker tie than party-membership, since party members were more ready to go to any extreme for any reason whatever. These parties were not formed to enjoy the benefits of the established laws, but to acquire power by overthrowing the existing regime; and the members of these parties felt confidence in each other not because of any fellowship in a religious communion but because they were partners in crime.'[42]

This grave indictment, delivered by a man remarkable for his detachment, shows the disastrous results of the class-war in Greece. Because of its competing claims men forgot their respect for law, for the family, for the gods, for the city. The balance on which Greek civilization was so delicately built was broken, and the spirit of personal ambition, nursed in an atmosphere of grievance and conspiracy, came naked to the surface. Thucydides describes a situation similar to another described three hundred years earlier by Hesiod, who tells of the horrors of the Age of Iron:

> Father and child will quarrel and bring the end,
> Guest with host will quarrel, and friend with friend.
> No brother will claim from brother the love once claimed,
> And parents will quickly age, dishonoured and shamed,
> And men will scorn them and bitter words they'll say,
> Hard-hearted, no longer god-fearing. They'll not repay
> The cost of their nurture, but might their right they'll call,
> And ravaging men will break through a city-wall.[43]

Just as this age was a parody and a perversion of the Age of Heroes which preceded it, so civil strife in places like Corcyra was a hideous travesty of the system of personal honour and of the right of the individual to be himself.

Thucydides ascribes this breakdown of order and decency to the demoralizing influence of war, and he is certainly right. Greek states lived at so bare a level of subsistence and were held together by so slender ties that a long war had a devastating effect on them. It meant that men were deprived of much to which they were accustomed, and took every step in their power to regain it. It also meant that the machinery for enforcing the laws was undermined by the absence of men on foreign service and by new openings made to the more reckless and more unscrupulous elements in the population. Just as in Athens the sober foresight of Pericles yielded to the fanatical frenzy of Cleon, so in other cities it was the more violent politicians who came to the fore because in such a time their very violence made an appeal to people stupefied by effort and privation and brutalized by bloodshed. The liberty which the circumstances of Greek life almost forced upon it could too easily turn to anarchy when the restraining influence of law was weakened.

Yet, though civil discord was an endemic and perhaps irremediable disease of Greek life, it was none the less possible to maintain for considerable periods a working balance between the need for public order and the demands of the individual to do as he pleased. In the sixth century the oligarchies succeeded, despite considerable troubles, in providing a generous measure of dignity and honour at least to the privileged minority; in the fifth century the democracies maintained their ideals in practice until they broke themselves in over-exertion and by asking for too much. Constitutional government, perilously poised between tyranny on the one hand and anarchy on the other, had always to be on the watch in its own defence, and it is not surprising that the Greeks were extremely suspicious of men who seemed likely to attack it. The violence of their political emotions is a tribute to their belief in their systems of life and the claims of their traditions. The mood in which the Athenians banished Themistocles or the Spartans Pausanias, whom Thucydides calls the two most renowned Greeks of their day,[44] might look like base ingratitude, but it was none the less a testimony to a determination to see that the frame of society was not undermined by personal ambition and delivered to the indescribable horrors of civil war.

Though Greek history abounds in political failures and disasters, and though its courageous experiments were to close in the absolute monarchies of the Hellenistic kings, yet it has its own grandeur. Greek politics were at least

founded on the conviction that men have a right to live
for their own sake and not for the sake of some exalted
individual or supernatural system. It was indeed difficult to
decide whether this should be applied to a whole people or
to a privileged section, but the mere fact that it existed
is a tribute to the Greek respect for human personality.
Even more impressive is the way in which this ideal was
translated into fact through the rule of law. Law guaranteed liberty, and even if it imposed limitations on what
the individual could do, these were not irksome in view of
the assurance which it gave to him that he could pursue
his own life in his own way. The Greeks saw that liberty
cannot exist without law, and that only in their combination
can a man realize himself among other men.

# CHAPTER V

# THE GOOD MAN AND THE GOOD LIFE

---

WHEN ARISTOTLE SAYS that 'good' has as many senses as 'being',[1] he shows that the Greeks found as much difficulty as we do in defining it and applied it to all kinds of subject with a wide variety of meanings. But in one fundamental respect they differed from us. In English 'good' has, among its multifarious tasks, a special function in relation to conduct and to people with reference to their conduct. A 'good' man or a 'good' action is a man or an action that satisfies our moral standards and wins our approval for that reason. The Greeks, too, applied 'good' to men and actions, but the approval so indicated was dictated by somewhat different considerations. In principle, just as a thing was good in their view if it fulfilled its function properly, so a man was good if he fulfilled the possibilities of manhood in certain directions. They started with a clearer assumption on the nature of goodness than we do, and they came to conclusions about its application which contained much that we should accept but much else that we should regard as outside its sphere. In the fourth century Aristotle gathered together many strands of traditional thought and presented his own impressive philosophy of the good, but, though he embodies much ordinary opinion and bases his doctrine largely on accepted beliefs, his theory is his own creation, a masterly organization of many half-conscious or unelaborated views into a philosophical system. The ordinary Greek notion of the good was uncritical and unphilosophical. We might explain this by the absence of sacred books prescribing the whole duty of man, but it is probably wiser to assign it to the practical and experimental character of Greek thinking, which tended to reach conclusions only after it had tested theories by experience.

The Greeks distinguished between the good man and the

good life, and gave to each its own associations and vocabulary. If we begin with the good man, it is noteworthy that for Homer the notion does not, as such, exist. A man is called good because of his proficiency in this or that activity. He may be 'good at the war-cry', like Menelaus; or 'good in strength', as Hector wishes his small son to be; or 'good in boxing', like Polydeuces.[2] He may be a good king, like Agamemnon; or a good doctor, like the sons of Asclepius; or a good squire, like the squire of Achilles.[3] This use of the word applies the notion that goodness lies in the fulfilment of a function, but the idea that man as such can have a function and fulfil it is not mentioned. Perhaps, if Homer had been pressed on the point, he would have said that a good man is one who excels in all the qualities which a heroic age demands of its great men, and that of this type Achilles is the pre-eminent example. But he says nothing of the matter, no doubt because he is sufficiently absorbed by his vision of a heroic ideal to feel no need to analyse or amplify it. But later generations, who saw that the heroic ideal had to be brought up to date in a changed world, were more explicit. The calls of the city-state fostered a conception of the good which was more conscious, more detailed, and more social than anything adumbrated by Homer.

The basis of this was the assumption that there are four cardinal virtues—courage, temperance, justice, and wisdom. The English words do not quite represent their Greek originals, and we must not read too many associations or subtleties into them. The establishment of this quartet is thought to have been the work of Pythagoras, and even if he inherited it from traditional wisdom, he may have given it a neater form and a wider currency. In any case it endured from the sixth to the fourth century and even later; it was known to Aeschylus, approved by Pindar, explained by Socrates, subjected to a far-reaching analysis by Plato and Aristotle, and strong enough to survive the disintegration of Hellenism and to play a basic part in the new ethical doctrine of the Stoics. It embodied what the Greeks admired in theory and sought in practice, and most of them would have thought that, if a man exercises these virtues and applies them to each situation as it arises, he does as much as can be expected of him.

The list is not canonical and has no special authority, but it represents average opinion on character and conduct and is a fair guide to the standards by which the Greeks judged each other and themselves. Originally, perhaps, the list looked at men from four different angles, physical, aesthetic, moral, and intellectual, and reflected the concept of the 'four-square' man in all its fullness and balance. Physical courage was highly valued at all times by a people much given to war, and we cannot doubt that the average man would not trouble himself with niceties about its nature, but respond with admiration to its imaginative appeal, as Aeschylus does when he speaks of the Seven against Thebes:

> Those hearts were iron-proof; there burn'd the clear
> Spirit of war unquenchable; they seem'd
> Lions, whose eyes are even as gleaming swords.[4]

Temperance was largely a matter of style, of doing things without display or vulgarity, of behaving without arrogance. If it was highly regarded in aristocratic circles as an essential element in good manners, it was also something that Pericles praised in the Athenians: 'Our love of what is beautiful does not lead us to extravagance; our love of the things of the mind does not make us soft.'[5] Justice is essentially a moral quality, the natural tendency to obey the rules and laws of a civilized society and to treat other men to their deserts, and is well described by Simonides as 'rendering to every man his due'.[6] It is primarily social in its application. The word *dikê*, which we translate 'justice', seems to be derived from the boundaries of a man's land and conveys metaphorically the notion that he should keep within his own sphere and respect that of his neighbour. Wisdom is certainly an intellectual quality. In early days it is applied to any activity of the mind and denotes skill in the arts, to say nothing of capacity for philosophy, science, or politics. Obviously it was not easy to find all four virtues equally prominent in a single man, but it was not impossible, and a respect for them certainly indicated a well-balanced view of what a man ought to be.

This straightforward conception received a new depth from its application to civic life and the needs of the city-state. When courage was prized both for its own sake and for its use to the city, it was seen that mere physical bravery was not enough and that a man was the more admirable if he faced danger in the knowledge that he fought for a cause and was for that reason ready to sacrifice his life. This lies behind Pericles' words on the Athenians who have died in battle: 'The man who can most truly be accounted brave is he who best knows the meaning of what is sweet in life and what is terrible, and then goes out undeterred to meet what is to come.'[7] Temperance was naturally associated with the doctrine of the Mean and with the precept of the Delphic Oracle, 'Know thyself', which implied that if a man really knew himself and his limitations, he would curb his ambitions and his pride. If a man had peace in himself, he would help to maintain it in the city, and Pindar shows what this means:

> If a man would set the common good
> Of his townsmen in calm weather, let him search
> For the bright face of great-hearted Quiet,
> And uproot from his mind angry Strife,
> Giver of poverty, hated nurse of the young.[8]

Since liberty depended on the rule of law, justice was inevitably associated with the possession of good laws and obedience to them. So, perhaps somewhat regretfully but conscious of the time in which he lives, Simonides sets up against the old ideal of the four-square man the ideal of the good citizen:

> Who is not base, nor too helpless,
> If he knows the right that helps a city,
> Is a sound man.[9]

Justice passes imperceptibly from social relations to political and covers almost every aspect of government under law and the qualities which it requires. Wisdom too had a significance for politics. Not without reason were the Seven Wise Men all politicians of one kind or another, and Thucydides shows what it meant in his time when he praises Themistocles because he 'was supreme at doing just the right thing at the right moment' and admires Pericles for his foresight and correct forecast of events.[10] In these several ways the old heroic and aristocratic virtues were given a new significance in political life and made to conform to its demands.

The growth of philosophy in the fifth and fourth centuries meant that various attempts were made to bring the four cardinal virtues into a more comprehensive whole, either by finding some common principle behind them or by subordinating three of them to a fourth. It was seen that courage could exist elsewhere than on the field of battle and might be more admirable if it were moral than if it were physical. Democritus thought that the truly brave man must have some understanding of justice: 'By understanding and knowledge of just actions a man becomes both brave and right-minded.'[11] Socrates advanced from this to the view that courage is a

form of knowledge,[12] and Plato came to the conclusion that
the highest form of courage is to face the seductions of
pleasure without yielding to them,[13] and thus made it almost
a form of temperance. In fact it was soon realized that temperance, justice, and wisdom were so closely related in any
responsible person that they were ultimately indistinguish-
able, and though Socrates regarded knowledge, and Plato
justice, as the unifying and central principle, there is very
little to choose between them, since both views assume that,
if a man has a right judgment on himself and his circumstances, he will be in a good position to be just to others.
Once wisdom, in this sense, took pride of place, the concept
of it could be developed in new directions. If Heraclitus was
right in saying, 'Wisdom consists of saying what is true',[14] it
followed that the pursuit of truth was a good in itself, until
Aristotle, like Pythagoras before him, regarded it as the
highest kind of life, comparable to the contemplative activity
of God. But the ordinary man was probably content to avoid
such attempts at systematization and to accept the four
virtues as a reasonable guide to behaviour, especially since
they allowed him both to realize his individuality and to take
a full part in the life of his city.

If the four virtues stood for an ideal of a balanced and
controlled personality, their antithesis lay in those faults
which destroy such a balance and work havoc both in individuals and in societies. If one of the four was lacking, it was
likely that the others would be impaired. It is, for instance,
typical of Greek thought that Aegisthus, who seduces Clytaemestra and plots with her the murder of her husband, lacks
not only temperance, as an adulterer, and justice, in his
bullying arrogance, but also courage. He leaves Clytaemestra to kill Agamemnon and from Homer onwards is
called 'cowardly'. In general it was thought that not only the
individual virtues but their unity and balance were destroyed
by *hybris* or arrogance. It might well reflect an inner lack of
courage; it certainly meant a defiance of self-control and temperance; it led inevitably to injustice in its disregard for the
rights of others; it often ended in folly when its possessor
thought that he could by unjust methods secure the impossible. The Greeks gave this vile eminence to arrogance because, more than anything else, it defied their ideal of a
harmonious and restrained self, and their deep political distrust of it was equalled by their moral condemnation. They
saw that it grows with feeding and creates other evils as
great as itself. To this process Aeschylus gives almost a
mythology:

> Ancient Arrogance loves to bring forth
> A young Arrogance among the evils of men,
> Soon or late, whenever
> The appointed birth-hour comes,
> And a fiend for her companion,
> Irresistible, unconquerable,
> Unholy Recklessness,
> Two black curses in the home,
> Like the parents that begat them.[15]

Unbridled arrogance shocked the Greeks morally, politically, and aesthetically. It was, in their view, quite different from legitimate ambition, since this was possible only with a large degree of self-control and even of self-sacrifice. At all periods from the heroic age to the fourth century arrogance was regarded as the worst of evils, because it made chaos of all attempts to achieve balance and harmony in the self and because it scorned the social obligations on which the city-state depended.

The conception of the four cardinal virtues may seem strange to us, because, even in its philosophic form, it goes well beyond the limits of mere morality and appeals to intellectual and other considerations. But that is simply to say that the Greek conception of the good was more generous than our own and embraced much that we admire but shrink from exalting to the dignity of a virtue. Such a creed was well suited to the Greek character because it encouraged its more positive and more creative qualities, and has indeed its relevance to any society which respects the intellectual virtues and thinks that they are worthy of pursuit for their own sake. It had, of course, its limitations. It excluded any high degree of specialization. A man should be good at his job, but that must not prevent him from being a good citizen and conscious of his civic duties. He could not shirk his responsibilities by retiring from the world, and anyone who did this would be regarded as 'either a god or a beast'.[16] The Greek system did not allow for solitary contemplatives, and when philosophers, like the followers of Pythagoras, wished to develop a doctrine which had certain mystical implications, they none the less took part in politics. Nor did men of letters and science live in untroubled seclusion. Thales, who was so accomplished a pioneer of astronomy that he foretold the eclipse of 28th May 585 BC, took a prominent part in urging the Ionian Greeks to unite and resist the advance of Persia;[17] Aeschylus' epitaph, possibly written by himself, mentions that he fought at Marathon, but not that he wrote tragedies;[18] Sophocles acted as a general in the Athenian expedition against Samos in 440 BC;[19] Empedocles was not only a scientist and a religious reformer, but a courageous leader of the democratic party in Acragas;[20] Plato tried bravely, if unsuccessfully, to put his political ideas into practice in Syracuse. Most Greek writers and thinkers were amateurs, but their work, so far from suffering from this, gained much from its association with the living scene and the thoughts and doings of ordinary men. They were fortunate to live in an age when specialization was not necessary, but they took full advantage of the busy world about them to enrich their work and to keep in touch with contemporary events.

A more serious criticism of the Greek conception of the good man is that it applies almost exclusively to the naturally gifted and leaves the rest out of account. It demands not only intelligence but inborn qualities of courage and even temperance, which are not given to everyone. With this the Greeks themselves would not have disagreed. They thought that goodness, in their sense, was indeed not possible for everyone, nor did they see any reason why it should be. Since they did not believe very strongly in the salvation of individual souls or regard a special form of goodness as necessary for this, they felt no need to assume that all men should have an equal chance of being good. For them it was a privilege allotted by the gods, just as the gods allotted good and bad fortune. But it was still open to a man, who had the right gifts, to make the best use of them and to deserve the adjective 'good' because of his moral and intellectual eminence. They did not feel that such an ideal was ultimately impracticable, and they were quite ready to accept approximations to it. They felt not indeed that every man is free to fashion his own destiny, but that, being what he is, he should make the most of himself, and in this sense Heraclitus was right, when he said 'Character is destiny'.[21] Such a belief gave great importance to the individual and allowed him to develop in his own way. The important thing was that he should reveal his powers in *aretê* and became the kind of man who is at once a full human being and a healthy member of society.

When we turn from the notion of the good man to that of the good life, it is clear that the word 'good' has another sense. We may take as our text an Attic drinking-song which lays down the four best goods:

For a man health is the first and best possession,
Second best to be born with shapely beauty,

And the third is wealth honestly won,
Fourth are the days of youth spent in delight with friends.[22]

It is a question not of what a man is but of what he has,
not of his essence but of his accidents. The standard of judgment is different from that applied to the good man, and the
results appeal more directly to happiness as the end. None
the less the qualities of the good man are to some degree pre-
supposed and taken for granted, and it is unlikely that one
who was not a good man in the Greek sense would enjoy the
good life. Indeed, the song points to this when it says that
wealth must be honestly won, and the connexion with the
good life is clearly stated by Sophocles, when he gives a
somewhat similar list of admirable things:

> The fairest thing of all is to be just;
> The best to live without disease; most sweet
> Power to win each day the heart's desire.[23]

This binds the two notions together. It shows that the good
life is impossible for a man who disregards the rights of his
fellows, and hints that happiness is not tenable with a bad
conscience. But once we admit this connexion, we can
analyse the good life on its own merits. The drinking-song
is not to be taken as gospel, but it represents common opinion and stands for much that was highly valued. To its four
blessings we may perhaps add good fortune and fame, which
are also highly and commonly praised, but the first is im-
plicit in the whole notion of happiness and the second is
almost a necessary result of it. If we examine the song in
the light of Greek thought, we shall see that it goes to the
heart of the matter.

What the Greeks felt about health may be seen from a
Paean written by Ariphron _c._ 400 BC:

Health, best of the Blessed Ones to men,
May I dwell with you for the rest of my days,
And may you be kind and stay with me.
For if there is any joy in wealth or in children,
Or in royal rule which makes men like the gods,
Or in the desires which we hunt
With Aphrodite's secret snares,
Or if men have any other delight
From the gods of respite from their labours,
With you, blessed Health,

All things are strong and shine with the converse of the
Graces,
And without you no man is happy.[24]

The Greeks prayed for health as the first of blessings because
not only did the lack of it ruin happiness as they conceived
it, but they were at the mercy of disease. Medicine had indeed begun to make an impressive appearance by the end of
the sixth century, but though it approached its task in a
strictly scientific spirit, it had much to learn and could not
cure all evils in a society which had almost no hygiene and
fell an easy victim to any new infection. How appalling a
disease could be can be seen from Thucydides' account of
the plague which attacked Athens in 430 BC and has been
variously identified with typhus and with measles. He himself suffered from it, and allows nothing to interfere with his
precise, factual analysis of its symptoms and its results. The
whole picture is of an appalling devastation fallen on a people
which seemed to be secure from such an act of the gods and
then found itself faced by a catastrophe which it could neither control nor cure. Its confidence was undermined, and it
is not surprising that the Athenians behaved as Thucydides
describes: 'The most terrible thing of all was the despair into
which people fell, when they realized that they had caught
the plague; for they would immediately adopt an attitude
of utter hopelessness, and by giving in in this way, would lose
their powers of resistance.'[25] If health was a gift of the gods,
it was all the more frightening that they should take it away.
It was the indispensable basis of all the physical prowess in
which the Greeks delighted, and when they lost their sense of
its security, they felt abandoned indeed.

The desire for health was inextricably connected with the
Greek cult of the body. This was essentially a religious
activity. Through their bodies men resembled the gods, and
the gods guided and guarded their development. August presences watched over the birth of children, and what the
Greeks felt about them can be seen from Pindar's address to
the goddess of childbirth:

Eileithyia, seated at the side
Of the deep-counselling Fates,
Daughter of strong and mighty Hera, listen,
Bringer of children to birth.
Without you we see not the day or the black night,
Nor find your sister, bright-limbed Youth.[26]

The new-born child was protected by Hera, who was accompanied by the Hours to symbolize his coming days.[27] When

he was a little older, he passed under the care of Artemis, the
goddess of all young and growing creatures. To her temple
by a stream outside Sparta nurses brought young boys and
consecrated them to her, and her feast was celebrated with
dances, masquerades, and sacrifices of loaves and sucking-
pigs.[28] At the Attic feast of the Apaturia, boys offered locks
of their hair to her, and it was she who helped the growth
of girls and looked after games and sports.[29] When boys
reached the verge of manhood, they passed into the control
of Apollo and cut off their long hair as an offering to him.[30]
The whole process of birth and growth was directed and
watched by gods, and at each stage it was the young body
that called for their care, whether it was strengthened at the
beginning by being passed over a fire or later by being exercised in games and dances, or tested by initiation ceremonies.
If health was the first of good things, it was because the
gods gave it and fostered it in those whom they loved.

The belief in health passes imperceptibly into the belief
in beauty, which is equally derived from the notion that
through it men and women resemble the gods. Indeed, the
Greeks could not think any physical form beautiful unless it
was healthy. They had no morbid taste for decay, and old
age was for them not beautiful but either impressive or
pathetic. The beauty which they admired and celebrated with
many statues of naked young men and well-clothed maidens
was that of the body when it is passing into manhood or
womanhood. Their masculine prepossessions did not by any
means blind them to the beauty of girls, and in the seventh
century at Sparta Alcman writes words for girls to praise one
of their company:

> On the hair
> Of my kinswoman Hagesichora
> Is a bloom of unsullied gold.[31]

In Lesbos competitions in girls' beauty were held in connexion with the shrine of Hera, and Alcaeus, who witnessed
them, shows that they were uninhibited in their sense of a
joyful occasion conducted with full divine approval:

> Where the Lesbian girls, judged for their loveliness,
> Pass by, trailing their robes, and all around them rings
> Wondrous sound of the holy clamour
> Loudly raised by women in ev'ry year.[32]

Both these occasions were patronized by goddesses and reflect the conviction that they delight in physical beauty and are happy to see it.

Beauty in men was no less honoured, but it must suggest capacity for action, and that was one of the chief reasons why the Greeks were so attached to games. Not only were games celebrated at the great festivals of Zeus at Olympia and of Apollo near Delphi, but hardly less renowned were those of Zeus at Nemea and of Posidon on the Isthmus of Corinth, and the young men who took part in them were thought to be types of the beauty which belonged to the gods. Victory in the games was the realization of health and grace. If the competing athletes wore no clothes because it was more comfortable, it was also a means of showing them as the gods had made them. If they were successful, their beauty was all the more appreciated, as Bacchylides praises Automedes of Phlius for his perfect command of his body:

> In the Five Events he shone
> As the brilliant moon of the mid-month night
> Makes the rays of the stars turn pale;
> So in the boundless concourse of the Greeks,
> He showed his wonderful body,
> As he hurled the round quoit.[33]

At such a moment a man fulfilled the promise of the body which he was given at birth, and deserved honour for making it do its utmost in grace and skill and strength. He was indeed close to the felicity of the gods whom he resembled in his beauty and his success. That perhaps is why Philip of Croton, who was a victor in the Olympic Games and 'the most beautiful of the Greeks of his time', was after his death honoured as a hero at Segesta and had sacrifices offered to him.[34] Indeed, so great were the honours paid to victors, and such the almost superhuman regard in which they were held, that Pindar feels compelled to point the lesson that no man should seek to be a god,[35] but none the less in athletic prowess he saw one of the most enviable fortunes that fall to men. When serious critics like Xenophanes[36] and Euripides[37] attacked the rewards and privileges given to successful athletes, on the ground that they brought no good to the city, they failed to appreciate that victory in the games was a triumphant manifestation of those physical gifts in which men can sometimes approach the flawless physique of the gods.

The Attic song names wealth as the third good. The Greeks

enjoyed the pursuit of money as much as any men, and had an undoubted talent for it, but it was thought mean to treat it as an end in itself, nor were the rich respected just because they were rich. A normal attitude was that a good man needs money to help him to lead the good life, as Cephalus said to Socrates: 'If it is true that a good man will not find it easy to endure old age and poverty together, no more will riches ever make a bad man contented and cheerful.'[38] It followed that the Greeks saw no virtue in poverty and regarded it as a condition which degrades those whose lot it is. Theognis, who lost his lands in political revolution and knew what it means to be poor, says that it is worse than old age or shivering ague and that to avoid it a man should fling himself from a precipice or drown himself in the sea, since it robs him of all freedom in action or speech.[39] It was a commonplace that a man who lost his money lost his friends, and Pindar quotes the proverbial case of Aristodamus of Argos:

'Money, money makyth man', he said
When he lost his possessions and friends together.[40]

Wealth, like birth, with which it was frequently associated, had its own obligations. If prodigality was regarded as stupid, generosity was almost a duty. This was natural enough in a country where it can never have been easy to make a large fortune, and where a wealthy man, living under his neighbours' eyes, was subjected to critical scrutiny. If the gods had given him wealth, it was for him to share their gifts with his fellows. But more powerful than this was the conviction that the sweetness of life is not possible without some degree of wealth. In their love of beautiful things, the Greeks needed money with which to procure them, and Aristotle hits the mark when he says of his 'magnificent man', that he 'is like an artist; for he can see what is fitting and spend large sums suitably',[41] and by 'suitably' he means with taste and style and distinction.

If wealth was necessary to the good life, it had also an imaginative appeal for a people which had long delighted in making delicate golden objects and began to use gold coins in the seventh century. In its beauty and brightness and permanence, gold is indissolubly associated with the gods, whose palaces, thrones, chariots, lyres, arrows, and armour are made of it. They themselves, and even their horses, are 'golden', because of the divine light which shines from them. The legendary time when men came closest to the life of the gods was called the Golden Age. Because gold recalls the radiance of the gods, it is regarded as in some sense divine. Pindar not only calls it 'child of Zeus', because neither moth nor weevil devours it,[42] but gives to Theia, the august daughter of Heaven and Earth, who sheds grace on many human actions, credit for the honour in which it is held:

> Mother of the Sun, many-named Theia,
> Because of you men think that gold
> In strength and power surpasses all other things.[43]

Because of its divine associations, gold had a symbolic value, and when Pindar wishes to stress the splendour of something, he calls it golden, whether it is the victor's crown of wild olive[44] or the opening of a song.[45] Gold stood for wealth in its most magical and least prosaic form, for the radiance with which it invests the art of living and for the graces which it makes possible.

This attitude was strengthened by the niggardliness of natural resources. When the Aeolian and Ionian Greeks, who lived on the seaboard of Asia Minor, came into contact with the wealth of the Lydian kingdom, they were impressed and delighted and responded with enthusiasm to new openings in elegance and luxury. Sappho mentions such minor extravagances as a special kind of Lydian shoe and a 'royal' ointment.[46] But, though Lesbian society may well have profited from contact with Lydia to find new graces for social life, there is no evidence that its essentially Greek character was affected, or that its people lost any of their vigour. Even if we feel that in Sappho's poetry there is an unexpected love of ease and comfort, that is less likely to be due to Oriental influences than to her writing for the society of women. In Ionia the situation was rather different, at least in the sixth century. Xenophanes, who was a keen critic of social conditions, complained that his fellow Colophonians became a ready prey to conquest and tyranny because they learned 'useless luxuries from the Lydians', and by this he meant that they wore purple garments and golden ornaments and were so given to drink that they never saw the sun either rise or set.[47] What shocks him is not so much the luxuries themselves as their result, which begins with arrogant display and ends with an irresponsibility that plays into the hands of their enemies. The grace of Ionian life, visible in sculpture and ornaments and pottery, seems indeed to have been maintained by an advance individualism at the cost of public spirit. The Ionians were easily conquered by the Persians, and when they tried to revolt from them, they failed to enforce

discipline in their own ranks and paid for it in the test of
battle.[48] Serious Greeks were afraid of wealth because it
might breed self-indulgence and sap the sense of public and
national obligation.

A more sensational lesson was drawn from Sybaris, a city
on the eastern side of the toe of Italy. Its people became a by-
word for luxury, and tradition told of their dislike of noise,
which made them forbid not only the din of the smithy but
the crowing of cocks, of their luxurious apparel, and especially the purple garments and golden ornaments of their children, of the Sybarite who visited Sparta and said that he
would rather die a cowardly death than live such a life, of
their horses, which were taught to dance to the flute and were
for this reason an embarrassment in battle, of their fondness
for pets such as dogs and apes, of the high regard in which
they held their cooks.[49] They were said to have become so
self-indulgent and so overbearing that when, in 510 BC,
they provoked their neighbours of Croton into war, the Cro-
toniates not only won easily but were not satisfied until they
had obliterated Sybaris by turning the waters of the river
Crathis on to it and burying it in silt. To us the luxury of
Sybaris suggests almost a golden age of style and grace, and
it is hard to believe that it was ever showy or vulgar. Indeed,
if we may judge by its colony at Posidonia (Paestum), where
a temple of the early sixth century combines an archaic Doric
dignity with a remarkably original plan (see Plate 1), the
Sybarite sense of style was in no way impaired by love of
comfort. Nor does any richer treasure-trove await the
archaeologist than the remains of Sybaris hidden many feet
below the surface in what is now a fever-stricken forest.
But the condemnation of Sybaris by the Greeks shows that
even on wealth they had stern ideas and were not tolerant
of any marked departure from the accepted rule of austerity. They would allow that wealth is indispensable to the good
life, but they saw that it had its dangers, and would agree
with Sappho that 'wealth without virtue is not a harmless
neighbor'.[50]

The fourth good named by the Attic song is to be young
among friends, and what this means can be seen from the delight which Greek sculptors and painters take in representing
the pastimes and indulgences of young men. They keep their
bodies fit by wrestling, playing ball, practising what looks
very like hockey, jumping over sticks, and throwing the discus
(see Plates 25, 26, 27). They exercise horses in a field or listen,
in unashamed dandyism, to a lyre-player. They have also
their convivial relaxations. A party gathers and soon becomes

gay. The young men rush to the mixing-bowl and fill their cups. They play on flutes to each other or to girls, who dance for them. In the end it is too much for them, and they pay for it by vomiting, while fatherly elders or decorous girls look after them (see Plates 74-77, 80). The Greeks did not expect young men always to behave with restraint and were content that at times they should release their ebullience in happy abandonment. This was part of the glory of youth, and it was not without its parallel on Olympus. It is true that the gods do not get drunk, but they enjoy feasting and laughter, and there are times when they dance, not indeed wildly, but with a lofty, high-stepping gaiety:

Now dance the genial Hours and the long-haired Graces,
Harmonia now and Hêbê take their places
With heaven-born Aphrodite, all in a ring
Joined hand to wrist, and merrily round they swing.
And one nor plain nor lowly is choiring there,
Mighty in stature, fair among the fair,
Artemis, shooter of arrows, Apollo's twin.
There makes the War-god merry; and following in,
The watchful Slayer of Argos takes his pleasure.
But Phoebus Apollo treads the loftiest measure,
Harping the while, in a dazzle of glory thrown
By the flash of his feet and the flirt of his damask gown.[51]

If the gods take pleasure in this way, men are entitled to find a human counterpart to it in their own relaxations.

The Attic drinking-song provides a summary of the good life as the Greeks understood and liked to practise it, but we may well object that it concerns only the young and that for the old it seems not to exist. There is some truth in this. Many Greeks certainly regarded youth and early manhood as the prime of life and looked upon what comes after as at least an anti-climax. With women it may well have been, and it is not surprising that the carefree time of girlhood should be contrasted with the anxieties of marriage and motherhood:

The delicate plant grows in the sheltered place
That is its own. And in the sun-god's heat
Shakes not, nor rain, nor any wind that blows.
It lifts its life up in untroubled joys
Till that day when a maiden takes the name
Of wife and finds at night her share of cares,
Afraid for husband's or for children's sake.[52]

But something at the same level was also felt about men. Theognis complains that men are fools to weep for the dead and not for the flower of youth as it perishes,[53] and his views are derived from what seems to have been almost a philosophy in Ionia in the seventh century, when Mimnermus laments that youth is menaced by the twin dooms of old age and death, and of the two he thinks that old age is perhaps the worse.[54] This was natural enough in a world where the old had few alleviations for the failure of their physical powers, and the memory of youth might only make age the more bitter:

> Youth is always dear to me;
> Old age is a load that lies
> More heavily on the head
> Than the rocks of Etna.[55]

Yet though the Greeks recognized the justice of such complaints and sympathized with them, they did not treat them as if they were universally valid.

Though the Greeks admired youth because then, and perhaps only then, men can approach to something resembling the joy of the gods, yet they saw that the passage of years transforms experience into something which is even more worth having. By maintaining their health through outdoor life the Greeks remained active to the threshold of old age. When Socrates fought at the battle of Amphipolis in 422 BC, he was already forty-seven years old, and soldiering in those times had no comforts. Nor was he in the least out of the ordinary, since most Greeks were expected to serve in war until the age of sixty. This implies a high level of health and strength, and the impression is confirmed by the long spans of life which fell to some of the greatest Greeks. Gorgias died at over 100, Xenophanes at over 92, Democritus at over 90, Sophocles at 90, Plato at 82. All these were busy to the last and suffered no diminution of powers. It was all very well to complain that

> All evils are ingrained in long old age,
> Lost wits, unprofiting actions, empty thoughts,[56]

but there were at least sufficient exceptions to this rule to justify a more cheerful view of the passage of time and its meaning for men.

The best solution was not to complain of the passing of youth and its opportunities, but to ask what advantages come

38. Marble Apollo, central figure from the west pediment of the temple of Zeus at Olympia. About 460 B C. Larger than life size. *Olympia Museum.*

39. Marble figure of Athene killing a giant, from the pediment of the Hekatompedon at Athens. Late 6th century B C. Larger than life size. *Acropolis Museum, Athens.*

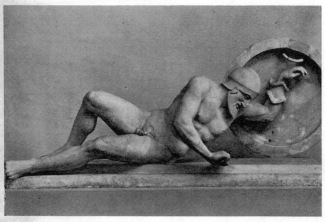

40. Marble recumbent warrior (restored) from the east pediment of the temple of Athene Aphaia on Aegina. Early 5th century B C. Life size. *Glyptothek, Munich.*

41. Woman struggling with a Centaur, from the west pediment of the temple of Zeus at Olympia. About 460 B C. Larger than life size. *Olympia Museum.*

42. Prone Lapith, from the west pediment of the temple of Zeus at Olympia. About 460 B C. Larger than life size. *Olympia Museum.*

43 & 44. Four drawings of the Parthenon made by a Flemish painter, 'Carrey', in 1674 A D, before the explosion of 1687. The two upper drawings are of the west pediment and show the struggle of Athene and Posidon; the two lower are of the east pediment and show the birth of Athene.

45 & 46. Marble frieze of the battle of Gods and Giants, from the Siphnian Treasury at Delphi. Middle of the 6th century B C. Smaller than life size. *Delphi Museum.*

47. Young men on horseback, on a marble frieze from the
Parthenon at Athens. 447–432 B C. In original position.

48. Water-carriers, from the same. In original position.

49. Seated gods, on a marble frieze from the Parthenon at Athens. 447–432 B C. In original position.

50. Marble grave-stone of a warrior. Early 5th century B C. *National Museum, Athens.*

51. Marble grave-stone of Aristion, by Aristocles. About 510 B C. *National Museum, Athens.*

52. Marble grave-stone of a young man with a small girl. About 550–530 B C. *Metropolitan Museum, New York.*

53. Marble grave-stone of an old man handing a cicada to a dog, by Alxenor, from Orchomenus. Early 5th century B C. *National Museum, Athens.*

54. Marble grave-stone of a girl with pigeons. About 460–450 B C. *National Museum, Athens.*

55. Marble grave-stone of Hegeso. Second half of the 5th century B C. *National Museum, Athens.*

56. Bronze statuette of a horse. About 480–470 B C. *Metropolitan Museum, New York.*

OPPOSITE:

58. Bronze statuette of a goat falling on its fore-legs, from Dodona. Early 5th century B C. *Staatliches Museum, Berlin.*

59. Statuette of a goat resting. Early 5th century B C. *British Museum, London.*

57. Bronze statuette of a goat standing. About 460–450 B C. *Museum of Fine Arts, Boston.*

60. Bronze statuette of a deer, from Sybaris. Late 5th century B C. *Louvre, Paris.*

61. Bronze figurine of a man and a centaur. About 8th century B C. *Metropolitan Museum, New York*

62. Flying heron, on a chalcedony gem, carved by Dexamenos of Chios. Enlarged. Second half of the 5th century B C. *Hermitage, Leningrad.*

63                           64

63. Left: *a–c.* Deer browsing and walking, engraved on sards.
Late 5th century B C. 22.5 mm long. *Museum of Fine Arts, Boston.*
*d.* Boar running, on a chalcedony gem. Early 4th century B C. 27
mm long. *Metropolitan Museum, New York.*

64. Right: *a.* Plunging bull, on a chalcedony gem. About 400
B C. 23 mm long. *Museum of Fine Arts, Boston. b.* Flying goose,
on an onyx gem. Second half of the 5th century B C. *British Museum, London. c.* Dog scratching himself, on a carnelian gem.
About 475-450 B C. 12 mm long. *Museum of Fine Arts, Boston.*
*d.* Dolphin, on a chalcedony gem. Second half of the 5th century
B C. 35 mm long. *Museum of Fine Arts, Boston.*

65. *a.* Pegasus on a coin of Corinth. 6th century B C. *British Museum, London.*

*b.* Octopus on a coin of Eretria. About 511–490 B C. *British Museum, London.*

*c.* Crab on a coin of Acragas. Second quarter of the 5th century B C. *British Museum, London.*

*d.* Nymph's head, surrounded by fish, on a coin of Syracuse. Soon after 480 B C. *British Museum, London.*

*e.* Sepia on a coin of Koresia, Ceos. End of the 6th century B C. *British Museum, London.*

*f.* Marsh tortoise on a coin of Aegina. About 404–375 B C. *British Museum, London.*

*g.* Posidon with trident on a coin of Posidonia. 6th century B C. *British Museum, London.*

*h.* Bull on a coin of Sybaris. 6th century B C. *British Museum, London.*

*i.* Ear of corn on a coin of Metapontum. About 500 B C. *British Museum, London.*

with the advance of years, and the answer was that, though
a man may lose the good things of life, he can still be a good
man with increased power and confidence and experience. He
may not be able to enjoy himself so much as before, but he
can make more of himself and become a more controlled and
more complete being. To each of the four traditional virtues
experience brings its special enlargement. Courage becomes a
form of patient endurance, as the old Oedipus, worn by
blindness and suffering but still noble and majestic, says of
himself:

> Contentment have I learned from suffering,
> And from long years, and from nobility.[57]

Temperance is easier for those whose passions have grown
feebler, as Sophocles, on being asked by his friend Cephalus
if he still had sexual desires, said: 'Don't talk in that way. I
am only too glad to be free from all that; it is like escaping
from bondage to a raving madman.'[58] Justice, in its full
civic sense, is recognized as the right task of the old in such
a proverb as 'Deeds for the young, counsels for the elder.'[59]
Wisdom profits from the years by drawing more fully on the
divine capacity which lives in every man:

> The wise never grow old; their minds are nursed
> By living with the holy light of day.[60]

To each of the four cardinal virtues age brings a new distinction and a richer usefulness. The man who has left behind
him youth and its good things, or can enjoy them only fitfully,
attains a new dignity through his renewed opportunities of
being a good man.

In some such way as this the Greeks, not very consciously or very carefully, related the concept of the good man
to that of the good life. The two remained separate, and the
good man was not necessarily he who led the good life. But
in a single lifetime the two could be combined, and if the
four best things belong especially to youth, the four cardinal
virtues are best displayed by experience. The distinction conforms to the ambivalent nature of man and his ambiguous
position in the universe. In so far as he can share the pleasures of the gods, he partakes of the four best things, but in so
far as he differs from the gods and has to fulfil his purely
human nature and obeying limitations, he must conform to
the four virtues, which are indispensable to the ordered maintenance of civilized society. The peculiar nature of man de-

termined the Greek notion of pleasure. They had no ascetic or puritanical hostility to it; in some respects they regarded it as a supreme good. But at the same time they felt that it must be kept in its place and not be allowed to upset the harmony of either the individual or the city. They felt too that the strongest pleasures are suitable mainly for the young, and that in due course a man passes beyond them to others which are less exciting. This distinction follows the general distinction which the Greeks made between men and the gods. If the gods enjoy power and freedom, men have responsibility, and through their use of it attain their own dignity, which is different from anything available to the gods. The advantage of this system is that it combines a natural taste for enjoyment with a real respect for proved capacities in action and in thought. Paradoxically, it may mean that in what seems to be his more human side, man is closer to the gods than in what wins him honour and respect. But it also means that goodness and happiness are brought together in a balanced harmony; for the Greeks believed not only that if a man is good he is happy, but also that if he is happy he is good.

# CHAPTER VI

# MYTH AND SYMBOL

A MYTH is a story which aims not at giving pleasure for its own sake but at alleviating perplexities which trouble pre-scientific man because his reason is not yet ready to grasp them. Before men advance to general concepts, they think in individual, pictorial images, and if they are to come to terms with something puzzling or unfamiliar, it must be brought into the orbit of such imagery and acclimatized to it. Faced by a world in which most things happen without a known cause, they need myths to explain them, and the explanation, which must suit their own special range of experience, is more emotional than rational and works not by describing cause and effect, but by associating one kind of experience with another and suggesting a connexion or similarity be-tween them. The solution so found makes it easier to face and accept phenomena by making them seem less absolutely alien. This process has naturally much to do with religion in so far as in primitive society religion provides the chief means for the understanding of nature, and most myths have some religious element in them. It is hard for us, who are accustomed to look on the world with the eyes of science, with its laws and its abstractions, to enter into a mentality which insists that everything is concrete and individual, but for primitive man this is the only way to shape the worries that beset him. He sees gods and spirits at work everywhere, and if he is to feel that he has some approach to them, he can do so only through myths; for myths bring the unknown into relation with the known and help to break down the barriers between men and the intractable mass of phenomena which surrounds them.

The Greeks had an unequalled wealth of myths, but most of them have been subjected to some process of rationaliza-tion, and not all arise from a like origin or answer the same needs. Some, indeed, conform to the strict notion that a myth is a story invented to make sense of some ritual whose significance has been forgotten, if indeed it has ever been fully understood. Such myths need not be very ancient, though the rites behind them may well come from a much older world, where religious actions are sufficient in themselves and no explicit explanation of them is demanded. They appeal to the consciousness at an emotional level, and that is enough to justify them. If we can find what the original rite was, we can begin to see how the myth has been formed. Such is the case with the myth of Hippolytus, the virginal young man who rejects love and comes to a hideous end when he is torn to pieces in the panic of his own horses. Though the story, as Euripides dramatizes it, has later accretions, it reveals its origin in a rite, when at the end of the play Artemis says:

> To you, ill fated, for these sufferings
> Great honours shall I give in Troezen town;
> To you shall maids before their wedding-day
> Cut off their hair, and through the length of time
> You shall receive the tears of their vast grief.[1]

The rite is that before marriage the young women of Troezen dedicate a lock of hair to Hippolytus, and this symbolizes what they lose, the virginity which they must sacrifice. They offer it to Hippolytus because he stands both for virginity and for sacrifice, for the irreparable loss of something prized and treasured. The association of young women with him is based on this sense of irreparable loss, and this is enough for the rite to have a meaning and for a myth to be necessary to explain it. What is otherwise vague and inchoate is conveyed in a concrete case, and the emotional implications of a moving occasion emerge with force and intimacy.

A myth which explains a rite is not likely always to be so satisfactory as this, since the character of a rite may often have been obscured by the passage of time. When the Greeks became conscious of their rites and sought to explain them, they sometimes found it difficult to do so, and their efforts are not entirely convincing. For instance, when they offered sacrifice to the gods, they kept the best part of the meat for themselves and gave the gods no more than bones wrapped in fat. We do not know the reason for this, though it was sensible enough in a country where food was never too abundant. It clearly did no honour to the gods, and an explanation had to be found for it. The answer came in a story, told by Hesiod,[2] that Prometheus, who is not an Olympian but belongs to the older, dispossessed order of the Titans, has no

love for Zeus, and when he offers an ox to him, he covers
the bones with glistening fat with the intention of deceiving
him into taking what looks like a good portion but in fact is
not. Zeus takes it, but sees at once that he has been tricked.
But, since he has acted of his own choice, he accepts it, and
this is the portion that is henceforward offered to the gods.
The myth does not really get rid of the difficulty about the
dishonour which the rite does to the gods, but at least it
places its origin in the far past and gives it some sort of historical explanation. This commonly happens with aetiological
myths. The real nature of the rite is often too much for them,
and they must be content with a story which brings it into a
familiar orbit of experience.

A second class of myths is derived not from rites but
from a desire to explain natural phenomena through some
dramatic, cosmological tale. A very primitive example is
that of Uranus (Sky) and Gaea (Earth). Uranus does not allow the children to whom Gaea is about to give birth to see
the light, but hides them in her depths. The other children
shrink from attacking their father, but Cronus takes a sharp
weapon from his mother, falls upon Uranus when he is cov-
ering Gaea, cuts off his male member, and casts it into the
sea.[3] The story has a close parallel in Polynesia, where it
is told to explain the severance of heaven from earth, and
the Greek myth must have had the same purpose. After such
a catastrophe, heaven and earth can never be united as before,
and their separation is in some sense accounted for. The
barbarity of the story is unusual in Greek mythology, and
the subject found little favour with poetry or art, but it is
none the less an illuminating relic, which shows that the
Greeks began with myths as crude and clumsy as those of
any primitive people, but in due course left them behind
for others of a finer grace and aptness.

Such is the myth of Demeter and Persephone, which symbolizes the yearly coming and passing of crops on the earth.
That this was the work of the gods nobody would doubt,
but it was natural to ask why they ordained it as they did. In
the Homeric Hymn to Demeter, Persephone, the daughter of
the earth-goddess Demeter, is carried off by Hades, the god of
death and the underworld. Her mother seeks her in vain
through the earth, and while she does so, crops fail. At last
she finds out what has happened, and an agreement is made
by which Persephone is to spend the winter under the earth
with Hades and the summer on it with her mother. To the
unscientific mind this provides an admirable account of what
happens yearly to the earth, and it does so in a most effective

way. It presents the cycle of growth and decay in a spirit which is both imaginative and religious, or rather is imaginative because it is religious. Human joy in the spring and desolation at the winter are matched by Demeter's joy in regaining and grief in losing her daughter. The association of Persephone with Hades is an apt symbol of the interplay of life and death, and her decision to divide her time between her husband and her mother speaks in the language of affection and separation to our conviction that we must come to terms with life and death alike. So profound and so satisfying a myth is not likely to be very primitive, but it illustrates the Greek capacity for the vivid presentation of mysteries which were beyond the reach of precise analysis, but reveal all their implications in a concrete form.

These primary myths were supplemented, and to some degree displaced, by other stories which were not strictly myths, since their main purpose was not to explain, but to delight. The more ancient tales of the gods, which arose from their rites and their functions, provided a starting-point for many brilliant stories about them, which might indeed presuppose a ritual background or an aetiological purpose, but left them behind in the new form which they received. For instance, when Homer tells how Hera tricks Zeus into sleeping with her that he may not see what happens on the battlefield of Troy,[4] the story may possibly be derived from a rite of divine marriage, in which the king and the queen of the gods were honoured in a ceremony which suggested a wedding. An echo of this may be recognized in the flowers which grow around their couch, as befits a ceremony held in the spring. But Homer says nothing about its ritual character and was plainly not interested in it. For him what matters is the amusing, dramatic story, and nothing else. In another case Homer shows an equal indifference to a myth which must ultimately be aetiological. The companions of Odysseus are destroyed because, despite his prohibition, they eat the cattle of the Sun. Since these are 350 in number,[5] we can hardly doubt that they stand for the days of the year in a primitive calendar, and there is no reason for them to have a place in a tale of adventure. But Homer is not interested in their origin; what concerns him is that they provide him with a good motive for the destruction of the comrades of Odysseus and for his eventual return to Ithaca alone.

A second reinforcement came from folk-tales, from stories of unfathomed antiquity told simply to entertain and devoid of any theological or didactic content. Such Homer uses freely in the *Odyssey*. Some of these may be based on travellers' tales, which reflect a misunderstanding of unusual facts, like the floating island of Aeolus, the Symplegades or Clashing Rocks, which are derived from some strait made dangerous by shifting currents, the dark world of the Cimmerians, which is an echo of the long winter nights of the far north. Others are creatures of primeval fancy, like the one-eyed Cyclops and the trick with the name 'No-man', which outwits him, witches like Calypso and Circe, who hide the wanderer on his return home, monsters like Scylla, who belongs to the race of crakens and giant squids, the Sirens whose song lures mariners to their doom. Such stories may be found in many parts of the world and survive by their appeal to all who love the monstrous and the unknown. But they are acclimatized in Greek heroic legend and have become part of the story-teller's repertory. They do not stand for anything outside themselves or convey any lesson or interpret any mystery. They do not even exist in a special order of their own, but are introduced into tales of human beings who deal with them in a human way and keep them in their proper place.

Both authentic myths and supplementary stories were brought together in the spacious frame of heroic poetry. The long tradition, which culminates and survives in Homer, created a body of narrative which included all these elements and added its own distinctive contribution on the glorious doings of men, which it derived ultimately from historical events. So rich was this store that Greek dramatists drew almost all their material from it, and sculptors and painters used it as their main staple for the decoration of public buildings. In effect myths and folk-tales were combined with heroic tales, which had a foundation in fact. The great days of Mycenaean Greece in the fourteenth and thirteenth centuries provided many subjects for songs which were remembered for centuries as poets retold them and made their own generous improvements and additions to them. Of what was once a vast mass of oral poetry only the *Iliad* and the *Odyssey* survive, and we must try to imagine countless other poems, not necessarily so gifted or so mature, but similar in manner and in outlook, which told of the multifarious doings of a heroic generation. It was this poetry which provided the Greeks with myths in the widest sense, with stories which were honoured because they were the traditional heritage of a whole people. Into this frame the bards incorporated mythical versions of religion, history, and folk-lore, relics of real rites now inexplicable or misunderstood, and creations of fancy and fiction. The generous heroic frame absorbed them all with ease and gave to them the distinction and authority which come from being presented with a high style and a sense of heroic grandeur.

Much of this poetry is concerned with gods and their relations with each other or with men. It has indeed its elements of miracle and marvel, but it is noteworthy that these are nearly always the direct work of gods. When the horse of Achilles speaks or the shape of Odysseus is changed, it is Hera or Athene who is responsible. So far as men are concerned, they act by purely human means. It is true that they do far more than ordinary men ever could, but none the less it is by exerting their own powers to a prodigious degree. This is the more remarkable since in most primitive societies and in much primitive and not too primitive story the chief actor is not the hero, who relies on his human powers of head and arm, but the magician, who works miracles by enchantment. The Greeks seem to have passed through this phase but to have outlived it or to have relegated it to an unimportant corner. They had indeed their memories of famous shamans like Calchas, who died of chagrin because he was wrong, when his rival Mopsus was right, in giving the number of leaves on a tree,[6] but Homer has reduced him to a prophet whose main task is to interpret the will of the gods.[7] Another shaman may perhaps be seen in Perseus, who flies on winged sandals, wears a cap of darkness, and kills the Gorgon with the help of a magic mirror.[8] But he has been even more fully transformed and differs little from an authentic hero. This elimination of miraculous stories is the more remarkable because the Greeks did not lack men who made surprising claims to shamanistic powers. Aristeas of Proconnesus said that his soul could leave his body and survey the whole earth;[9] Epimenides slept for fifty-seven years in a cave;[10] Hermotimus obtained an unusual knowledge by letting his soul leave his body behind and go on far journeys without it, until one day he returned and found that enemies had burned his body.[11] Despite such oddities, the Greeks persisted in their view that men are limited to their purely human powers, and it is with these that many of their myths deal. This exclusion of magic was no doubt dictated by a feeling that it was beneath the dignity of heroes, and this in its turn was based on the peculiarly Greek conviction that men are honoured for what they do by purely human means.

In their primitive stage myths are the common property of a people and need no justification for their telling. But by the time when we see them in currency in Greece they have already reached a secondary stage, when they are indeed honoured as a national heritage, but no longer used for their original purpose of explaining rites or the workings of nature. Even the archaic and conservative Hesiod, who is not unaware of these purposes, collects and organizes myths for a different reason. He is concerned to see that they are known, that his own generation should be instructed in these sacred relics of the past, that a body of instruction, if not of doctrine, should be available in an attractive and easily remembered form. At this stage myths are honoured because they belong to religion and to the heroic past, and they never lost the prestige which this gave to them. Later religious teachers and reformers imitated Hesiod's method and produced other cosmogonies with their own peculiarities or did their best to rewrite remote history by reconstructing genealogies, while the devotees of Orpheus composed poems on his descent to Hades and his hideous death when he was torn to pieces by Thracian women. Such poetry helped to maintain the dignity of the mythical outlook and to show that it still had its uses in a world already touched by science and philosophy. Sculptors performed a similar task. Like the carvings and stained glass of medieval churches, the sculptures of Greek temples were often a kind of *libri pauperum*, a visual presentation of myths which concerned the gods and goddesses whose shrines they adorned, or heroes of the past, like Theseus and Heracles, who had connexions with them and exemplified qualities thought worthy of imitation. It was important that these things should be known, but it was also important that they should be so portrayed as to evoke a right understanding and interpretation of them. The Greeks were fortunate in having traditions which were delightful in themselves and appealed to all who loved bold actions and gallant gestures. Since the gods were embodiments of power, it was right to reveal this with all the clarity and firmness of vision which the artists could command. Such an art was certainly instructive, in that it told about the gods, but it was not concerned with purely moral issues. What mattered was to awaken awe and amazement before the irresistible might of the gods and the splendour of heroes who had the blood of gods in their veins.

In these ways myths played a considerable part in the education of Greek youth. But more important and more influential was their indirect impact, the formative effect which they had through their brilliance and liveliness and assured sense of human values. Though Homer points almost no moral and is as impersonal as Shakespeare, he radiates a humanity which is itself an education. His interest in his mythical figures is so lively and so understanding that they appeal to us as living men and women and become, if not models of conduct, at least examples of humanity in its authentic integrity. The world of his poems is indeed imaginary, but it is based on real experience and makes human beings more intelligible and more attractive by transposing them to a remote past. It gave inestimable service in making the Greeks regard men as a central subject for study, and the very skill and power of its presentation made this study more relevant and more insistent. The abiding concern of the Greeks with humanity was largely the result of the heroic tradition of poetry, and it was all the more secure because this tradition was deeply interested in the dealings of men with gods and implicitly with the worth of human actions and the notion that a man should exert himself to the utmost with his natural powers. If myths gave instruction, they did so in a generous spirit, with no attempt to preach. They helped to form character by clarifying issues of conduct in their dramatic presentation of them and in showing the place of man in the universe by telling of his relations with the gods.

A similar spirit can be seen in much Greek art, which aims at showing gods and heroes in action and displays their strength and courage. Even in Homer's own day, when vase-painting was still in its infancy, artists portrayed scenes like his own, such as sea-fights, funeral pyres, battle-scenes, chariot-races, and shipwrecks. In later centuries, when the heroic ideal had found a new significance in the city-state, artists made it convincing and contemporary by their presentation of old stories in new shapes. They delighted to show what heroes are in the full exercise of their strength, like the triumphant Heracles, who carries off the tripod which he has just wrested from Apollo in open struggle (see Plate 79), or the relentless Achilles, who kills the Amazon Penthesilea (see Plate 85). These works of art give pleasure in a Homeric way and with something of the same magnificence. The artist presents a familiar subject for its dramatic and pictorial appeal and incidentally and unobtrusively conveys a whole vision of manhood. There is no doubt of what he sees in the taut, muscular bodies, alive with purpose and energy, which awake an admiring pleasure and make us wonder what these men must have been in the living pride of their prowess.

This straightforward handling of myths fixed them in the Greek consciousness, made it feel perfectly at home with them, and rely on them to illustrate or justify different courses of behaviour, and prepared the way for developments in which they could be used with a more special intention. As the heroic ideal was transformed to suit the demands of the city-state, the Greeks turned their myths to more complex purposes. With the vast achievement of the epic behind them, and in the sure confidence that its stories were more or less familiar to everyone, they could read more into them, treat them more allusively, and use them to dramatize those issues of life and death which awoke their eager and profound consideration. The three Attic tragedians, Aeschylus, Sophocles, and Euripides, all used familiar myths for their tragedies, and nearly always drew on heroic stories. This too was an exalted art, to which nothing common or mean could be admitted. Greek tragedy was not always tragic in the modern sense; it did not necessarily end in disaster. In this it reflected the epic, which dealt indeed with disasters but realized its essence in a sense of the urgency and importance of human action. Attic tragedy is no less serious, and is in this respect the rightful heir of epic. But instead of aiming exclusively at exalted enjoyment, it sought to make its effects more impressive by relating them to fundamental issues in the relations of gods with men. Perhaps this was inevitable in an art which was performed at the festival of a god, but it is no less likely to have been due to the Athenian spirit, which believed that men are inextricably connected with the gods, and wished to explore this connexion with a bold and searching curiosity. Myth provided the framework of drama, which illustrated in a highly concrete and cogent way some important crisis or problem, and that is why Greek tragedy can be called symbolical. The old stories are indeed told again for their own sake, and there is no lack of dramatic tension and human interest, but they also exemplify some far-reaching problem, which is admirably presented in this individual shape. The heroes of the past keep their individuality, but also become types of human destiny and examples of men's dealings with the gods. Each man may see in them something which concerns himself, and though their presentation is always exciting and gives its own kind of pleasure, behind and beyond this lies some universal issue which is made more significant by the special form in which it is embodied.

The essence of a symbol is that it expresses in a concrete, particular shape matters which are otherwise almost beyond our grasp, because, even if they can be expressed in abstractions, we fail to catch their full significance, since much of it lies in their appeal to unformulated emotions and to half-conscious memories and desires. A symbol is almost indispensable when dealing with anything that belongs to some transcendental order of being. It makes it visible to the eye of the mind and evokes its character by hint and suggestion and allusive reference. Greek symbols differ from modern in one important respect. Since the Greeks believed that gods and men live in a single world, and resemble one another in many ways, symbols were required not to convey the mystery of some order beyond the senses, but to show how the divine element is at work in the familiar scene, how it transfigures or transfuses human actions and gives them an unsuspected significance, how it makes its presence felt in unexpected conditions and in unforeseen ways. Symbols were needed to convey the quality of divine intervention in a human society much occupied with its own activities. But because the Greeks saw their gods in human shape and had through their myths a clear conception of them, the symbols of Greek poetry are so definite and so complete that we scarcely think of them as symbols at all. They are hardly ever ambiguous. They are never purely emotional. Their strength is that they are both intellectual and emotional, that they clarify obscure issues by their firm approach to them and appeal to the whole gamut of human feelings through their stirring events. They are so well established that they catch the attention at once and hold it without effort.

The Attic tragedians were deeply concerned with current problems. They saw them, indeed, with a lofty detachment, but they none the less thought that what mattered for their own generation was the right material for tragedy. They transposed the disturbing problems and the passionate disputes of the Athenian democracy to the world of ancient myth and gave to them a distance and a dignity which made their issues clearer and set them above the confusions of ephemeral controversy. Torn from their contemporary context, these questions are revealed in their ultimate urgency and given a new life through the myths which enfold them. So in the three plays of his *Oresteia*, Aeschylus takes in turn the murder of Agamemnon by his wife, the vengeance exacted from her by her son, and his ultimate release by Apollo and Athene from the persecution of the Furies, who haunt and harass him on his dead mother's behalf. Each play is complete, and each has its own formative, imaginative plan. But the whole is more than the parts, and the three plays together provide in mythical form, inspired with an unfailing magnificence of poetry, a theme of first significance for Athens, the role of the state as the champion of justice. Aeschylus must have taken this subject because the Athenians had begun to see that, if requital for murder were left to the family of the murdered, a vicious sequence of blood-feuds must be the result, in which each death was in turn avenged by another and there was no end to mutual slaughter. To replace this by a system in which the state was an impartial arbiter was indeed a momentous reform. Aeschylus saw its far-reaching significance, and for that reason gave a prominent part to the gods. When he produces Apollo and Athene on the stage and makes them debate with the Furies, the powers of order and sanity are pitted against a primeval, frenzied thirst for avenging blood. His issues are presented so powerfully through his majestic and passionate words that they live in their own world of art, but in them vast issues are incarnate, and the notion of divine justice comes forth in manifest presence on the stage.

Since tragedy was a vehicle for displaying the nature of religious experience, it often dealt with questions and misgivings which assail men about the gods. In the *Prometheus Bound*, which is the first of three plays about the Titan Prometheus, who helped men by stealing fire from heaven and on the orders of Zeus was bound for it to a mountain in the Caucasus, Aeschylus faces the whole metaphysics of power which makes the gods what they are, and asks what it means in human terms. Zeus, who punishes Prometheus, is presented as an upstart tyrant; Prometheus, the friend of men, as a patient, outspoken, unyielding martyr. Our sympathies are almost wholly with him, since his compassion for the pathetic helplessness and ignorance of men is in sharp contrast with the heartless unconcern of Zeus. Aeschylus surely means us to feel this, but it is only one side of the picture; the other side was developed in the two lost plays, in which Zeus in the end released Prometheus and showed that the fulfilment of power is in reason and justice. In these plays Aeschylus transposed to a cosmic stage something which was disturbingly apparent in the new and vigorous democracy of Athens. After the Persian Wars, Athens tasted power and thirsted for more, and in the process lost some of its first generosity. Just as it soon began to use force against those allies who refused to submit to its will, so it turned on its own saviours and benefactors, like Themistocles and Aristides, because it was suspicious of their independence and candour. Aeschylus knew this, but saw far beyond it, and realized that it raised universal issues, which he made the subject of his drama.

With this play of the expanding Athenian Empire we may compare another which comes from its close. Sophocles wrote his *Oedipus at Colonus* soon before his death in 406 BC, when the end of Athens was near and the long struggle with

Sparta could only end in defeat. He chose his subject from local myth, from rites paid near Athens at Colonus to Oedipus as a demi-god who lived under the earth and was believed to have recently helped the Athenians in war. Sophocles' play tells of the end of Oedipus. The old man, blind and worn by much suffering, comes to a grove at Colonus and knows that his wanderings are over and his end is near. He prepares for his passing, and in his last ordeals he displays with increasing force the qualities of the demi-god which he is destined soon to become, until at last a voice calls him from the sky and, despite his blindness, he moves away unaided and disappears from the world of men. The play is rich in violent action and incomparable song, but it is shaped by the notion of an unseen presence which watches over Athens. Sophocles is concerned to show what a demi-god really is, and gives to Oedipus a terrifying majesty and force of passion. He conforms to the belief that such beings love their friends and hate their enemies; and that is why Oedipus both shows a loving solicitude for his daughters, who have been faithful to him in his sufferings, and an unforgiving savagery for those who have wronged him, like his treacherous son Polynices. Above all, in his friendship with Theseus, the king of Athens, he forecasts how after death he will protect Athens from the earth where he abides. Sophocles understood Greek religious experience, and in this play faced one of its more mysterious articles of belief. Because his myth is so clearly conceived, he is able to show what a demi-god means to those who honour him.

In these two cases the poets almost point a moral, or at least propound both a problem and their solution for it. But this was not necessary, and perhaps not even usual. One of the chief functions of tragedy was to present in concrete form issues that concerned men in their relations with the gods and with one another. In almost every extant play there is behind the individual action a universal situation or problem or question, which is presented in such a way that we see what it really means for human beings. The selection which the poet makes from mythology provides him not only with a dramatic subject but with a means to clarify something that absorbs or troubles his mind. The strength of his play arises largely from the degree in which he has thought and felt about this and what it means in terms of human action. Even if he has a solution for it, this is usually much less important imaginatively and poetically than the presentation of the situation which provokes it. For instance, in *King Oedipus* Sophocles faces the problem of a gifted and noble man, who through no fault of his own is hideously humbled and suffers a ghastly fate. He hints, indeed, that there is a solution for this, that the gods humble the great because they wish to warn men against the dangers of power and position, but this is kept till the end and has very little part in the play. What counts in the dramatic action is the appalling emotional impact which it has on us and which forces us to sympathize, in the full sense of the word, with Oedipus in his tragic situation and to think for ourselves about it. The drama moves in a world in which men think that they know something about themselves and their destinies, but they are the victims of illusion. They know nothing, and in the end the gods force the truth upon them. This is not a lesson, but a state of mind inculcated and impressed on us by the power of poetry and by the myth which Sophocles uses. In its simplest form the fall of Oedipus is that of a man who falls from prosperity to adversity, and the myth provides this for the poet to make use of. What he does is not only to dramatize it in such a way that every word and action makes an impression on us, but to show the frame of mind in which such a fall is possible, the errors which beset a powerful and successful man like Oedipus, and the even greater errors into which they lead him. Nor is this technique merely an adroit exploitation of a given myth; it is in itself a reflection of the mythical way of thinking. The issues which Sophocles dramatizes are best presented not as intellectual abstractions, but as living states of mind which we all know in ourselves and which become more urgent and more vivid when we see them on the stage. By relying upon myths for their plots, the Greek dramatists are able not merely to provide a stirring drama but to communicate to us something whose whole character and significance can be revealed only by this imaginative identification of the universal problem with the individual case.

A myth is no less useful when the dramatist is unable to see any solution to a problem and wishes to present it for its own sake, as something which troubles him and of which others should be at least aware. This is the clue to certain plays of Euripides. He was a man who welcomed new ideas of many kinds, but seems never to have settled down to any single system of belief or thought. In this he was perhaps typical of the latter part of the fifth century, when war accentuated the doubts and anxieties which men had begun to feel about traditional beliefs. Though he played with new ideas and brought them incidentally into his plays by making his characters give expression to them, he did not use them to give shape to his interpretation of myths. More than Aeschylus, more even than Sophocles, he was obsessed by a vision which was irremediably tragic because he saw no consolation and no comfort for the disasters and injustices which he dramatized. For him myths were an instrument by which he could show what these flaws in life really are, how easily they arise from human nature, and how hard it is to justify the part played by the gods in them. Even when he seems to approximate to an orthodox standpoint, he leaves us uneasy and speculating as to what he really means. So when, in his *Bacchants*, he follows tradition and shows how Pentheus is torn to pieces for mocking Dionysus, he might seem to agree with the old view that Pentheus deserved his fate, especially since he is an uncontrolled and arrogant prig. But none the less we are not quite convinced. Pentheus may be a poor creature, but Dionysus is almost a devil, fascinating indeed and alluring, but merciless when his pride is offended. Perhaps Euripides believed that the gods were really like this, or that Dionysus was a power in human nature, beyond good and evil, inexorable and ruthless. Yet what he excites in us is not awe or even fear for Dionysus, but something closer to horror. In a sense we may call this a lesson. It is, after all, what Euripides must have felt himself and meant us to feel also. But his effect is made entirely through the emotions and does not attempt to go beyond them. He presents the myth in what is probably an ancient, unelaborated form, and this makes his effect the more powerful. He makes us see what a god is really like for those who believe in him, and he marshals a whole host of violent and primitive emotions suitable to such a theme. Because the myth is faithfully treated and is itself so clear in its intention, it both attracts and repels. We yield to its absorbing excitement, and may well be carried away by it, only to find in the end that we recoil from it with something akin to dismay. Euripides uses his myth to secure a special kind of psychological conflict in his audience, and we can hardly doubt that this was what he felt himself.

Though the main outline of a myth was more or less fixed and familiar, a poet could take considerable liberties with its treatment and interpretation. This was indeed almost inevitable, since the tragedians were forced by convention to use stories which had often been used before, and could hardly fail to set a strong personal impress on them. How freely they could work can be seen from the three plays which Aeschylus, Sophocles, and Euripides wrote on the vengeance which Orestes takes on his mother Clytaemestra for the murder of his father, Agamemnon. In his *Libation-bearers* Aeschylus shows how after the vengeance Orestes is haunted by the Furies, which is a mythical way of telling how the killing of a mother so affects a man that it almost unseats his reason. In his *Electra*, Sophocles says nothing about the Furies. His play is concerned with revenge and punishment, and shows how, when so fearful an evil as the murder of Agamemnon has been committed, it can be cured only by another evil hardly less great, when the son slays the mother. But he insists that this is commanded by the gods, and behind the play lies the conviction that wickedness so breaks the ordered harmony of the world that this must be restored by means no matter how exacting, and that in the end hatred is redeemed in peace, and the favour of the gods is restored to men. Euripides takes almost the opposite view. When, at Apollo's command, Orestes kills his mother, he finds only misery and feels almost that he has been tricked. For such a state there is no solution, and the play leaves us with a truly tragic sense of waste and frustration, which are all the more painful because Orestes is still alive. Like Italian painters of the *quattrocento*, who painted again and again the familiar stories of the Bible, Greek tragedians told again and again the familiar myths of their people. Both gained greatly from it. They were able to take so much for granted that they could go straight to the main point without explanatory introduction and be sure that each new turn which they gave to an old story would be appreciated at once at its full value. They were thus able to produce works of striking originality in which they gave free play to their own ideas inside a traditional frame, which enforced its seriousness on them and made them live up to its demands.

If tragedy shows on an extended scale how myths can be used to interpret issues of wide range and most serious import, other forms of art also made use of them on a smaller scale. When the metopes of the Parthenon display the conflicts of men with Centaurs, they hint that in Athens men struggle heroically against the element of the beast which still thrives in humanity and is symbolized by the Centaur, who is half man and half horse; the metopes of Olympia, which portray the labours of Heracles, are an image of the toils which man must endure if he is to realize his powers in their full scope. The spirit behind the sculptures reveals itself at once and leaves no uncertainty about its intention. So too, with a finer subtlety and a more indirect approach, Pindar conveys many comments and lessons and assurances by his use of myths. He often introduces them with an air of nonchalance as if they were mere decorations and not very relevant, but they are always chosen with care and insight. To a young Thessalian he tells of the ageless Hyperboreans at the end of the world, who spend their days in dance and song under the patronage of Apollo and are an ideal counterpart to the young man and his festal companions;[12] to an Aeginetan, rich in the promise of a noble manhood, he recounts the wonderful childhood of Achilles, who foreshadowed his heroic future by killing lions when he was six years old;[13] to a wrestler from Argos he gives a classical example of devotion in the story of Castor and Polydeuces;[14] at Rhodes, to an athlete, whose family suffers from political misfortunes, he offers the consolation of three local stories, in each of which something goes wrong, only to end happily.[15] The tone of his myths varies from easy gaiety to almost tragic urgency, and he always strikes a note which is at once serious and detached. The myths enable him to sharpen his lessons and comments with an element of surprise, to shed a new light on them, and to magnify each present occasion by ranking it with high precedents from the east.

That poets and sculptors should use myths is natural enough, but we hardly expect them from philosophers. Yet they too saw that even for their special task myths had their uses. In the sixth century, when philosophy was still in its youth, it had to be related to its senior and more firmly established rival, poetry. The abstract thinker must sometimes express his thoughts in a mythical form, partly no doubt because it was natural for him to do so, but more because it brought home to a public trained in poetry the nature and the importance of his unusual task. So when Parmenides begins his formidable poem on the nature of Being, he uses a myth, but it is his own creation, skilfully compounded from other myths. He drives in a chariot through the sky, accompanied by the Daughters of the Sun. His axle flames as he travels by the 'Way of the Goddess', which recalls the Greek name for the Milky Way, and in this he resembles Phaethon driving the chariot of his father, the Sun. But, unlike Phaethon, Parmenides does not come to disaster. He drives up to a great gateway in the sky:

> There are the gates of the ways of Night and Day;
> A lintel holds them above, a stone threshold below.
> High in the air they are blocked by mighty doors,
> And avenging Justice keeps the double keys.[16]

The gateway is like that of Olympus, and when Parmenides arrives, he resembles Heracles arriving after death, knowing that he is to become a god. Parmenides' myth stresses the boldness, originality, and splendour of his quest for truth. In it he implicitly compares himself to a demi-god, and though we must not press this too far, there is no doubt that it is conscious and intentional, that Parmenides really believes his task to be far above any task of ordinary men. How seriously he treats it may be seen when he makes Justice, and not the Hours, keep the Gates of Olympus, and later, when he tells how a goddess welcomes him and instructs him on the nature of reality. Though Parmenides' myth makes remarkable claims for his philosophical task, at the same time it insists that it does not disdain or defy the gods, but is inspired directly by them.

In the later part of the fifth century myths found a new field with the growth of what is called the Sophistic Movement. The Sophists were popular educators, who were often original thinkers in their own right but made a living by bringing knowledge to the public in an attractive form. Among the subjects of their discourse ethics had a prominent place, and myths were useful in driving points home and in giving to certain assumptions, not otherwise easy to prove, the authority of revelation or dogma. A simple example is the tale, ascribed to Prodicus, of the Choice of Heracles. At a crossways Heracles is confronted by two women, of whom one has alluring attractions, while the other is shy and simple. The first promises him a life of ease and pleasure, to be won without effort and sustained by the fruit of other men's toil; the second offers him a life of struggle and sacrifice, of dedication to others through a stern mastery of his own body and mind. They are, of course, Vice and Virtue, and Heracles chooses Virtue.[17] The myth is a little simple for sophisticated tastes, and the critical may complain that it says no more than that it is better to be good than to be bad. But in effect it says a great deal more. It distinguishes between Vice and Virtue on the grounds of self-gratification and self-denial, and thus offers at least a clear basis for morality, and it concludes by showing that the first wins universal disapprobation and the second immortal glory. Its appeal is to the ordinary man, who would appreciate its distinctions and respond to the austere nobility with which the case for Virtue is presented. Other Sophists used myths to point more complex lessons. The myth which Plato ascribes to Protagoras about the beginnings of human society not only shows what it means to rise from the condition of the brutes, but shows what law means in human progress, and because it is both clear and imaginative, touches us at points where mere history would not. The myth of Atlantis, which Plato ascribes to Critias, is indeed incomplete, but presents a vivid picture of an almost ideal society before it has been corrupted by power and pride. Above all, Plato gives myths to his beloved Socrates, which must be at least the kind of story which he himself would have told, and they embody an indispensable element in Plato's system. In them he establishes, as he cannot by logic alone, his sense of values and supports it by visions of life after death where good and evil are revealed in their true character. He does not claim that they are literally true, but he means them to be taken very seriously and to appeal directly to the conscience. They touch us as mere argument never could. Even when philosophy had ousted poetry as the means by which the Greeks shaped their most troubling problems, myths still had a place in making fundamental issues vivid and intelligible.

If Plato developed myths for religious revelation, others found them useful for other purposes, especially for the presentation of ideas which hover on the edge of the unknown; and sometimes we can see how a myth moves into new spheres as alterations and additions are made to it. In the sixth century poets told how Orpheus, the singer whose music could charm all nature, went down to Hades; there he saw what happens to the dead, and returned to reveal his new knowledge to men. So far the story was the simple myth of a singer who was also a prophet, and it gave authority to the religious teaching associated with the name of Orpheus. To emphasize his powers it told that from the dead he brought back his lost wife, Eurydice. At first this was almost incidental, no more than an instance of his marvellous gifts, and was given no special prominence and caught nobody's imagination in words or art. But in the fifth century some poet, probably a tragedian, saw its possibilities. If Orpheus could win back his wife, yet it surely cannot have been for long, and he must, like Protesilaus, who was granted a like privilege, have soon been forced to surrender her. So the story was altered and made to tell that, after winning her back, he had to allow her to return to the dead. The crucial scene is depicted on a copy of an Attic relief, on which Orpheus turns back the veil from the face of Eurydice to look at her for the last time, and she, with a gentle gesture of farewell, lays her hand on his shoulder, while behind her Hermes, the guide of the dead, puts out his hand to take her away to Hades (see Plate 30). At this stage the story presents in mythical form the hopeless futility of any attempt to defeat death, who 'alone of gods does not love gifts',[18] and yields to no persuasion or entreaty. Later still even this story was altered, and it was told that Orpheus failed in the end to bring back his wife because, after persuading the lords of the dead to release her, he disobeyed their command that he must not look back at her until he reached the upper world. Overcome by desire, he looked back and lost her for ever.[19] Here some poet has introduced the ancient notion that men must always avert their eyes from gods or ghosts of the underworld. The story so refashioned is both tragic and rich in symbolical significance; for it shows that even the power of song, which can almost call back the dead, fails in the last test because it is at the mercy of the human heart, and even love is not stronger than death. By such adaptations the Greeks kept their myths alive. Even when the old religion had lost its hold, the stories derived from it could be put to new uses in a world which still needed them to unravel its mysteries.

The unfading youthfulness of Greek myths lies in their appeal alike to the intelligence, the emotions, and the imagination. They appeal to the intelligence because some solid consideration underlies their dramatic events, some positive assertion, concretely presented, about existence, which invites conclusions to be drawn from it. Their events are so striking and so unusual that they arouse the curiosity to ask what they mean and to extract from them some illumination for issues of every day. They appeal to the emotions, because what happens in them evokes horror or fear or admiration or delight and forces men to compare their own desires and aims with them and to wish to rival their moments of felicity or to avoid their moments of catastrophe. They appeal to the imagination, because every man needs some image against which he can set himself and see his own limitations, only to transcend them in the light which is shed on some familiar situation or in an unforeseen expansion of his faculties. Whether they guide his fancy to the golden mansions of the gods or the unfathomable night of the Furies or the stricken fields of long ago, they take him out of himself to another order of things, where his insight is sharpened and his sensibility purified. So long as the Greeks approached the problems and trials of living with their whole responsive natures, they needed myths not only in their arts but in their lives. Such stories were a leading discipline in their education, and through them they found a means to organize and interpret and expand experience.

# CHAPTER VII

# IMAGINATION AND REALITY

NO ESTIMATE OF THE GREEKS can afford to neglect the part played in their lives by poetry. Its roots lay in an unfathomable past, and though our earliest examples come from about 700 BC in the Homeric poems, these contain stories and phrases which may go back six hundred years to Mycenaean times. When the old writing disappeared *c.* 1200 BC, poetry continued to thrive on the lips of men through an oral tradition which spanned the centuries from the disappearance of the old syllabary to the arrival of the new alphabet after the middle of the eighth century. This encouraged men to write down verses, and how popular and widespread this soon became can be seen from lines painted or scratched on vases before 700 BC from places so diverse as Athens, Ithaca, and Ischia. The Greeks did not confine poetry to ceremonial occasions or esoteric mysteries; it was part of common life, honoured and enjoyed by a large number of people. It was needed for hymns and supplications to the gods and enjoyed the respect due to anything connected with them. It was a repository of stories for a people deeply interested in the superb achievements of its ancestors. It was needed at public festivals to celebrate the glory of a city when it rejoiced over a victory in war or the games. It gave its sanction to domestic occasions like weddings and funerals, and if individuals wished to unburden themselves of their loves or hates, a natural release was to transform them into songs, which would have a more vigorous circulation than any book or pamphlet. Above all, it was for a long period the chief means by which the Greeks sought to express their convictions and perplexities. As an artistic form, it was much older than prose, which came into its own in the sixth century with the demands of scientific inquiry, and even after this poetry continued to be the instrument by which the Greeks clarified and made known the issues which troubled or enthralled them. Of all their arts it was the oldest and had the most continuous history, and in their greatest days it spoke most directly of what most concerned them.

In primitive societies the poet is regarded as the instrument of an external power which possesses him and speaks through him with his own voice. He is a prophet, a seer, a man who speaks with tongues, an agent of unseen, incalculable forces. Art hardly belongs to him; for he depends on inspiration. He may see what others do not see; he may be a master of arcane knowledge, which he utters in dark and difficult words. But neither his knowledge nor his words are regarded as really his own. His statements call for interpretation, and can have more than one meaning. They are for men to make what they can of them, messages of hidden wisdom wafted from another order of being. In ancient Rome the word for poet, *vates*, was the same as for prophet, and in Hebrew poetry the rhythmical line is as often ascribed to God as to man. Not without reason did the oracle of Delphi deliver its mysterious messages in verse, or Hesiod speak of himself as one who knows things that were and are and will be.[1] The Greeks accepted these assumptions and did not deny that poetry was an inspired activity. Plato tended to think that all poets were in some sense possessed,[2] and the poets themselves paid their tribute to inspiration when they spoke of the Muse, the divine power, who directed their art. Homer begins each of his great epics with a summons to her to tell a tale, whether of the wrath of Achilles or of the man of many wiles. Hesiod, more emphatically, relates how he heard the Muses singing on Mount Helicon, and they gave him a poet's staff and told him of what to sing.[3] Pindar calls on the Muse to swell the gale of his songs or to come with him to Aegina.[4] The Muse is a divine power whom the poet invokes to his aid, and the assumption is that without her he is more or less powerless. She is outside his control, and she can do for him what he cannot do for himself. She is the personification of an indubitable fact—the extraordinary character of the power which from time to time visits a poet and fills his being.

This view of poetry as something divinely inspired might seem to be contradicted by another view which is no less common. The Greeks also insist that poetry is a form of craft, of practised skill, and their approach to it can be seen in their words for it. They have no single inclusive word for it. The word *poiêsis*, from which our own word is distantly descended, simply means 'making'. There were indeed words for different kinds of poetry, such as *epos* or epic poem, *aoidê* or song, and *molpê* or song combined with dance. But there is no single, specific word to cover all the branches of what we regard as a single art. If the Greeks wished to speak of them together, the word which they used is quite unexpected. It is *sophiâ*, which means 'wisdom' or even 'skill'. It is applied equally to all the fine arts, from poetry to sculpture and embroidery. It is also applied to activities so different as those of a helmsman, a builder, a general, and a cook. All these are not merely forms of 'wisdom'; they are even forms of technical skill. Pindar speaks of himself as a skilled craftsman and compares his poems to buildings or statues, the product of skilled hands. For him, as for most Greeks of his time, the poet practised a special skill. It had its own material—words —and its own rules in prosody, metre, and diction, but it was, in spite of everything, a craft to be practised by trained men who knew their job, and who, even if they were amateurs, were judged by high professional standards of ability and competence. If we take this view too literally by itself, it is a little alarming. We are so used to the view that poets are born and not made that we may resent the bland assumption that the creation of a poem is comparable to the cooking of a meal. Moreover, we know that in the experience of most poets the mere business of making a poem is not enough, that they rely more upon 'given' lines which seem to come from nowhere than on 'made' lines which are subsidiary and complementary to these. It is hard to believe that the greatest passages of Pindar or Aeschylus are of a purely manufactured kind, and we suspect that this theory of poetry as a craft cannot have been quite seriously held.

These apparently antithetical views of poetry are in fact two ways of looking at a single thing. In poetical composition both inspiration and craftsmanship are equally necessary, and the Greeks were well aware of it, even if at some times they stressed the need of the one and at other times the need of the other. Their respect for technical skill made full allowance for inspiration by assuming that all crafts have their presiding deities, and that it is from the combination of divine prompting and human labour that the special appeal of poetry is born. The Muse gives something to the poet which he cannot get for himself, but on this he must work with his own practised skill. He is no mere mouthpiece, no merely inspired instrument of the gods. He has his own task to do. Though the Muse is present to help him, he has his own verses to make. In this respect the Greek view of poetry is as different from the pure romantic notion that it consists of 'profuse strains of unpremeditated art' as it is from the so-called classical notion that it is simply a matter of polish and care. Between these extremes the Greeks struck a sane and happy mean, and known facts of the creative process are on their side. On this foundation they reared a splendid structure, and gave a special character to it. For the admission of the intellect, of the searching and inquiring mind, to the inspired realm of poetry was revolutionary and rich in unprecedented results. Instead of being confined to a few mysterious experiences, poetry could be made to cover the whole range of human consciousness and feeling. Instead of being simply the voice of a god, it was the voice of a man who had a god to prompt him.

This conception of the nature of poetry grew from the Greek view of its task. The primary impulse in the arts is to give permanence to the fleeting moment, to bid it stay because we cannot bear to lose it, to defy mortality by creating something which time cannot harm. The Greeks expressed this by comparing poetry to such inanimate objects as pillars or temples or gold or ivory or coral. But they saw too the paradox that, though it must have the permanence of such lifeless things, it is also in some sense alive, that it not only *is* but *does*, that it both exists in itself and affects us, that for all its finality of form it still moves and acts. That is why they also compared it to such living things as flowers, birds, bees, chariots in motion, and athletes at their games. But beyond this they saw something else, which they could express only in the imagery of fire or light. Poetry not only warms the heart but sheds a special radiance on the subjects which it celebrates, a celestial brightness which somehow brings man nearer to the enduring brilliance of the gods. It was an important means by which the Greeks sought to catch divine felicity. In its presence they felt that they indeed enjoyed an Olympian fullness of being, and in its ability to outlive themselves they saw something akin to the unageing security of the gods. For them poetry embodied something so unusual and so important that they could not but relate it to a superior order of things.

In considering what this means and what makes poetry so enthralling, the Greeks formed a conception which has so passed into common currency that we hardly pause to notice it. Yet the whole idea of the beautiful was their discovery, and played a central part in their approach to the arts. They knew as well as we do that it cannot be defined, and Plato reflected ordinary opinion when he said that 'it slips through and evades us'.[5] But they were none the less confident that they recognized it when they saw it and that without it poetry had no purpose. If we try to analyse what they meant by it, it is clear that it was not a subjective feeling which varies from man to man but something permanent in the nature of things, a universal quality, which poets and artists interpret and embody and which is within the reach of anyone who has eyes to see and ears to hear. They assumed that so mysterious a power has its own existence and is revealed through sudden illuminations when something catches and enthrals the attention. The metaphor of light illustrates its character; for just as light transfigures the whole terrestrial world, so beauty transfigures shapes and actions and gives them a new significance. When it reveals itself, we cannot but love it, and the Greeks expressed their feeling for it in the myth that at the wedding of Cadmus and Harmonia the Muses sang:

What is lovely is beloved; what is not lovely is not beloved.[6]

It was the task of the poet to catch the beauty which lurks in things both visible and invisible, to perpetuate in words the moments of rapturous illumination which he himself knew, and to share them with other men.

The Greeks interpreted the beautiful in a very wide sense. If its first and most obvious application was to whatever might attract and hold the senses, whether in the human form or in natural things, it was equally relevant to elements of character and conduct which are no less enthralling and obsessing. The Greeks made no attempt to restrict it to certain accepted categories, nor did they assume that certain classes of things are in themselves essentially and always beautiful. What matters is precisely the unique illumination which comes on each occasion to the poet and stirs him to write poetry. This generous and well-founded conception enabled them to write about many matters which might in ordinary opinion be thought ugly or painful. Whatever throws its enchantment on us is a fit subject for poetry, and both Homer and the Attic tragedians are equally justified in telling of dark and troubling events. Indeed, if we ask what Homer's conception of poetry is, the answer is probably that anything which really touches us deeply is a fit subject for song. From this he developed his own quiet but impressive theory of human suffering. So his Helen tells

Hector that the sorrows of Troy come from her and Paris, since Zeus has laid an evil doom on them

> that in the future
> Men in the ages to come may make of us stories for singing.[7]

By transforming even the ugliest disasters into themes for a high delight, song, which is inspired by the gods, makes some amends and gives some consolation for the wrongs and the failures of living. Such a belief would not be possible if Homer had not believed, as did other Greek poets after him, that poetry transforms experience into exalted joy and raises it far above the level of ordinary consciousness where we are at the mercy of our emotions and have no defence against the blows of chance. When later Aristotle said that tragedy effects in us a purification,[8] he may well have narrowed his definition unnecessarily, but he was in the true Greek tradition in seeing that the poetical presentation of events which would in ordinary life be painful beyond endurance transfigures them and sets them in a world which is somehow pure and delightful.

To catch the magical moment and hold it in enduring words demands no small degree of art, and just because the Greeks believed that poetry is a skilled profession, they paid much attention to its forms and were inspired rather than deterred by the challenges of its technique. They were happy to possess traditional forms of verse and to make the utmost use of them. They felt little call to invent new forms, and if innovations were made, they were more in detail than in general design, more improvements than reforms. Homer's consummate use of the hexameter is based on an ancient art which was devised for extemporary performance and provided him with formulaic phrases and devices to meet almost all the demands of his narrative, and his own skill lay in using these ancient elements with a new point and a special distinction. The songs of Sappho, Alcaeus, and Anacreon have indeed a wonderful range of melody, but behind them we can detect the influence of popular song with its age-old themes and its simple, direct candour. The elegiac couplet, which was used alike for inscriptions on graves, for dedications in temples, and for songs over the wine, owed much to the language of the epic and maintained its own devices as time had matured and canonized them. Even the remarkable art of choral song, practised by Pindar and Bacchylides, was no less traditional in its approach to its subjects and its maintenance

of a certain tone. Tradition dominated Greek poetry without
hampering its freedom in the smallest degree. Indeed, just
because it laid down the manner of art expected from a
certain kind of poem, it left the poet free to show his skill
in a given direction without troubling himself to invent
some new form or manner or approach.

Within these limits Greek poets developed the ancient
forms and enriched them in many ways. The choral lyric,
as we know it, has a long history behind it, and once it
must have been much simpler and less highly organized.
But the Greek genius for keeping an old form and making
something new and impressive from it can best be seen in
Attic tragedy and comedy, both of which were born of
primitive religious ritual. The word tragedy means 'goat-
song', and the first beginnings of the art are to be found in
a choral song to Dionysus, when a goat, which was thought
to embody the god, was at first torn to pieces and later
given as a prize for the best song. The songs told of heroic
or mythical events, and in due course a speaker would stand
out from the other singers and dramatize some incident in
the story, and from this tragedy was born. Even then it
kept some traces of its origins. The actors were never more
than four; the chorus took an important part, even if it
might interfere with the development of the action; gods
might appear on the scene, especially at the beginning or
the end of a play; conversation between characters often
took the form of stiff, single lines. Though the connexion
with Dionysus soon became tenuous, tragedy remained religious in its tone and its choice of subjects. Though it was
not always tragic in the sense of ending unhappily, it always dealt with serious questions concerning the relations
of men with the gods. The limitations of the form must have
put some strain on the dramatists and the actors. It was
not always easy to fit the Chorus into the action, and sometimes in moments of high dramatic tension it plays a su-
pine and slightly ridiculous part. The same actor might have
to take two or three different parts in a single play and
must have found it difficult to play all with equal conviction. Even when scenery was introduced, it cannot have
been extensive, and stage-effects were very limited in scope
and character. The ancient convention by which a character
spoke a Prologue and told the main facts of the situation,
and even of the forthcoming action, called for considerable skill to make it convincing. Yet, though the Greek
tragedians kept all these relics of the past and observed them
with respect, they usually turned them into something im-

pressive and noble. The old stories became a vehicle for pressing, present issues; the songs of the Chorus gave new chances for the expansion of lyrical genius; the limited number of actors meant that each part had to be firmly and clearly characterized. Greek tragedy has its own archaic formality, but that does not prevent it from rising to the most sublime occasions or being intensely moving and human and dramatic.

Something of the same kind is true of comedy. It too was born of a Dionysiac ritual, a fertility rite, in which a *kômos*, or riotous company, performed mimetic gestures to stimulate the fertility of the earth, and was quite unashamed in its use of phallic symbols and its unreserved language. The lewd mockery which pervaded such an occasion had indeed a religious purpose, in that it was meant to avert misfortune, but it was also enjoyable for its own sake and provided a fine nursery for satire and abuse. Comedy emerged from this rite and resembled tragedy in supplying actors to take parts and in keeping the old form of the choral song, but, unlike tragedy, it canonized ribaldry and licence and dealt not with the mythical past but with the immediate present, as a nimble imagination might transform it to make its absurdities more manifest. So while the songs of Aristophanes are pure flights of lyrical fancy and the movement of his anapaests has been compared to the gallop of the horses of the sun, his episodes draw freely on contemporary life and make more of it by transposing it to a world of impossible absurdity in which birds talk and men grow wings or ride on dung-beetles to heaven. Just because this art was based on a tradition of unlicensed speech, it used this liberty abundantly on all kinds of subject and was not deterred by any respect for the sensibilities of eminent persons. Even the phallic element kept its place. Many of the jokes of Aristophanes would expose a modern author to prosecution, and in the *Lysistrata* he turns the sexual instinct to a dramatic purpose in a play, which, despite its rollicking farce, is seriously concerned with the evils of war. Greek comedy has nothing to do with the drawing-room. It draws its strength from the ribaldry of the market-place and stands firmly on its right to make full use of it. Just as the old rite was thought to bring health and life to the soil, so comedy, which grew from it, purged its audiences of many troubles by making them laugh at them. If tragedy was born from the ritual of a god's yearly death, comedy was born from the ritual of his yearly birth, and provided a contrast and a counterpoise to all that tragedy stood for.

Greek poetry owes much of its abiding strength to a metrical system which allowed a variety of metres beyond almost all other languages. The basis of this is that Greek metric is not accentual, but quantitative. That is to say, the rhythm is based on units in which the balance of syllables is dictated not by the loudness, or stress, with which each is spoken, but by quantity, or the time taken to speak it. Even so simple a form as the dactylic hexameter has a precision and a formality which are almost impossible in accentual verse; for no accent is quite strong enough to do what quantity can, and English hexameters too often limp or languish. The quantities of a Greek word are fixed and known, but the English accent can be shifted according to taste; the Greek division of syllables into longs and shorts is absolute, but we can never be quite sure how strong an accent is or which syllable carries it. For this reason Greek has a variety of melody beyond the reach of accentual languages. It is just possible to write English hexameters, and with some difficulty to produce Alcaics and Sapphics, but it is quite impossible to compose anything resembling the complex metres of Greek choral poetry like that of Pindar or the songs of the tragedians and Aristophanes, for the simple reason that the English accent falls so dubiously and hesitantly that we can never quite know what the rhythm is, whereas in Greek it is perfectly clear and emphatic from the start.

The extraordinary variety of Greek lyric metres and their ability to take new forms undoubtedly owe much to dancing and music. The elaborate stanzas of this poetry were part of a complex unity in which dance and music were as important as words and all three elements formed a single harmonious whole. The word 'foot', which we still use of metrical units and in so doing follow Greek precedent, indicates some kind of dance. Individual 'feet', whether dactyls or anapaests or iambs or trochees, were based on the rhythm of dancing steps and the balance between short and long movements. In action such steps were matched by a music which marked and fitted their character, and from this combination Greek lyric metres were born. Greek dances were performed not by couples but by individuals collaborating in a company, and each performed an elaborate sequence of steps, which might become more elaborate as the dance proceeded and the music altered with it. This not only trained the ear to respond to all kinds of rhythmical motion, but forced the accompanying song also to follow them. But while such a dance allowed a wide variety within a certain range, it also insisted on a dominating formality, and this is what we find in the structure of a choral ode. Though each of Pindar's odes has a different metrical pattern, the structure is always such that every main section, however new and ingenious in itself, corresponds with every other section in an undeviating precision. Just as the Greeks classified their music into different kinds and attributed to each its own temper and mood, so in their metric we may distinguish at least between Dorian and Aeolian rhythms, of which the first was noted for its robust virility, the second for its melodious sweetness. This means that Greek lyric song was not only strictly lyrical in the sense that it was sung to the lyre, but was part of a combined activity of voice, dance, and musical accompaniment. If the element of dance gave to the words that living force which the Greeks demanded from poetry, the formality of the whole gave that sense of structure and permanence which was no less indispensable.

With this technique at their command Greek poets were ready to write poetry about any subject which seemed to have the necessary element of the beautiful, and their work has an unusually wide range. In narrative it tells of humble and unimportant things no less than of fierce passions and violent actions. Homer sees the appeal not only of Hector's last fight and the slaying of Penelope's Suitors but of such quiet activities as the scudding of a ship over the sea in the evening, the heating of water for a bath, the folding and hanging of a garment before going to sleep, the washing of linen in a river. The lyric poets may often write in the white heat of passion, but that does not prevent them from writing also about such simple matters as flowers and trees, the mixing of wine for a party, the flight of birds, or the vagaries of the weather. Such subjects pass easily into verse because the poet feels that his art is no isolated activity which is confined to a special class of subjects, but must respond to whatever touches or moves him. Greek poetry, indeed, sometimes deals with matters from which modern poetry shrinks. We are afraid, for instance, of anything didactic. In spite of the *De Rerum Natura* and *The Prelude*, we are suspicious of any verse that savours of instruction. Instead of public and political themes we prefer the undeniable poetry of the emotions and the sensibility. We look for songs and not for sermons. Not so the Greeks. Hesiod used poetry to write about a plough; Parmenides for a stiff exposition of the unity of being; Archestratus for table delicacies; Empedocles

for the nature of the elements. In almost every poet there
are moral maxims, stated almost baldly, as if for our good.
They sometimes sound platitudinous, sometimes almost child-
ish, but they are never insincere, never repellent. The Greeks
are free from any suspicion of trying to impose on us; they
may evoke an occasional smile, but not dislike or irritation.
Nor need we complain that they wrote of what we regard
as unpoetical subjects. It is true that the nature of a plough
or of the universe may well be displayed in prose, that fish
may thrive in the pages of a text-book, but there is much to
be said for writing of them in melodious hexameters. The
measure and the style give them a new dignity and charm,
and the poet exerts himself to enliven them with the traditional decorations of his craft.

This happened because the Greeks allowed reason a large
part in poetry, but there is another side to this, more important and more illuminating. Because the Greeks regarded
poetry as a rational activity, they brought to it a remarkable
source of strength. They put into it their own pondered and
serious view of life, and they thought it their duty to say
what they really meant. For this reason they infuse it with
the power which comes from long and intense thought. When
Aeschylus constructs a tragedy, he makes his action illustrate
the divine laws which operate through human life. His view
of these laws is not only original; it has been reached by a
deep consideration of human affairs, and his presentation
of it comes vastly enriched by all the imaginative and emotional attention which he has given to it. These are no conventional judgments, lightly adopted and hastily presented.
They are what experience has forced on him, and in his
majestic and searching treatment of them there is an uncommon power because he is desperately concerned with the
truth. Unlike him, Sophocles keeps his own views in the background but lets them emerge through the personalities and
fortunes of his characters. But the fortunes of these characters present instances of problems which have long troubled
his mind—the vast difference between human error and divine knowledge, the conflict between heroic and merely
human standards of conduct, the illusions which beset those
who are unworthily in power. He sees the issues with extreme
clarity and has thought so hard about them that they have
become part of his consciousness and, when he puts them
into poetry, they are enriched by the associations and the
special strength which come from sustained personal familiarity.

Such honesty and seriousness of purpose show themselves

in the concern which the Greeks felt for the truth of poetry.
This question has been much discussed, and many different
answers found to it. But the Greeks were insistent that poetry
must have a strong element of truth. Though Homer says
nothing of it, and we do not know how much of his historical
tale he thought to be true, yet he was at least careful on
some points where we can check him. The plain of Troy still
looks very much as he says that it did, and even Ithaca,
scarred battle-ground of higher critics and archaeologists, is
still in many respects much as his Odysseus knew and loved
it. Hesiod faces the issue more directly, when he claims that
the Muses said to him: 'We know how to tell falsehoods like
the truth, and we know, when we choose, how to speak the
truth.'[9] The vital point in this admission is the recognition
that poetry cannot entirely dissociate itself from truth and
falsehood, even if it does not always distinguish between
them. Once the question was raised, there was but one answer, and Pindar is an instructive example of a poet who
feels it his duty to tell the truth. Tradition demanded that in
his odes he should tell of gods and heroes. To this he ad-
hered, but he was careful to tell only what he believed to be
true. If an old tale of the gods placed them in an unfavourable light, he told a new version which he thought more probable. If story told that Apollo heard some news from a raven,
Pindar corrected it; for he knew that Apollo, the lord of
prophecy, needed no raven to tell him anything.[10] He felt,
indeed, that the old stories contained much that was false,
and that is why he was never fully sympathetic to Homer, of
whom he says:

> On his falsehood and his winged cunning
> A majesty lies. Art tricks and deceives us with tales,
> And blind is the heart of the multitude of men.[11]

But he trusted that time sorts out the true from the false
and that the wisest witnesses of all are the days to come.[12]
His natural piety forbade him to acquiesce in any story which
brought discredit to the gods, and he asserted his right to tell
the truth as he saw it.

This attitude is of course most obvious in poets who speak
in the first person about their own views, but it could be applied without much difficulty to epic and tragic poetry. If the
tragedians did not always believe in the literal truth of the
myths which they dramatized, still less in their own additions and variations to them, they certainly believed in the
importance of the issues presented through the dramatic

action and in their own handling and interpretation of them. Greek poets had their own notion of the kind of truth which their art demanded. In the fourth century Aristotle faced the issue candidly and squarely and, in discussing the difference between history and poetry, came to a clear conclusion: 'It really lies in this: the one describes what has happened, the other what might. Hence poetry is something more philosophic and more serious than history; for poetry speaks of what is universal, history of what is particular.'[13] No Greek poets would have used precisely this language, and most of them would have been surprised to hear their work called philosophical, but they would certainly have thought it serious. But Aristotle is right to call it philosophical, because in its own way it is concerned with the revelation of truth. The truth in question, as he saw, is not of particular facts, but of universal principles or tendencies or characteristics. Even if, as is perfectly possible, there was once a historical Achilles, the importance of Homer's presentation of him is irrelevant to his existence. The Achilles whom we know is indeed universal in the sense that he embodies in a convincing and satisfying form qualities which are to be found in many men, but seldom so clearly or so forcibly as in him. To find this universal element the poet must make a severe selection from reality and present it with decisive discrimination. Just as sculptors emphasized what they thought to be the essential characteristics of their subjects at the expense of the incidental and the accidental, so poets emphasized what they thought to be the essential characteristics of human beings and showed how these led to certain kinds of result in action and suffering. They saw too that behind the infinite variety of human behaviour and fortune there must be forces at work which could to some degree be understood and presented in a concrete form. Their idea of truth was to find out these principles and forces, which were indeed at work in individuals but could best be grasped if they were abstracted from the particular case and displayed through situations which manifested more clearly their significance and their reality. In this pursuit their notion of poetical truth was generous and capacious. They saw that it lay not merely in revealing powers at work in and above human nature, but in a sympathetic understanding of irrational and emotional elements which must be portrayed in their authentic force, that there is a truth of the heart as well as of the head, and that poetry works equally through both. Though this certainly calls for hard thought and perceptive insight, it calls also for powers more instinctive and less rational, for an immediate and imaginative response to the innumerable winds which sweep through the human soul and drive it to incalculable ends.

This sense that unseen forces can best be understood if they are presented in concrete and visible forms means that Greek tragedy is, in its own way, realistic. It deals with real emotions, and its characters are swayed by motives which we know in ourselves. It presents its events with a careful regard for their fundamental verisimilitude. Though it tends to eschew the miraculous and the romantic, there are times when they are necessary to the plot, and then they are made as convincing and as life-like as possible. When Aeschylus presents on the stage the ghost of the Persian king Darius, he makes him speak with commanding accents, as befits the King of Kings, and shows that even after death the great warrior and administrator has not lost his care for his people's welfare. The shirt of Nessus, with which Heracles comes to a ghastly end, is indeed a work of witchcraft, but its havoc on him is told in almost medical words.[14] The madness which Hera sends to Heracles is all the more tragic and convincing because it takes the form of making him kill his own children in the belief that they are the children of his enemy Eurystheus.[15] The monster which rises out of the sea to destroy Hippolytus is hardly described, but we are left with a terrifying nightmare of a monstrous bull.[16] In an art whose material dates back to a time when the boundaries between fact and fancy were not clearly defined, the tragedians did their utmost to put blood into ghosts and to bring the supernatural and the miraculous as close as possible to the workings of human nature.

The subject of Greek literature is human beings, and of course gods, because gods belong to human life and play an indispensable part in it. They had indeed stories of animals, but though these belong to an unpretentious art, they too told of human beings in the sense that different animals display human qualities in the form of fables, like those attributed to Aesop. It is true that Achilles' horse speaks once when it foretells its master's death, but that is because Hera has given him speech for this time only.[17] Horses and dogs have indeed their place in literature, but it is the same as in life. Hector summons his horses to a great effort in recognition of the barley and wine which Andromache has given them,[18] and the old dog of Odysseus, lying full of ticks in the midden, recognizes his master after twenty years and then dies.[19] Even in the legendary and fanciful world of Odysseus' wanderings there is a tendency to apply to human beings what a

less sophisticated art would apply to animals. When Odysseus
is cast up from the sea on Scheria, he is saved by the king's
daughter, Nausicaa, and at every point she lives as a girl on
the edge of womanhood, courageous, resourceful, sensitive,
and young. This story is known in a much earlier Egyptian
version, but there the castaway is saved not by a princess but
by a gorgeous snake, thirty ells long, with a skin of gold and
lapis lazuli. Even Polyphemus, who is indeed an odious monster, has his human side, when he speaks affectionately to his
ram. The monstrous queen of the Laestryonians, who is as
'big as a mountain', is brought into a human setting when
the poet comments of Odysseus' comrades that 'they loathed
her'.[20] Like the gods, animals and monsters are fitted into a
human frame and made to comform as far as possible to it.
Their actions are almost intelligible, and they are treated as
if they were accustomed to the ways of men.

In their interest in human beings the Greeks saw them
simply and directly, and presented them in the epic or on
the stage with a keen eye to their main characteristics. Their
sense of personality was different from ours, in that they were
less interested in the subtleties and oddities of character
than in its dominating traits. Homer's heroes are fully differentiated from one another, and each has his own marked
personality, which we know from his words and his actions.
These show the thoughts and the emotions which guide him,
and through them we feel that we know him. The same is
true of the tragedians and of Aristophanes. The enormous
impact which the Clytaemestra of Aeschylus makes on us is
not from any rare complexity in her psychology, but from the
magnificent effrontery of her behaviour and the ringing words
with which she first deceives and dominates her husband and
then glories in his murder. Though Antigone goes to death
on a point of conscience, she is so simply conceived that she
has not even thought out her own motives very clearly, but
acts as she does because she knows, without argument, that
it is right. When Euripides presents in Medea the tragic figure
of a barbarian woman humiliated by her Greek husband, he
understands the full frenzy of her violent desire for revenge,
but it rises naturally from what she has suffered. There is
nothing in Greek literature to compare with the complexity
of Hamlet or Richard II, still less with the searching psychology of Tolstoy or Proust. No doubt this is partly because it
operates on a relatively small scale. Tragedy and comedy,
even the epic, had to make their effects rapidly within a
limited space, and must leave no doubt of their intention.
But we must also attribute something to what the Greeks

looked for in a man, and this was an essential part of their whole outlook.

Their first interest in man was as a being made and given to action, and they examined with care the motives of action and the kind of man who will act in this or that way. Their concern was not with 'humours' but with thoughts and emotions, and their combination in promoting certain results. This is true even of their more precise and more detailed analysis of character and their anticipations of a systematic psychology. When, in Plato's *Symposium*, Alcibiades delivers his brilliant speech in praise of Socrates, what concerns him are the real motives which prompt Socrates to act in the extraordinary way that he does, and his explanation contains nothing which is not straightforward and sensible. When Theophrastus (*c.* 372–287 BC) wrote his *Characters*, he was indeed interested in the oddities of human behaviour and sketched them with a good eye for significant eccentricities, but his purpose is simply to show that even people like these act from some central principle in their nature. The Greeks were well aware of the vagaries of our flesh and blood and often amused or interested by them, as when Herodotus says of Candaules, king of Lydia, that 'this Candaules fell in love with his own wife',[21] or Aristotle says of the extravagant man that 'he gives a club dinner on the scale of a wedding banquet'.[22] Such observation is indispensable to literature, and the Greeks had their full share of it. But at a certain point they stopped. They were not deeply interested in the hidden conflicts and contradictions of human character, and they shrank from analysing themselves on any exacting scale. It is significant that they hardly ever wrote confessions or autobiographies. It is true that in the fifth century Ion of Chios wrote reminiscences, but they seem to have been more about others than himself, and the first human soul revealed to us in the Greek language with searching intimacy is that not of a Greek, but of a Hebrew of the Hebrews, Paul of Tarsus. The Greek concern with human beings was indeed strong, but it was not directed towards the less easily discernible currents in their souls. It liked men to be up and doing, and then it was able to see them as they really were, without any distracting or disturbing analysis of their inner contortions.

This concern with reality as it is embodied in human beings means that Greek poetry is in no sense a poetry of escape. The poets felt that their task was to interpret experience by presenting it in individual shapes which anyone could relate to his own life. To retire into dream was to shirk a primary duty, and no Greek ventures such prolonged flights of fancy as Ovid's *Metamorphoses* or Ariosto's *Orlando Furioso*, in which dream and reality are inextricably fused in a golden haze. They had indeed their desires for escape, but they knew what they were worth, and used them circumspectly, as when a Chorus of Euripides, appalled by the horrors which take place around them, wish that they were birds and could fly away to the world's end.[23] But they know that the wish is only a wish, and they turn back from it to reality. When the Greeks wished to reach the furthest edge of fancy, they imagined some simple scene like that of Sophocles:

> Beyond all seas and earth's last boundaries,
> The spring of Night and heaven's vast expanse,
> Apollo's ancient garden.[24]

All is clear, almost on the map. In their efforts to envisage things beyond mortal ken the Greeks made them as life-like as possible. They concentrated on their brightest, clearest aspects; they selected details with care, and in the end the picture was, if not actually of life, at least like life, and certainly alive. Even the cosmic travesties of Aristophanes, in which the laws of nature are often set at naught, are peopled by solid men and women with robust appetites and homely vocabularies. In their wildest flights of imagination the Greeks never lost their grip on reality. Indeed, the farther they travelled from it, the more they were concerned to keep in touch with it, as if poetry ceased to be itself if it lost its connexion with the actual characters and doings of men.

For this we may suggest at least one reason. The Greek poet knew very well that his hearers were not a select circle of adepts like himself, but a public in whose life poetry had an accepted place and belonged to its normal round of interests. It was not an exotic or unusual thing, calling for a specially adjusted frame of mind. The poet sang for people of multifarious tastes and activities, who were concerned with their own problems and expected him to tell them something which was not unreal or absurd, but had some relevance to their own experience. His stories might well have highly unfamiliar elements in them, but his task was to make them as actual and as credible as possible. In his *King Oedipus* Sophocles tells the old grim tale of a man who discovers that he has unwittingly killed his father and married his mother. Modern taste might shrink from the stark horror of such themes as well as from their inherent unlikeliness. But not so Sophocles, who shows exactly how they must have happened. Oedipus tells how he killed his father in a lonely place, not knowing who he was. The old man threatened him, and the young man defended himself in the heat of his youthful blood. Even as he recalls the encounter he cannot but recapture some of its excitement. We see his mother on the stage after he has married her, and the relation is true and tender-hearted between them. Jocasta looks after Oedipus as a wife older than her husband may, and when she sees him tormented by dark doubts and suspicions, tries to comfort him with soothing words. She is at once his wife and his mother, who speaks to him with unfaltering affection and is anxious only that he should not suffer. Nor can anything be more essentially true to such a nature than when Jocasta realizes the appalling truth that she has married her own son, and leaves the stage to kill herself, saying:

> Alas, alas, ill-fated one, that name alone
> I give you, and none other any more.[25]

Sophocles does not acquiesce in the improbabilities of the old story. He tries to see how it can have happened, what elements of truth can be found in it. He presents it as it may really have happened, we might say as it only can have happened. And his audience, full of life and the knowledge of life, would see that he was right and understand what he meant.

It would be wrong to suppose that the great Greek poets sacrificed anything for a popular appeal or to make themselves more easily understood. On the contrary, sane and solid as they were, they expected their audiences to rise to their own level. They made no concessions to tickle the ears of the groundlings. Their independence and their integrity may be seen in their rigid adherence to their own views and convictions, in their determination to state the truth at all costs, and above all in their style. All three of the Attic tragedians wrote in what can only be called a poetical language. Each has his own special characteristics, but each is equally removed from common speech. Indeed, it is hard for us to see how an audience could at a first hearing take in a choral ode of Aeschylus. The compressed, heavily loaded sentences, the abundant and forcible metaphors, are hard enough for us, with all the resources of scholarship and unlimited time at our disposal. How much harder, it might seem, they must have been to ordinary men hearing these words sung—and for the first time. And yet Aeschylus was not merely respected, but loved, so much so, indeed, that Aristophanes can quote casual words from him in the knowledge that they will be recognized, and pay him that tribute which can be real only when a poet is known and admired—parody. His parodies of the Aeschylean manner must have raised a laugh among most of the thousands who heard them. They were made in all affection and reverence, and they came with the more force because the audience was able to laugh at something which it knew and respected.

The Greeks certainly understood their poets, and the mere fact is remarkable enough. They were of course very intelligent. Of that there can be no doubt, and equally no explanation. But there are many intelligent people who do not understand poetry, and the Greeks' understanding of it, even in its most complex forms, was due not only to intelligence but to being trained from childhood in it. In their education they learned no foreign languages, almost no natural science, little geography or history, and no economics. But they learned music and poetry, and when they listened to a poet's work, they understood it with that almost instinctive ease which comes from early training and prolonged practice. They were prepared, as very few peoples have ever been, to understand almost as experts the intricacies and difficulties of a mature art. Because the poets knew that they would be understood, they gave of their best and drew much of their strength from feeling at one and at ease with their public. They had no cause to apologize for their art, for being poets. They need waste no time in explaining their position. Such preliminaries were taken for granted. The poet agreed on essential issues with his audience and did not feel, as poets have felt at other times, that his age was hostile to the arts and that this prevented him from doing his best.

The popularity of poetry in Greece is the more remarkable, since it was usually written in what can only be called an artificial language. Apart from a few lyrical poets, such as Sappho, Alcaeus, and Anacreon, who wrote more or less in their own vernaculars, all Greek poetry is written in a language which was used for poetry and for nothing else. Our first reaction to this may well be unfriendly, since we may feel that the very word 'artificial' condemns and that the truest poetry is to be found in 'native woodnotes wild'. Now Greek poetry is indeed capable of sublime simplicities, of advancing beyond all imagery and metaphor to those bare and splendid heights, where decoration is left behind and passion goes forth in its naked power. So, when Oedipus begins to find out the truth about his destiny, he cries out:

O Zeus, what have you planned to do with me?[26]

When in his death-hour Hippolytus knows that his protectress, Artemis, cannot help him, he says:

Lightly you leave our long companionship.[27]

But these high moments of simplicity are themselves the product of an artificial style, and their effect is all the greater because they have been distilled from it. Most Greek poetry is written in a language which combines archaic words, foreign words, new compounds, and words from different dialects. It exults in metaphors and similes; it is not above periphrasis and tropes, as when Aeschylus speaks of 'dust, thirsty sister and neighbour of mud'[28] and Pindar calls inspiration 'a shrill whetstone on the tongue'.[29] Even Homer, master of directness and candour, uses a language which can never have been spoken, but was created entirely for heroic hexameters. Centuries of creative discrimination had fashioned for him his wonderful epithets, like the 'loudly-resounding' sea, death 'which lays at length', the 'rosy-fingered' dawn, and the 'long-shadowing' spear, and provided him with a large number of synonyms and alternative forms to suit almost every possible demand of his metre. Greek poetical language was a product of artistic creation and far removed from Wordsworth's ideal of poetical style.

The essence of the grand style—and such the Greek style is—is that it aims at exalting an experience beyond ordinary views of it. It is of course exposed to its own perils. Even before the close of the great age we find absurdities in Timotheus, who calls teeth 'glittering children of the mouth' and oars 'mountain-born feet of the ship'.[30] In such pretentious pomposities the grand manner decays into awful mannerisms, but at its best it need not be judged by them. Fine words chosen for their sound and associations can do something that plain words cannot always do. They give an air of strangeness and majesty; they show that the poet's experience is not that of other men, and needs special means of expression. Such words need not be ambiguous or obscure, and in Greek they seldom are. The grand style can keep in touch with facts and show them in their true grandeur. When Homer makes Achilles say that between him and his home lie 'shadowy mountains and the echoing sea',[31] he uses words far removed from conversation, but they are apt and right, and they are grand. It is not merely that the adjectives are well and truly chosen; the whole sweep of the phrase conveys an irresistible effect of distance and separation. It is such mountains and such a sea that lie between Achilles and his home. This style was traditional, but it was not fossilized, and had in it great possibilities of development. Each new poet worked on the lines of his predecessors, but re-made his vocabulary afresh and employed the old phrases in new contexts and with many happy variations. So the grand style avoided its greatest danger—ossification. It remained lively because it was used by men who knew that its purpose was to achieve an effect, to delight and enthral others who were trained to listen to poetry, and to expect from it a special exalted pleasure.

The long tradition which sustained Greek poetry, and the outlook which took the need of it for granted, were closely related to religion. Poetry not only served religion by telling of the gods, but made it more real and more relevant by its concrete presentation of invisible forces at work within and without man. This in a sense is what poetry always does. It presents in a vivid, palpable shape what cannot be expressed in the plain speech of every day. The Greeks were able to give it a peculiarly wide scope because their world was full of unseen presences which they wished to understand and to grasp as their own. Even their most factual poems suggest vistas beyond the immediate scene and undefined forces which defy precise analysis. Part of the strength of Greek poetry comes from the effort to catch these forces and to show them at work in a convincing and intelligible way. The passion and the sincerity of such an endeavour cannot but enhance the enchantment of poetry and strengthen those qualities which make it unique. But the search for the unknown was as strong as it was only because the Greeks were enthralled by the visible world, and especially by the world of men. It was this embracing and energetic curiosity about what they saw around them that forced them to look for principles behind it. When they found these principles and set them forth in majestic words, it was the visible scene that gained; for it was revealed on a foundation of indestructible forces, and this justified men in their unfailing delight in it and their desire to understand it with the full force of their imaginative reason. The unusual strength of Greek poetry comes from its eager concern with the living world and its desire to see this in all its depth and richness, to pass from the immediate situation to what lies behind it, and to enjoy the illumination which this brings to common and familiar things.

# CHAPTER VIII

# THE PLASTIC VISION

THE PLACE OF POETRY in Greek life was matched by that of the visual arts. Though neither was subordinate or inferior to the other, and each went its own way within the limits of its own medium, yet the Greeks recognized that there was something fundamentally in common between poetry on the one side and painting and sculpture on the other. This was succinctly stated by Simonides when he said: 'Painting is silent poetry; poetry is painting that speaks'.[1] This assumes a common task and a common end, and admits that both painting and poetry are alike branches of *sophiâ* and appeal to us in ways which are not ultimately dissimilar. Like poets, sculptors and painters were regarded as craftsmen, whose first task was to master their technique. If poets depended for their inspiration on the Muse, artists were the servants of Athene, who stood by them to instruct or encourage. All alike dealt with the same kind of subjects. If much painting and sculpture treated the world of heroic myth, they resembled epic and tragedy; if they honoured individual men and women and chose scenes from every day, they had a counterpart in lyric poetry and comedy. If by their very nature the visual arts cannot show any close parallel to the high, artificial language of most Greek poetry, they secure a similar effect of detachment and distance by their avoidance of excessive realism or melodramatic display. Though they are based on the living scene and draw freely from it, they aim at something beyond it, and try to reveal this by their selection of what they think to be really relevant and significant. When in the fourth century Plato elaborated his theories of art, he applied them equally to poetry, painting, and sculpture, and in so doing he followed the traditional notion that they were all closely related and must in any consideration of their social and ethical uses be treated together.

Painting and sculpture, like architecture, which is closely

155

related to them, developed later than poetry and lacked that unbroken connexion with the Mycenaean past which favoured the growth of the epic. They called for good tools, but once these were forthcoming, physical conditions favoured a rapid progress. Unlimited supplies of hard limestone and marble can be turned to almost any need of builders and sculptors. Anything made of them flouts the assaults of the weather and gains new shades and tones and texture from the passage of time. The clearly defined outline which such buildings present against the sky makes them an appropriate and impressive background for a life passed largely out of doors, and the varied configuration of the landscape provides dramatic sites for temples on ledges above deep valleys, like that of Apollo at Delphi (see Plate 8); or on promontories facing the sea, like that of Posidon at Sunium (see Plate 3); or on rocky hills rising abruptly from the plain, like that of Athene at Athens (see Plate 5); or on a mountain among other mountains, like that of Apollo at Bassae. In the colour and texture of their material Greek buildings proclaim the land from which their stones were quarried and rise in congenial affinity with it. The fine polish of their surface catches the rays of the rising or the setting sun and takes new hues from it, while in storm and shadow it keeps some of its brightness in defiance of the shifting elements above and around. So too Greek sculpture, which was commonly placed in the open air or on the exterior of temples, shows its full depths and varied planes against the searching light. Painting, which is essentially an indoor art, began with a limited range of colours, perhaps because materials had not been discovered to provide much variety, but subordinated them to sharp, clean drawing and relied on the Greek light to abate what would in cloudier climes be too violent effects. The Greeks normally painted their stone statues, and in so doing brought sculpture closer to painting. Shape, colour, and line alike were in harmony with the natural setting and appealed to the eye which had been trained on it.

Though Greek art owes many of its subjects to myth and legend, it is not in any strict or narrow sense literary. It relies not on any second-hand evocation of associations from poetry, but on presenting scenes directly to the eye for their own visible sake. Its works are complete in themselves, and those for whom they were made would respond instinctively and immediately to them. This is not to say that it appeals only to the sense of design or that it cares for nothing except the schematic arrangement of bodies in space. It does indeed care for them greatly, but only as parts in a larger whole. In its own way it often tells a story, or at least presents some vivid moment of vigorous action. But its appeal is different from any that comes from story-telling in words. It depends on our whole-hearted response to certain visual impressions and presents these in such a way that we grasp their essential character and significance through the simultaneous operation of our eyes and our minds. No matter how recondite or interesting or dramatic its subjects may be, what matters is the complete effect which their representation makes on us. An Attic relief of a soldier who is 'all out', conveys an overwhelming sense of exhaustion in every part of his body, in his drooping head, his arms clutching at his breasts, his bent knees (see Plate 50). When Achilles kills Penthesilea, his irresistible strength and her helpless collapse are shown in the relentless grip of his arm and the sprawling relaxation of her body (see Plate 85). For the Greeks the body could speak as well as the face and had its own many varieties of expression. If Poetry provided many subjects for painting and sculpture, that did not mean that it imposed its own point of view, or that it led men to look at them as mere illustrations of books. Poetry and the visual arts were complementary to one another in a common vision of life, but they remained distinct and exerted their own powers in their own spheres. So long as the visual arts kept to their proper realm, there was no need to make them do any more than appeal directly to the eyes.

Greek sculpture and painting raise in a special way the question of the place of the emotions in the fine arts. They certainly display them at work, and even arouse them in us. But our responses are not ultimately emotional. What we feel about a dying warrior on a pediment from Aegina (see Plate 40) or Actaeon devoured by his own hounds (see Plate 36) is not in the final resort anguish or sorrow or pity. These may be our first, immediate reaction, but they are soon transcended in something else, which is in fact an exalted delight. Greek art, at least in its archaic and classical periods, so masters its subjects that it passes beyond realistic or naturalistic representation to another sphere. What might be unbearably painful is so controlled and transformed that it does not distress, but exalt. The fundamental experience which it gives is indeed derived from the living scene, but this is so arranged and ordered that it affects us as no living scene would. Nor indeed are the successes of Greek art confined to the human body. The long folds of the dress of the Delphic Charioteer (see Plate 22) or of the women on the

Ludovisi Throne (see Plate 28), are curiously expressive
and absorbing, even if they have no element of drama or
passion in them. In them an inanimate material, which or-
dinarily we might not notice, is given a new harmony, and
through it a new appeal. Even human subjects need not always
be in themselves very exciting or unusual. The Calf-bearer
from the Acropolis (see Plate 14) calls up no myths or
legends and suggests no personal history, and yet it is su-
premely satisfying. The simple details fall into a dominating design; the pervading temper of calm strength is manifest
alike in the face and the confident grip of the arms; the
calf is as true to its own nature as the man is to his. But
beyond this lies the hold which it takes of us, and in the end
this defies analysis. We may call it significant form or
what we please, but we can only say that it appeals to the
sensitive eye and through the eye to the whole being. Ultimately this depends on the way in which physical nature
can at times grip us and hold us with an inexorable enchantment. Greek artists understood this and selected from
nature the subjects which touched them most deeply. Just as
in poetry the final experience is inexplicable because it is
somehow beyond our emotional responses, so Greek painting and sculpture move more obviously and more directly
to something which is equally inexplicable and constitutes
their chief claim on us.

The Greeks were conscious of this when they tried to
represent in visible form something to which the usual man
is normally blind. In the arts, as in poetry, they called it the
beautiful and were on the whole content to leave it at that,
even if they sought to relate it to some abiding reality behind
the world of changing appearances. Just as poetry sought to
embody in concrete form issues beyond the reach of ordinary thought, so did painting and sculpture. Their first concern was with living creatures, and their chief aim was to
interpret these in their essential nature. That is why inanimate
nature plays almost no part in Greek art and is never depicted for its own sake before the landscape-painting of the
Hellenistic age. If it appears, it is as a background which is
thought to be indispensable to the main, human subject, like
the two trees from which a man tries to snare birds (see
Plate 72) or the tree from which a girl picks an apple (see
Plate 86). This means not that the Greeks lacked interest
in nature, but that they did not regard it as a first subject
for art. The same tendency can be seen in their poetry,
which shows no lack of love for natural beauty, but hardly
ever concentrates on it and keeps it as a background for

human actions. Unlike modern lovers of nature, the Greeks were never far enough from it to develop a romantic longing for it as a haven and a refuge, and, though they peopled it with gods of all kinds and degrees, it was the gods themselves, rather than their habitations, which aroused their interest. The chief subjects of Greek art are beings in human shape, whether gods or men, as was indeed appropriate to the conception of a single universe in which the two classes are sufficiently alike to behave in much the same way. An honourable place is also given to animals, who are often depicted for their own sake or as accessories, necessary or merely ornamental, to men. Not very different from them are the monsters, on whose importance tradition insisted, and who had their own place in myth and symbol. Greek artists were drawn to any subject which possessed life and movement and embodied *dynamis* or inherent power. In a sense this limited their scope, but within these limits they had a wide choice, and were able to give to their chosen subjects the special attention which comes from love and admiration.

The Greeks agreed that art was in some sense an imitation or *mimêsis*. The common word for a statue, *eikôn*, means literally 'likeness' or 'image', and a Hippocratic author echoes common opinion when he says that 'sculptors make an imitation of the body'.[2] But imitation is a vague word, and tells us little more than that the Greeks created figures which were recognizably like living originals. It does not tell us what qualities or aspects they thought most worthy of imitation, and since all art depends on a selection from a given mass of possibilities, we ought to find out what Greek artists chose and what they rejected. That their art was not merely naturalistic or realistic in any narrow sense is clear from two facts. First, they often represented gods and monsters whom they had never seen. In this there is no imitation in any real sense. The artist embodies his own vision of what a god or a monster ought to be. If he puts into a god the highest degree of power and beauty that he can imagine, and derives this from his observation of human beings, he is still not imitating any individual, any more than in making his monsters as monstrous as possible by combining disparate limbs and features in them he is imitating anything real in the animal world. Secondly, we can hardly doubt that Greek artists sought to represent human beings not as they would appear to any casual observer, but with some feeling for what is most interesting and important in them. That they allowed themselves a considerable degree of freedom is clear from the remark of Socrates, which was accepted by the painter Parrhasius: 'When you copy types of beauty, it is so difficult to find a perfect model that you combine the most beautiful details of several, and thus contrive to make the whole figure look beautiful'.[3] We cannot doubt that Greek artists took considerable liberties with their sitters and felt no obligation to depict them 'warts and all'. Nor would they have done this if they had not felt that the representation of human beings in stone or paint must conform to certain assumptions on the nature of art.

It is said of the sculptor Polygnotus that he depicted men as 'better than they are',[4] and though the word 'better' is tantalizingly vague, it does not necessarily mean that he made them more beautiful, as Zeuxis was said to have done.[5] It suggests rather that he tried to get the best out of them, and, since he was renowned for his skill in depicting character,[6] we may assume that this played at least some part in his creation of superior beings. Polygnotus seems to have tried to make the most of his subjects, to show them as most truly themselves. And this is on the whole what Greek sculpture does. We can see this spirit at work even in the archaic art of the sixth century. It is not in the least clumsy or incompetent, but confines itself to a narrow range of effects, as if it felt these to be the most important. The first figures of *kouroi*, or naked young men, are certainly stiff and formal, as they stand with their left feet forward, their arms hanging by their sides, their heads held erect, and their faces lit by a curious smile (see Plates 9-11). The formality of their stance may owe something to Egyptian precedent, but it is not likely to have been accepted without good reason. They walk with a firm and springy step because that is how young men display the balance and control of their bodies; they are dignified and restrained because their statues are usually placed in the precincts of temples or in some public place hardly less honourable; their archaic smiles are a kind of good manners, the expression of their youthful happiness and sufficiency. The artists have a clear idea of what a young man is, of what is most characteristic and essential in him, and have translated this into stone. If this is imitation, it imitates only certain carefully chosen qualities and concentrates on these at the expense of others. What matters is the guiding vision, the firm discrimination, which decides that a young man should be portrayed in this way. If it is an image, it is also an *agalma*, the earliest Greek word for a statue, which literally means 'delight'. The task of such statues is to give pleasure, and they do so by conveying

66. Bronze crater, possibly of Peloponnesian origin. 6th century B C. At Vix, France.

67. Funeral scene on a large Geometric amphora. 9th–8th century B C. *National Museum, Athens.*

68. Warriors fighting over a dead body, on a Rhodian plate. 7th century B C. *British Museum, London.*

69. Soldiers carrying a dead body, on a Laconian plate. Third quarter of the 6th century B C. *Staatliches Museum, Berlin.*

70. Fish, on a Laconian bowl. Late 7th century B C. *Museo Nazionale, Taranto.*

71. Dionysus in a ship, on a cup by Exekias. Third quarter of the 6th century B C. *Staatliches Museum, Berlin.*

72. Bird-nester in a tree, on an Attic-Ionic bowl. Early 6th century. *Louvre, Paris.*

73. Priam and Hermes leading Hera, Athene, and Aphrodite to Paris, on a Pontic amphora. Second half of the 6th century B C. *Glyptothek, Munich.*

74. Young men listening to a lyre-player, on an amphora by the Andocides Painter. Late 6th century B C. *Louvre, Paris.*

75. Man holding horses, on a cup by Epictetus. End of the 6th century B C. *Staatliches Museum, Berlin.*

76. Young man on a horse, on an Attic black-figure vase. Late 6th century B C. *British Museum, London.*

77. Symposiasts, on a cup by Epictetus. End of the 6th century B C. *British Museum, London.*

78. Young men jumping, on a cup by the Panaitios Painter. Early 5th century B C. *Museum of Fine Arts, Boston.*

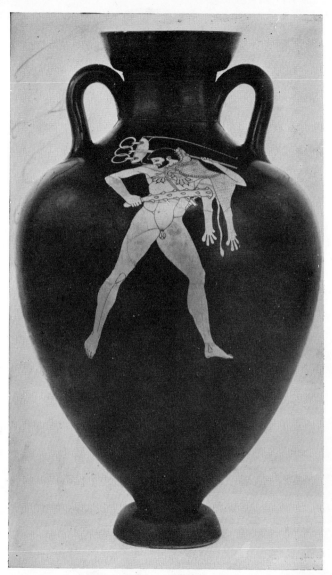

79. Heracles carrying off the Delphic tripod, on an amphora
by the Berlin Painter. Early 5th century B C. *Museum of the University, Würzburg.*

82. Artemis killing Actaeon, on a crater by the Pan Painter. About 470 B C. *Museum of Fine Arts, Boston.*

OPPOSITE:

80. Young man and girl, on a bowl by the Brygos Painter. About 500 B C. *Museum of the University, Würzburg.*

81. Dawn carrying the dead body of Memnon, on a cup by Duris. Early 5th century B C. *Louvre, Paris.*

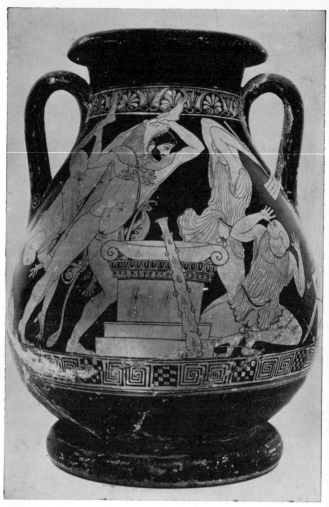

83. Heracles and Busiris, on a crater by the Pan Painter. About
470 B C. *National Museum, Athens.*

84. Aphrodite riding on a swan, on a cup by the Pistoxenos Painter. About 460 B C. *British Museum, London.*

85. Achilles killing Penthesilea, on a cup by the Penthesilea Painter. *Glyptothek, Munich.*

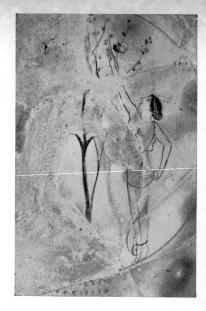

86. Girl picking apples, on an Attic white-ground cup, by the Sotades Painter. About 460 B C. *British Museum, London.*

87. Warrior and seated woman, on a *lêkythos* from Eretria. End of the 5th century B C. *National Museum, Athens.*

88. Maiden playing a lyre, on an Attic *lêkythos*. Late 5th century B C. *Private Collection, Munich.*

89. Boy with a toy cart, on an Attic *lêkythos*. Late 5th century B C. *Metropolitan Museum, New York.*

b

90. *a*. Warrior seated at a tomb, with a man and woman, on an Attic *lêkythos*. End of the 5th century B C. *National Museum, Athens. b.* Detail.

a

the permanent qualities of young manhood. Behind the personal idiosyncrasies of their subjects the sculptors find something more enduring which makes them what they are.

This tendency to interpret a character by selecting certain marked traits became more pronounced as the improved technique and wider vision of the fifth century encouraged a greater variety of positions and a greater freedom of movement. When these statues are of gods, it is easy to see why they are presented in their full youth and strength, but it is significant that the same qualities are sought in men. Even if they are more faithful portraits than in the previous age, the artist still makes them conform to his idea of what a young man really is, and it would not be an exaggeration to say that the qualities so sought are those in which a man most resembles the gods. These statues are not abstract types. They have often their personal traits, like the shy, quiet gaiety of the 'Critian Boy' (see Plate 17) or the troubled seriousness of the 'Blond Boy' (see Plate 24), but what they all have in common, what seems to be indispensable, is their youth and freshness, their lithe grace and well-formed limbs, their air of being in possession of a form in which they cannot but delight. The sculptors sought in their subjects what is most charming and attractive in them, and this was to be found in more than the shape or expression of their faces. The Greeks were such connoisseurs of the body that they appraised with an expert eye much that we might miss, and what counted with them was the whole form as more than the sum of its parts. In the balance and relation of their limbs such figures express their whole character, mental as well as physical, and reveal their central being, the radiant reality of youth in its heyday, when for a few brief years its possessors resemble the unageing gods.

What the naked body does for a young man, her dress does for a young woman. Just as Homer delights to tell how Hera dresses herself to attract Zeus, so Greek sculptors begin by portraying women in full and elaborate dress. They were certainly aware of their naked charms, but the normal practice was to make full use of dress as something delightful in itself and intimately appropriate to any idea of womanhood. Women were normally seen fully dressed, and only in Sparta did girls resemble boys in playing games naked. It was proper that, when statues of women were put in public places, the same decencies should be observed as on Olympus. The series of *korai,* or female figures, from the Acropolis at Athens conforms to this notion, despite considerable variety in size, hair-style, fashions of drapery, and colour. The common form is for the figure to stand erect, with her right arm at her side and her left stretched out with some offering like an apple, and her dress reaching to the ground. Little of her form is revealed except her head, neck, shoulders, and arms, and on these the sculptor can work with as much care as if he were portraying a naked young man. They give the right, sufficient suggestion of her young body, but the air of proper modesty is secured by showing no more. This gives a special importance to the dress, which both reveals the character of its wearer and has its own charm and distinction. How well the archaic sculptors understood their subjects may be seen from 'Acropolis 679' (see Plate 15), the statue of quite a young girl, whose half-way state between girlhood and womanhood is seen in her small breasts and her charmingly self-conscious dignity. Just as her hair is neat and trim, so her dress has no elaborate folds, but hangs closely round her body. We may compare with her a somewhat later figure, 'Acropolis 686' (see Plate 16), where the face has much more character, partly because the sculptor is more experienced, partly because the girl herself is a little older, and the dress, whose pleats and folds are carved in more detail, accords well with her appearance. Greek female figures present a counterpart to male in embodying the essential qualities of their sex as the Greeks saw them, and they are presented in this way because it was thought to reveal what was most characteristic and most distinctive in them.

In contrast with human beings, animals can hardly be given a distinction which shows their kinship with the gods, but the Greeks were so well acquainted and passed so much time with them that they knew them as they really are without any false or idealizing sentiment. The horse was part of their daily life, but since it had a special prestige in racing and might be regarded as most itself on the racecourse, images of horses take note of this and show light, wiry, well-built animals, eager to move and lifting their legs gaily and confidently (see Plates 47, 56). Dogs were bred not for show but for use, and may seem gaunt and bony in comparison with more languid breeds, but there is a reserve of strength in them, whether they lie watchfully at rest, or scratch themselves with abandoned self-indulgence, or go to their tasks with a will (see Plates 12, 64, 36). Animals less subservient to man reveal their independent spirit, like bulls, which plunge or butt (see Plates 64, 65), or goats, which with ungainly obstinacy fall or lie down or wait for something to happen (see Plates 58, 59, 57). Wild

animals like the lion, which was not at all familiar and
tended in archaic art to become a fabulous monster, show
their self-sufficiency when they lie at rest and their deadly
attack when they got into action (see Plates 10, 20, 29).
The boar might be no less formidable and was certainly
better known, whether on the run or standing at bay (see
Plate 63). In contrast with him the wild deer is all grace
and gentleness, standing surprised at some unexpected sight
or browsing quietly in peace (see Plates 60, 63). Animals
might be friends or foes of man, but in either case they
were very much themselves, and had their own personalities, which they revealed in rest or action. They were not to
be interpreted by any 'pathetic fallacy', which ascribed human feelings to them, and the artist's task was to catch
what was most characteristic in them and to show them in
their essential nature.

The same thing could hardly be done for the monsters
of whom Greek legend had a fair stock. In dealing with
them dependence on nature was something of a hindrance,
since it did not allow artists to draw too boldly on their
fancy. So they compounded their monsters as best they
could from natural sources. Sometimes, it must be admitted,
the task was too much for them. The chimaera, for instance, which was a lion in front, a goat in the middle, and
a snake behind, may sound well enough in Homer's poetry,
but becomes absurd when it is visualized. Monsters in
general depend for their horror on being vague and dimly
conceived and are usually ineffective in any art which
insists on making them realistic. Such a creature as the
Gorgon, which was believed to turn men into stone by its
mere look, can never be adequately portrayed by human
hands, and though Greek Gorgons indeed make ugly grim-
aces (see Plates 21, 37), they hardly freeze the blood. The
Sphinx, which was once an emblem of death, loses its en-
scrutable fearsomeness when, as the national symbol of
Naxos, it sits, a dignified and almost friendly figure, on the
top of a pillar at Delphi (see Plate 13). The old 'Tricorpor',
or snake with three human heads, is less frightening than
friendly in the gravity of his smiles and the stylish spirals
of his tail (see Plate 19). Centaurs, who were partly men
and partly horse, present a more interesting case. In archaic
art the human side is emphasized, and they are men with a
horse's body and hind legs (see Plate 61). As such they have
an uncouth charm and recall the admirable Chiron, who was
the schoolmaster of Achilles. Later the animal side became more prominent, when only their trunks and heads

are human, and they have a savage animality as they fight with the ferocity of wild beasts and the cunning of men (see Plate 41). The winged horse, Pegasus, was never intended to be fearsome, and artists took the opportunity to create a swift, elegant creature, whether he gallops over the ground and wears his wings as ornaments, or caracoles before ascending into the sky (see Plates 35, 48a). Monsters fell rather outside the orbit of Greek art because their essential nature was not easy to grasp or portray. Tradition insisted that they should have their place with gods and heroes, but they belonged to an earlier world, for which they had indeed some relevance, and meant little to a later age which concentrated on gods and on men made in the image of gods.

The forms of Greek painting and sculpture, like those of Greek poetry, were largely dictated by external and sometimes irrelevant considerations. The wonderfully accomplished art of painting scenes on vases was necessarily circumscribed by their shape, which was in its turn determined by their function. A bowl or a jar or a plate or a jug offered different spaces for the artist's use, and each presented its own problems. Sculpture had a like problem when it was used for the decoration of buildings in pediments, metopes, and friezes. It was no easy matter to fit a group of figures into an isosceles triangle with acute angles at the base, and the first pediments show that the artists had not fully resolved the difficulties. In the archaic pediment from Corfu the figures in the corners are a little awkward, but the artist has already seen the possibilities of the form when he sets his gigantic Gorgon in the middle and makes her dominate the scene (see Plate 37). This solution was taken up by other sculptors, whether in providing two figures to hold the centre, like Apollo and Heracles on the Siphnian Treasury (see Plate 2), or a single figure, like Apollo at Olympia (see Plate 38). Once this was done, it was a matter of no great difficulty to fill the corners with prone figures and to complete the ascending scale of height with other figures sitting or kneeling. The triangular frame imposed its demands on sculptors, but did not prevent them from making a good use of it. The metope, being a square, meant that a simple, self-contained design was almost indispensable. The earliest metopes, like those from Temple C at Selinus, conform to their architectural background by using straight lines with considerable effect, as in the scene of Heracles and the Cercopes (see Plate 32), which is nearly all perpendicular lines and right angles, while the metopes of Olympia, notably those of Heracles holding the sky or battling with the Cretan bull (see Plates 33, 34), show how the artist takes advantage of his frame to create a well-balanced and self-sufficient pattern. The frieze, on the contrary, allowed so much freedom that the question was rather how to make the best use of it. In the Siphnian Treasury the sculptor varies his design by combining a tumultuous scene of battle with seated figures of the gods, and the same happy combination appears on the Parthenon where the human figures at a national festival are varied by the gods sitting on their thrones (see Plate 49). The essential quality of a frieze is its continuity, but this must not be allowed to become monotonous. Not only must different kinds of action be displayed, but, while each scene must have its own character and completeness, it must fit into the general sequence to which it belongs. Even here liberty is controlled and made part of a mastering plan. In sculpture, as in poetry, the existence of certain forms was not a hindrance but an inspiration. It told the artists within what limits they had to work and fired them to make a new and distinguished use of them.

Painting and sculpture differ from poetry in the important point that they have no connexion with music or dancing. But rhythm played so large a part in the Greek consciousness that it could not fail to make some appearance in the visual arts. Though they could not move, they could at least embody rhythmical elements in their fundamental patterns, and it was characteristic of the Greeks, who associated music with mathematics, that this rhythm should be found in what may be called a geometrical foundation in design. If the followers of Pythagoras sought an ultimate reality in numbers and thought that even such matters as the scale of colours can be explained by them, most Greeks had a natural feeling for their neatness and clarity. In creating works of art Greek sculptors, painters, and architects seem often to have been dominated by a sense of geometrical pattern and order. This was, as we might expect, most obvious in architecture. If tradition insisted that the design of a temple must be simple, the desire for geometrical order dictated that a rectangular design should be maintained at all costs, and that if variation was needed, it should be secured by the inclusion or addition of other rectangles. Level sites for temples are not easy to find in Greece, but instead of accommodating their buildings to the terrain, the Greeks made the terrain suit the buildings by levelling it to take them in their full regularity, as if anything else would interfere with their essential nature. Even the Propylaea at Athens, which is a secular building on a steep slope, makes few concessions to it and asserts its majestic and orderly mass over the irregular rock (see Plate 6). This was indeed appropriate to an art which relied for its first appeal on the use of straight lines. If the main plan was oblong, the roof, with its low pitch, meant the construction at either end of a pediment with acute angles at its base and an obtuse angle at the top. The variations on this severe plan were provided by pillars. If once these were no more than wooden props, they soon developed a marked character. They were tubular, tapering, and fluted perpendicularly, and though they did not in fact taper regularly, they were made to look as if they did by a swelling in the shaft which deceives and satisfies the eye. The triumphant step in their career was when they were promoted from being used only in porches to forming an essential feature of the whole exterior, as they are in the Parthenon, between the horizontal lines of the foundation below and of the architrave above (see Plate 5). This means that a Greek temple is equally satisfying if we look at it horizontally or vertically. In the first case the unity of design depends on the firm use of straight lines which plant the building on the landscape and stress their difference from it in their severe simplicity; in the second case the pillars take the eye upward and give the impression of a mass rising majestically from the earth. Circles and straight lines are brought together with the precision of a problem in geometry, and, though they are kept distinct, their combination gives a unique character to Greek architecture.

This architecture is functional in the sense that it does just what it is required to do. So far from pretending that it is anything else than it is, a Greek temple proclaims itself from miles away. But this does not mean that the Greeks eschewed decoration. They were indeed careful to exclude it from the more strictly functional parts of a building, but they favoured it elsewhere. The pediments, the metopes, and the inner wall were all made to carry sculpture in the round or in relief. But the sculpture is not allowed to interfere with the essential dominance of lines and curves. The only compromise is in the capitals of pillars, which, whether Doric or Ionic, allow not indeed decoration but at least a concession to the alliance of different kinds of line in their use of flat curves or volutes. How important this fidelity to line was can be seen from the few cases where it is not observed, notably in the invention of Caryatids, or female figures, who act as pillars to support the pediment of the porch in the Siphnian Treasury at Delphi and the architrave in the shrine of Erechtheus at Athens (see Plate 7). However admirable they may be in themselves, they spoil the abstract purity of the design by introducing an alien and discordant element. If mathematical designs and human shapes were to be combined successfully, it was not by such means as this. A closer and more subtle combination was necessary, and was found in painting and sculpture.

In its beginnings Greek painting, which survives chiefly on vases, resembles architecture in being literally geometrical. The ground is covered with parallel lines, squares, key-patterns, swastikas, circles, and semi-circles. When *c.* 800 BC rudimentary figures appear, they have triangular bodies and fit happily into the abstract patterns around them, as on the great vase from the Dipylon at Athens, where the dead man and his mourners are all straight lines and sharp corners (see Plate 67). It was indeed a sensational move when the Greeks took to delineating natural, and especially human, forms, and it might seem to indicate a revolution in their outlook. But they reduced the presentation of human figures to an order in which geometry still had a place. Though purely geometrical patterns become much rarer from the seventh century onwards, figures are disposed with an eye to balance and order. At its simplest this may mean no more than a row of vertical figures at regular intervals, like a row of gods and goddesses hurrying to some Olympian gathering (see Plate 73). This can be varied by cutting the vertical lines by a horizontal, either at the top, as when a dead warrior is borne by four men (see Plate 69), or in the middle, as when Dawn carries the body of Memnon (see Plate 81). Straight lines can be diversified, as in architecture, by circles, as on a plate from Rhodes, where the two round shields of warriors balance each other in the middle and their erect forms provide a vertical balance outside (see Plate 68). Circular plates inspired a happy use of circular or concentric designs, as when Dionysus, sailing in a ship, is surrounded by fish (see Plates 70, 71), or Aphrodite rides on a swan (see Plate 84). Such fundamental patterns could vary from extreme simplicity to a complicated balance of triangles and circles, but in nearly all Greek painting we can discern under the lively forms of men or animals a geometical skeleton through which the design acquires a special neatness and balance and satisfies the Greek desire for an intelligible, dominating order.

This sense of order owed much to a sense of space. Just as the figures of geometry exist isolated in space and reveal their shapes in the absence of competition, so Greek design often isolates figures of men or animals against an empty background and fixes our undivided attention on them in their completeness. This may have been stimulated by the Greek landscape, in which natural features, like mountains and islands, stand alone in clear outline against the sky and can be seen in full contour and perspective. The physical configuration of Greece tends to isolate the main elements in their individuality of shape and height, and an eye trained on them would naturally seek to do something similar in art. Just as a lack of open vistas in lands thick with tangled vegetation may account for the crowded character of Mayan or Khmer sculpture, which reflects the forest or the jungle in its pullulating pressure, so conversely in Greece open spaces and differences of elevation promote a desire to set an object against an empty background. Greek coins, which display local gods or emblems, not only aim at depth by the use of full relief but place their subjects neatly in a circular frame with a separating space between them and it, and this gives its own distinction to Pegasus or an ear of corn or an octopus or a sepia or a crab (see Plate 65). So too gems naturally wish to make the most of what is engraved on them and use space to fix our gaze on a goose or a heron in the air or a dolphin in the sea (see Plates 62, 64). Though vases sometimes reflect large-scale painting in depicting complex or crowded scenes, at other times they give a special emphasis to a theme by setting it against an empty background, as when Heracles, carrying off the Delphic tripod, strides majestically alone in full possession of it (see Plate 79), or a maiden, playing the lyre, sits happily by herself (see Plate 88). The design is concentrated in the single figure, and the surrounding emptiness stresses its individuality. It needs nothing to complete it and lives splendidly in its own right.

The Greek landscape also disposes its features in natural patterns in relation to one another. Mountains are separated by valleys or the sea; promontories balance one another before bays or inlets, but the sky and the sea keep them apart and allow to each its own character. Space provides the means by which a complex scheme is held together, and from the artists learned the value of space in their own designs. They saw that *horror vacui* had no terrors so long as they made a nice use of empty intervals between their different figures. This was particularly natural and appropriate for figures out of doors. So much of Greek life was passed in the open, and so many subjects, whether heroic or athletic, imply room for movement that artists could not fail to take notice of it and turn it to their own ends. Even early in the sixth century, when sculpture was still experimenting with new designs, and there was a tendency to crowd the allotted ground with figures, the Siphnian frieze uses empty intervals to suggest the passage to and fro across a busy battlefield (see Plates 45-46), and when classical art brought a greater freedom and economy, space was exploited more dramatically and more ingeniously. When on a vase a young man holds two horses (see Plate 75), the intervals between them suggest that they are in a field, and this makes the figures complete and separate and yet subordinate to a single design. When young men jump over a stick (see Plate 76), the isolation of their bodies both marks the various stages of their sport and stresses that they are all concerned with the same thing. When this technique is applied to marble reliefs, it creates many openings for a happy balance, as on a statue-base from Athens young men play ball (see Plate 26). Each of them has his own part to play, and is differentiated by the pose of his head and arms and legs, but they are all brought together by a rhythm which makes full use of the intervals between them. In this the organizing mind of the sculptor is well aware of the formal patterns to be united in a single design which holds and transcends them. Anatomy and geometry are fused into one, and each does something for the other.

The Greeks probed this question and tried to clarify it by looking for mathematical proportions, which governed visual works of art. Though their answers are not final, they throw light on Greek aesthetic theories. Writing about art in the third century AD the philosopher Plotinus says: 'The general opinion, I may say, is that it is the interrelation of parts with one another, and with the whole, together with the additional element of good colour, which constitutes beauty as perceived by the eye; in other words, that beauty in visible things, as in everything else, consists of symmetry and proportion.'[7] This theory goes back, probably through Plato, to at least the middle of the fifth century. The importance of proportion is clearest in architecture, where buildings like the Parthenon or the temple of Apollo at Bassae seem to be based on the 'golden section', that is the division of a line in extreme and mean ratio. This means not that architects worked *a priori* from a preconceived theory, but that they deduced conclusions from practice and applied them as rules. In architecture this is easy enough, but it is more remarkable that something of the same kind was applied to sculpture. When Polyclitus wrote his manual,

*The Canon*, he said: 'Beauty consists in the proportion not of the elements but of the parts, that is to say, of finger to finger, and of all the fingers to the palm, and of these to the forearm, and of the forearm to the upper arm, and of all parts to each other.'[8] Though Polyclitus does not, in his surviving words, say what proportion is required, and though the lack of any authentic works by him prevents us from testing what he means from his own practice, it is clear that he attached importance to his view that beauty lies in proportion. It was no great step to exalt this to metaphysics and to claim, as Plato did, that the universe itself is built on geometrical proportions.[9] Such a notion would help to explain what is otherwise inexplicable in art and relate it to the scheme of things. But though this notion endured, and though proportion was always important in Greek art, it does not explain everything. Beyond it lies the appeal of the actual works both in detail and as wholes, and this eludes any explanation by proportion alone.

The Greeks felt this, and that is why perhaps they maintained to a late date an early, almost animistic idea that statues are in some sense alive. Myth sanctified this in stories that Hephaestus[10] and Daedalus[11] made images which moved of their own accord, and this embodies the belief that the image, for instance, on a man's tomb was somehow the man himself. That is why inscriptions not uncommonly make the image speak in the first person. To simple people this may well have meant something; for it had analogies in statues of the gods which were thought to incarnate their living presences, and it was supported by the feeling that an image of a dead man must be more than a mere piece of stone or metal. Yet most men would find it hard to believe that a statue or a picture was really alive in the same sense as the man whom it represented. Democritus went to the point when he said that 'images are a bright spectacle in their clothing but heartless',[12] and when Aeschylus tells of the stricken solitude of Menelaus when he is abandoned by Helen, he knows that statues are a poor substitute for the living beauty:

> The grace of shapely statues
> Is hateful to her husband,
> And in the eyes' starvation
> All love drifts away.[13]

Socrates applied a similar criticism to painting, when he complained that it was unable to take part in that art of conversation to which he gave his life: 'Its offspring stand like living things, but if you ask them a question, they are wonderfully and completely silent.'[14] The old view broke down because it failed to satisfy the affections, and its failure prompted a revival of the view that art is after all no more than an imitation of reality, and this received a new meaning as art became more naturalistic. That it did not answer every question is clear from the painter Parrhasius, who, on being asked by Socrates if he could paint an imitation of the soul, replied: 'How can it be imitated, since it has neither shape nor colour . . . and is not visible at all?'[15] His point is that imitation is not enough and that a man's soul or personality can be suggested only through the way in which his features are represented. Yet the notion that art is imitation had enough truth to win adherents, and it is significant that Aristotle adopted it when, in describing tragedy, he argued from an analogy in the visual arts: 'Though the objects themselves may be painful to see, we delight to look at the most realistic representations of them, the forms of the lowest animals, for instance, and of dead bodies.'[16] There is truth in this, but it is not the whole truth, and we begin to see its limitations when Aristotle goes on to say that our pleasure in art consists of recognizing that a picture is of such-and-such a person. This may be a legitimate pleasure, but it is not the only or the chief pleasure which art has to give. Nor would most Greek sculptors and painters have agreed with him. Despite all their desire to represent a subject faithfully, they sought always something beyond mere imitation of the transitory self.

This approach not only provided Greek art with the limits in which it worked and kept it from being purely geometrical, but also provided it with an aim. This aim was to present its subjects in their essential nature, in their timeless essence. If it fell short of reality by being unable to make them speak or stir affection, at least it transcended the transitory world of sensations by catching something permanent and essential. If its works were not alive, at least they suggested a life more real than that of mortal men, and if they were heartless, that was because even the affections can be transcended in something larger and wider than themselves. The Greeks delighted in works of art, but saw in them not so much an extension of the living scene for its own sake as a connexion between it and something else. It appealed to their desire to find an abiding reality behind the gifts of the senses. This reality was not separate from its appearances, but could itself be known only in and through

them and gave to them their special character and power.
Artists sought to catch and express the essential nature of a
subject, whether divine or human, high or humble, tragic or
convivial, heroic or salacious, because they felt that the
conviction of the beautiful which came to them in inexplicable and inspiring visitations was derived from a higher order
of being and must be treated with a full awareness of its
haunting and possessing presence. For this reason they presented in a special way what they saw, stripping it of its
trivial or confusing accessories and concentrating on its inner strength and central being, which itself belonged to the
central being of things. If the Greeks saw their gods in the
glorified likeness of men, it was a tribute to those qualities
by which the gods could be known and understood, and,
conversely, when they tried to see men in their most abiding and most characteristic qualities, it was a tribute to their
kinship with the unchanging gods. It was this sense of a
connexion between the seen and the unseen, between the accidental and the essential, between the transitory and the
permanent, which provided Greek art with a guiding ideal
and a welcome discipline and ennobled it with an exalted
detachment and a consistent, self-contained harmony.

This outlook made Greek art what it is and accounts alike
for its special qualities and for its lack of much that we like
and admire in the art of other peoples. In its archaic and
classical periods its most marked characteristic is that,
though it is always concerned with the search for beauty, it
makes this familiar and at home in its presentation of it.
There is nothing alien or violent or unapproachable in its
visions of gods and heroes. They are related to the known
world and, even if they are nobler than anything in it,
they have somehow a place in it and seem to belong to it.
So far from making us feel that there is a gap between things
as we see them and as they really are, Greek art insists
that they are one, that each stresses the nature of the other
in a single unity, which reflects a complete and single world.
To make its creations fit into the common scene, it takes end-
less pains to make them real in their own way. Nothing must
be shirked or skimped. The folds of the dress of the Delphic
charioteer may not be visible inside his chariot, but they must
none the less be modelled with a full and faithful sense of
their quality; the figures on the pediments of the Parthenon
are seen only from one side and from some distance below,
but they too must be shaped fully and carefully in the round.
To the eye it is shape that counts far more than anything

else, and every shape, whether in main design or in small detail, must have its own character and its own significance. To make concessions to realism, in the sense of depicting things for their more obvious but not more essential qualities, may mean that the sense of shape is lost or spoiled, that our attention is drawn to some petty triviality instead of to what really matters in the pose of a limb or the muscle of a body. In their later days the Greeks attempted a dramatic realism, but in such works as the Farnese Bull or the Laocoön, we miss the harmony which belongs to earlier work just because it makes each part speak for itself without claiming anything at the expense of the rest. The later realism is far removed from the air of reality which we find in classical art; it is more sensational, more violent, more unrestrained. And just for this reason it misses the majesty and the balance which come from not trying to say too much but allowing the design to suggest an infinitude of possibilities through the hints which it gives of them. Just as Greek poetry achieves some of its most impressive results by saying almost the least that can be said on a subject, so Greek painting and sculpture practise a similar economy and restraint, and seem to go out of their way to prevent us from being troubled by having to absorb more than we can with ease and comfort. If the real reason for this was a desire to depict living beings in their essential nature, its result was an art which can appeal to almost everyone in its simplicity and candour. Indeed, just because the Greeks saw things in this way, they achieved a style which is, in the best sense of the word, grand, in that it makes no concessions to vulgar sensation and concentrates on purity of line and significance of shape.

The Greeks were not a nation of artists, still less of aesthetes, and the reason for this was largely that the arts played so large and so accepted a part in their lives that they did not feel any call to apologize for them or to take up a defensive position about them. If the artist was a craftsman, he was also a citizen, who took his part in civic life and carried out his national tasks. He put into his art his own vision of things, but he shaped this, unconsciously and instinctively, by living among other men whose ideas and tastes he shared and whose support encouraged him in his work. His aim was not so much to show his originality and difference from other artists as to display his skill in doing the kind of thing that they did but he hoped to do better. He was bound by many conventions, by religious propriety, by social manners, by artistic rules of balance and proportion.

Yet in these he found not a handicap but a help. Since he knew so well within what limits he had to work and was not troubled by having to evolve too many new expedients, he had time to perfect his own technique and to make the most of his given task. The rapid development of Greek art must of course have owed much to the originality of its artists, but there is no reason to think that they sought to be very original. Their advance was rather a matter of solving problems as they suggested and of trying to do a little better what others had done before them. In this they were sustained by a public which both knew about art and knew what it liked. That is why in its great days Greek art is essentially national and strikes us less as the revelation of individual personalities than as the expression of a whole society and a whole civilization.

In their love of art the Greeks were conscious that they must not set too high a value on it or ask from it more than it had to give. It was indeed a means of defeating time, of keeping memories alive, of sustaining glory after death, but even if it did all these things, it could not do them for ever and was not beyond the reach of chance and change. There were moments when belief in it might encourage high hopes of its powers, as when Cleobulus of Rhodes, who was reckoned as one of the Seven Sages, wrote an epitaph on Midas:

A bronze maiden am I, and I lie on the tomb of Midas.
So long as water flows and tall trees flourish,
And the sun rises and shines, and the bright moon,
And rivers flow, and the sea swells high,
Here in this place I shall remain on this much-wept tomb
And tell to passers-by that Midas is buried here.[17]

To us this might seem to make claims no more exorbitant than many artists and poets make for their own work, and the boast is founded on a natural trust that a monument will indeed defeat the years. But even this met with disapproval. Simonides knew the lines and criticized them sharply:

Who that trusts in his wits would praise
Cleobulus, who dwelt in Lindos,
When against the everlasting rivers and the flowers of the
    spring,
The flame of the earth and of the golden moon,
And the eddies of the sea,
He set the might of a grave-stone?

For all things are less than the gods,
And a stone even mortal hands can smash.
The man who thought this was a fool.[18]

The monuments of men had indeed their own beauty and
glory; they were often tributes to the gods and to men like
the gods. But beyond that it was unwise to go. Art had its
proper place in life, which was honourable enough, but there
was no call to claim too much for it or to pretend that it did
not suffer from the limitations set on all things made by
men.

The comparatively modest claims which the Greeks made
for the place of art in life emphasize the disturbing paradox
of Plato's views on the subject. He was not opposed either
to painting or to poetry as such, but he thought that a large
part of both was perniciously misguided, and he wished
greatly to restrict their scope. He accepted the view that art
was essentially imitation, and he argued that, since it imitated
particular things which are themselves imitation of ideal
Forms, it was at a third remove from the truth. This doctrine
is all the more remarkable because Plato was acutely sensitive to the appeal of the arts and was in his own craft of
words an incomparable artist. It is not enough to say that
what he condemned was the representational and realistic art
of his day, since it is clear that he passed an equally damning
verdict on the art of the fifth century, and his reasons were
deeper than any distaste for current fashion. He was pas-
sionately concerned with discovering the fundamental truth
about reality, and he believed that reality was to be found
in an ideal order which only the intellect could grasp. He
was also moved by the conviction that much art brought discredit on the gods by telling stories about them which he
could not believe to be true. Both intellectually and morally
he was stirred to demand rigid restrictions on the content
of the arts because only by such means could he fit them
into the order which he wished to impose on society. Yet
despite the eloquence and the sincerity of his arguments, he
was wrong on both points. Artists and sculptors were no less
concerned than he was to find an ideal order behind appearances and to make it known to men, but they believed
that this order revealed itself not so much to the dispassionate intellect as to the whole sentient self. Nor was their purpose less serious than his. The difference was that their view
of the gods was less exclusively ethical and that they sought
to make men better in a wide sense, not by inculcating some

specific morality, but by exerting an influence which would make them more aware of great issues and more able to respond to their challenges. In painting and sculpture, as in poetry, the Greeks saw that there are other and more effective instruments than argument and precept to awake awe and wonder before the beauty of the world.

# CHAPTER IX

# THE PLACE OF REASON

IN THEIR ARCHAIC PERIOD the Greeks expressed their most significant speculations in poetry, and even when this was reinforced by sculpture and painting, their outlook was still largely shaped by their poetical education and the principles which it implied. Even if the traditional myths left much unexplained, and even contradicted each other on important matters, they provided an approach to experience, a way of thinking in concrete images, which satisfied a people who had no reason to doubt that the gods were at work everywhere and that a knowledge of them explained most phenomena, both physical and mental. But by the beginning of the sixth century a new spirit had been born, which grew and matured until it touched many branches of inquiry. This was a desire to understand things more exactly, to penetrate the mystery which enveloped them, to explain them in rational language, and to find principles and rules in nature rather than the inexplicable whims which myth ascribed to the gods. Such a movement was perhaps inevitable in a people so intelligent as the Greeks, but it was stimulated by social and political changes. It began in Ionia, and its first exponent was Thales of Miletus. The disappearance of the hereditary monarchies and their replacement by a new ruling class, which soon turned its attention to foreign trade, meant that the intellectual horizon was enlarged with the physical, and the establishment of trading-stations, like Naucratis in Egypt, brought Greeks into contact with an unfamiliar, if narrow, range of applied knowledge. At home building, sculpture, and metal-work posed technical problems which called for solution; the increased activity of sailors, who penetrated to the far western end of the Mediterranean, demanded a more than mythological acquaintance with geography and astronomy; the popularity of athletics encouraged a proper knowledge of the human body, if only to mend broken limbs and heal sprains. Events fostered a new spirit of inquiry

177

into the visible world, and this inquiry took three main forms. Though there was some overlap between them each maintained its special character and obeyed its own laws of growth.

The first was mathematics. This was not a Greek invention, but had already been practised with some skill in Babylonia and Egypt, and it is from Egypt that Thales was said to have brought it.[1] That perhaps is why he was able to determine the height of a pyramid by measuring its shadow.[2] Egyptian mathematics seem to have been more practical than theoretical, and Thales marked the special character of Greek studies when he proved that a circle is bisected by its diameter[3] and forecast the direction in which mathematical proof was thenceforth to move. The Greeks raised mathematics beyond the practical application which the Egyptians had given to it for such matters as building and emphasized its theoretical character. Just as in their arts they sought some reality behind appearances, so in mathematics they sought permanent principles which could be applied wherever conditions were the same. The possibilities of such an inquiry caught the imagination of Pythagoras and his disciples, who saw in numbers the key to most problems and asserted, 'Things are numbers'.[4] If we do not take this too literally, it marks an important stage in intellectual development, since it establishes the principle that a large mass of phenomena can be understood if we can discover mathematically the laws which govern them. It is one of the surprises of history that Pythagoras was impelled towards mathematics by the study of music. He was concerned with establishing fixed relations between the several notes on a musical scale, and he saw that this could be solved as a matter of arithmetical proportion. From it he seems to have moved to the theorem, which still bears his name, that the square on the hypotenuse of a right-angled triangle is equal to the sum of the squares on the other two sides. This was known in a limited and practical form in Egypt and is said to have been discovered independently in India, but the Greek demonstration was a triumph of pure mathematical thinking without reference to practical considerations. Greek mathematics began with geometry and remained faithful to it through its long career.

The second form taken by the new movement was philosophy. This too was an attempt to find the reality behind phenomena, but its instrument was not numbers, but words. At its start it seems to have posed the question: 'What is the primary substance of things?' and Thales answered that it was water, Anaximenes that it was air. Such an inquiry was cosmological in that it sought to find a more satisfying theory than myths which told that Chaos gave birth to Light and Darkness and that each had its own appropriate progeny. In fact this question really contained two questions, 'what is the *origin* of things?' and 'what is the *nature* of things?' The philosophers faced both, and came to their several answers. But they agreed that these questions were indeed fundamental and could be answered by hard thought. In this way they laid the foundations of logic, of correct thinking, in which any contradiction between one proposition and another means that one at least of them is false. Though the philosophers might appeal to phenomena for the illustration and confirmation of their theories, the theories themselves were built on a coherent system of argument from assumed or accepted beginnings. In this respect they resembled the mathematicians, and though in its early stages philosophy was less abstract than mathematics, it certainly believed that no theory of being was adequate unless it was throughout coherent and consistent.

The third form was natural science. If this had something in common with philosophy in its desire to discover and explain the nature of phenomena, it differed in its methods. It believed not so much in the establishment of a consistent theory as in observation and experiment, and though in astronomy it relied largely upon mathematics, it controlled this by careful attention to established facts. Its most practical, most successful, and most strictly scientific inquiry was medicine. From the start medicine seems to have broken free from the presuppositions which underlay other branches of science and to have kept itself in well-defined limits. In replacing the traditional apparatus of magic by controlled diet and nursing, the doctors began a far-reaching revolution. Their task was to study the causes of disorder in the human body, when, on the analogy of music, its *harmoniâ*, or attunement, was broken, and to try to restore it to its normal state. In the fifth century Greek medicine, under the leadership of Hippocrates of Cos (479–399 BC), broke with the past and its belief in supernatural cures and developed a whole system based on scientific method. The writings of Hippocrates and his followers show a minute care in the examination of pathological symptoms. Every part of the body has to be examined, every unusual colour or movement or temperature noted. The doctor must find out about the patient's sense of taste and smell, his sleep and his dreams, his appetite or lack of it, his pains and his itches, his stools and his urine. Once the evidence had been collected and the symptoms compared with other recorded cases the physician felt that he could proceed to diagnosis and treatment, confident that he knew all that he could about the case and that he could within limits prognosticate what was going to happen:

'It is necessary to learn accurately each constitution of the seasons as well as the disease; what common element in the constitution or the disease is good, and what common element in the constitution or the disease is bad; what malady is long and fatal, what is long and likely to end in recovery; what acute illness is fatal, what acute illness is likely to end in recovery. With this knowledge it is easy to examine the order of the critical days and to prognosticate from it. He who knows these matters can know what he ought to treat as well as the time and the method of treatment.'[5]

Here the spirit of scientific inquiry relies on careful observation and is able to give some forecast of what is likely to happen. The author does not claim that, even when he knows what the disease is, he can cure it; he is content to diagnose it and avoid errors in its treatment. The principles of Greek medicine were those of natural science today, and it is appropriate that the Greeks made this momentous revolution through their care for the human body.

Though mathematics, philosophy, and natural science had their separate assumptions and principles and methods of work, they had also a good deal in common and shared certain basic characteristics which belonged to the age of Greek enlightenment. First, they were not in their early days in conflict with religion. Since, like religion, they dealt with questions of the nature and origins of things, it is not surprising that Thales should say, 'All things are full of gods',[6] or Anaximander call the air a god.[7] Such language was suitable in a society which saw gods everywhere and was not too troubled to define their exact spheres of activity. Just because the Greeks believed that the world of gods and of men is one, they had no difficulty in believing that what they saw around them had a divine as well as a physical side and that ultimately the two are not distinct. In their desire to find some universal principle, they assumed, as religious thinkers did, the existence of a cosmic order, and in elaborating their ideas of this they used the old language which ascribed divine control to various spheres of reality. Even if they could not finally unravel what laws governed phenomena, they could at least claim that such laws existed, and use mythical language to show what they meant. The first glim-

merings of laws of nature were themselves derived from
divine laws, and we can well understand how, when Anaximander wishes to display the balance of opposite forces as
central to reality, he says: 'Things give satisfaction and
reparation to one another for their injustice, as is appointed
by the ordering of time',[8] or when Heraclitus speaks for
the regularity of the sun's movements, he says: 'The Sun will
not overstep his measures; if he does, the Erinyes, hand-
maids of Justice, will find him out.'[9] So long as the gods
were taken for granted, it was not difficult for philosophers
to fit their ideas into a system which was tolerably elastic
and quite happy to welcome new functions for its gods.

These branches of inquiry all presuppose that it is both
possible and proper for man to discover the truth about the
nature of things and would in principle accept the saying
of Heraclitus: 'Wisdom is one thing. It is to know the
thought by which all things are steered through all things.' [10]
But at the start this was contrary to much common belief
that, since the gods treat men as they please, it is impossible
to be certain of anything. Pindar and Sophocles alike make
men's ignorance of their own destiny a cardinal point of
difference between them and the gods. But as science and
philosophy developed, this idea was modified and fitted into
the new ideal of knowledge. In the sixth century, Solon, who
was well versed in traditional wisdom, follows a kind of
ascending scale from utter ignorance to reasonable expecta-
tion. If the merchant and the farmer are at the mercy of the
weather, which they cannot forecast or control, the craftsman, poet, seer, and physician have at least a divine patron
who instructs and protects them and fortifies them in their
knowledge of their own business.[11] They may of course make
mistakes and can never be quite sure what will happen, but
they do not work in utter ignorance. Indeed, the possession of
such knowledge was one of the means by which men could,
no matter at what distance, become more like the gods and
more able to control their own destinies. The practical answer was that, though men cannot hope for certainty, they
can make good surmises, as the doctor, Alcmaeon of Croton
(fl. 500 BC) says: 'About what is invisible, about what is
mortal, the gods have clear knowledge, but to us as men,
only inference on what is coming is possible.' [12] This takes
the old idea and gives it a practical application. Inference
is after all something and may well be useful. Within limits
a man may seek to resemble the gods, and if he remembers
the vast difference between their powers and his, there is no
reason why he should not regard knowledge as an attainable

end, provided that he confines it to certain spheres and does not claim too much for it, especially in trying to forecast the future or to know what is reserved for the gods alone. This was a delicate position, and not always easy to hold, but if it was kept within certain limits, it avoided any overt breach with religious faith.

Philosophy and science had to come to terms with religion, if only because they themselves made similar assumptions. It was of course possible to adopt a purely negative position and dismiss science as futile, as Pindar did when he said that natural philosophers 'pick a useless fruit of knowledge'.[13] This was natural enough for him, since the knowledge which he valued was much less of the physical world than of the gods. But few men seem to have gone so far as this, and even the devout Sophocles was at times touched by scientific notions,[14] though they did no more than confirm his already strong religious faith. In fact the early philosophers treated their task in almost a religious spirit and aimed at presenting it as in some sense a revelation, not similar indeed in content to the old beliefs, but like them in its spirit and its methods. Though Heraclitus rejected with angry contempt the stories told by Homer and Hesiod, he proclaimed his own insight into the *Logos*, or Word, which directs all things.[15] Parmenides not only asserts that his knowledge was given to him by a goddess but speaks of himself as one initiated into special mysteries and of his system as a Way.[16] Pythagoras sought to find in numbers an instrument of salvation as well as of geometry. Greek philosophers were not in the beginning irreligious. Rather they proposed reformed versions of traditional assumptions and offered these in a language which ordinary men could understand. In this they were quite sincere. They believed that they had something to say which was divinely inspired and that their task was to present it in all its seriousness and urgency.

A special claim and characteristic of this task was the pursuit of truth through inquiry. The old view that truth was given in revelation by the gods was not actually denied, but quietly replaced by the conviction that men can find it out for themselves. It did not take a scientist to recognize that revealed truth is not always satisfactory. The Muses, who were credited with telling men about the gods and the past, were notoriously untrustworthy, and even Pindar admits that poetry creates illusions:

> Beauty, who creates
> All sweet delights for men,

Brings honour at will, and makes the false seem true
Time and again.[17]

The traditional position was that men should be content
with what truth they have and hope that time will reveal
more to them. The scientists and philosophers emended this
by insisting that truth is a first duty and that no effort must
be spared to discover it. Xenophanes denies the old notion
when he claims that in fact men find out things for themselves: 'The gods have not revealed everything to men from
the beginning, but men by searching find out better in
time.'[18] Truth has its own appeal and makes its own claims
on its servants, as Democritus saw when he said that he
would rather find out the cause of a thing than have the
kingdom of the Parisians.[19] It was indeed recognized that the
pursuit of truth might be a high, even the highest, form of
conduct, and Heraclitus implicitly rejects old views of *aretê*
for his own conception of it: 'To think is the greatest virtue
(*aretê*) and wisdom consists of speaking what is true and
acting in obedience to nature.'[20] The climax was reached
when Socrates propounded his paradox that virtue is wisdom,
and inspired far-reaching theories by it. The seriousness with
which philosophers sought truth had indeed a religious
earnestness and, when Anaxagoras built an altar to Truth,[21]
he showed what it meant to him. Such a spirit was not at war
with established religion, which gave a welcome to new
divinities even of this abstract nature, and anyhow it could
hardly complain that men should wish to understand the nature of things and be humble in the presence of its mysteries.

Mathematics, philosophy, and natural science also shared
a belief in the value of observation and experiment. They
might differ greatly in the degree in which they used them,
but none of them felt that they could entirely dispense with
them. Because their sharp eyes were trained on the visual
arts and took pleasure in noticing details, the Greeks were
naturally keen observers and regarded observation as a
human activity which called for no apology. Without it no
important questions could be either posed or answered, and
because it was natural to them, it stirred their intelligence
and their speculations. In the sixth century Anaximenes noticed that clouds are formed from air and in turn by conden-
sation become water.[22] He concluded that the primal substance is air, and that everything is ultimately made from it.
The theory was too simple to be true, but it was at least an
attempt to answer a question forced on him by his own observation of facts. So too when Anaximander noticed that

the structure of fishes is like that of human beings, he propounded, in advance of Darwin, the theory that life began in the sea and that men are descended from animals of another species.[23] It was a bold idea, and he could not have foreseen its future justification, but at least he knew what his problem was and propounded his solution with a proper regard for what he had himself discovered. If theories of this kind seem to us to be insufficiently based and to be no more than inspired or ingenious guesses, we must remember that we know of them almost by accident and have almost no information on what evidence was put forward in their support. But there are indications that the first Greek scientists took trouble to collect facts which seemed relevant to their questions, and saw that proof is more than a stroke of happy insight. When Xenophanes tried to elucidate the relation of land to sea, he noted the presence of shells in inland districts and on hills, the imprint of a fish and of seaweed in the quarries of Syracuse, the form of an anchovy in the depth of the stone on Paros, and flat impressions of marine creatures on Malta. This shows a man who knew what to look for and took pains to find it, who was at once observant and systematic, a collector and a thinker. He came rightly to the conclusion that earth and water are not ultimately separate, and that they somehow invade one another. The conclusion is less interesting than the method, which shows that Xenophanes was a true inquirer in his assumption that the observation of hitherto unnoticed facts may be used to advance theories of far-ranging import.

These early investigators also did something to control observation by experiment. In this their efforts may look rather primitive, but they were at least a beginning and showed the right approach to their subject. This happened even in mathematics, when to demonstrate that the pitch of a musical note produced by a taut string depends on the length of the vibrating medium, the Pythagoreans used a movable bridge to vary the length of the string, and not only proved their point but found a means for measuring precisely a physical phenomenon. In philosophy Anaxagoras wished to show that the accuracy of the senses cannot be trusted beyond a certain point; he took two vessels, filled one with a white liquid and the other with a black, and mixed them drop by drop, until the eye could no longer distinguish between them.[24] The same spirit prevailed both in the physical and the biological sciences. Empedocles demonstrated the corporeal nature of air by thrusting a funnel, with the upper end closed, into water and showing that the water could not get into it until the obstruction was removed and the air set free.[25] In his inquiries into sense-perception Alcmaeon of Croton practised vivisection and dissection and came to the conclusion that the brain is the central organ of perception. If we make allowances for the almost complete lack of apparatus and for the absence of many materials which we have at our disposal, we need not be surprised that experiments were not conducted on a more elaborate scale. Their importance is their revelation of minds so vigorously at work and so certain what their problems are that they were able to add to observed facts by supplementing them with new facts of their own creation.

Greek thinkers had their own notion of the social implications of their task. They were not only convinced that their own form of activity was the best in itself but they maintained that it made men better morally and intellectually and that the pursuit of knowledge imposed social responsibilities and lessened the differences between man and man. The Hippocratic Oath, still used by doctors, shows how seriously the pioneers of medicine regarded their own task and how well they understood both its dangers and its duties, and it is no accident that a Hippocratic writer says, 'Where the love of mankind is, there also is the love of science',[26] as if the knowledge of nature and the love of humanity could not ultimately be kept apart. No less striking are the words of Euripides on the happiness which comes from the study of nature:

> Happy is he who has knowledge
> That comes for enquiry. No evil he stirs
> For his townsmen, nor gives himself
> To unjust doings,
> But surveys the unageing order
> Of deathless nature, of what it is made,
> And whence, and how.
> In men of this kind the study
> Of base acts never finds a home.[27]

In the troubled conflicts of his time, when the old certainties were being shaken and the old balances broken, Euripides turned to the philosophic and scientific calm promised by inquiry into nature. In its detachment and its peace he saw a new hope for mankind and a cure for the ugly passions which were bred by political and social disorder.

Greek mathematics, philosophy, and science all survived the collapse of Athens in 404 BC, and all made some of their most notable contributions after it. Though mathematics never lost its connexion with astronomy, yet it remained largely 'pure' and *a priori*. This indeed was its glory. For the Greeks worked out a system by which mathematical proof can be conducted, and it has never been bettered. It begins with definition, and the definitions, as they survive in Euclid, are still models of conciseness and clarity. Next, it established analysis, in which, after making an assumption, we ask what the results will be, and so make the problem clear. Thirdly, it fashioned the form of exposition which still prevails in geometry, because it is ruled by strict logic. On these foundations the Greeks achieved their magnificent performance in mathematics, by which geometry not only was used for all that we now associate with it, but came near to performing operations like the integral calculus and founded statics and hydrostatics. The great genius of Archimedes (*c.* 287–213 BC) covered an almost unbelievable range of achievement, and long after him Greek mathematicians pursued his methods in the discovery of trigonometry, the theory of numbers, and the beginnings of algebra. When Plato had inscribed over the door of his Academy the words, 'Let no man enter who knows no geometry', he was not being eccentric, but paying his tribute to the Greek conviction that through geometry the world could be known as a rational whole. Because they were trained in it, the Greeks were able to make fundamental discoveries in astronomy, which culminated in the anticipation of Copernicus by Aristarchus of Samos (*c.* 310–230 BC) when he argued that 'the fixed stars and the sun remain unmoved, and the earth revolves about the sun in the circumference of a circle, the sun lying in the middle of the orbit'.[28]

Like mathematics, Greek philosophy tried to grasp the world as a whole, and though its conclusions are not so final as those of geometry, it imposed on posterity its notion of what philosophy is and what problems should concern it. To it we owe such fundamental distinctions as those between the one and the many, reality and appearance, knowledge and opinion, being and not-being, form and matter, universals and particulars. In making such distinctions the Greeks tried to solve the discord between the infinite multiplicity and variety of phenomena and the need for some permanent reality behind or in them. They realized that for so precise and delicate a task words are by no means an ideal instrument, and they did their best to establish a vocabulary which should be both clear and consistent, and to see that the functions of words were understood as well as their meanings.

With such an instrument they hoped to show what the sum of things is and how it works, and though their speculations might indeed carry them into bold constructions, they argued each step with a mathematical precision and tested their hypotheses with examples and instances which anyone could understand. In such a task they were inexorably forced beyond the visible world to a world of abstractions, which was for some more real than the common reality. Though the basis of their system was logic, they were not afraid of applying it to ethics, politics, and religion, or of summoning faith to their aid when argument had reached its limits and could do no more. Yet the strength of Greek philosophy lies not so much in its range as in its assumption that there is no problem which cannot be solved by hard and careful thought. It assumes that words are the instruments of thought and that thought is about things, no matter how remote or impalpable or complex.

Natural science did not in Greece have anything comparable to its present range, but in two main directions it laid the foundations of what we now think. The first is the atomic theory as it was propounded by Leucippus (*fl.* 440 BC) and Democritus (*c.* 460–370 BC). It has little in common with atomic physics as we know them, but is none the less their remote ancestor. It began as an attempt to solve the ultimate nature of things. The early answers that everything is derived from a single substance, such as water, air, or fire, were not satisfactory, nor was Empedocles' doctrine of the four elements, water, earth, air, and fire, since it left too much unexplained. The strength of the atomists was that they took note alike of the infinite variety of nature and of its ordered regularity. They put forward a theory of atoms, which are so small as to be invisible, and though all are made of the same stuff, they have an incalculable variety of shapes and sizes, and their relations with one another produce the variety of phenomena. The strength of the theory is that in it the physical universe is really physical, operated by natural laws, or, as Democritus said, 'necessity', and to this there are no exceptions. Even the gods belong to the phenomenal world and are explicable on the same principles as other phenomena. In effect the theory conforms to certain principles which lie at the heart of most scientific thinking. First, it assumes that all knowledge begins with the senses, and that without them no knowledge is possible. It is therefore not *a priori* and insists that theories must be verified by observed facts. Secondly, it dismisses the idea of any external power for that of inherent laws which operate absolutely everywhere and can for this reason be discovered. Thirdly, it treats even the human mind as a natural phenomenon, which can also be examined and discussed and explained. Fourthly, though it assumes the existence of a void in which the atoms move, a concept not easy to hold and liable to cause trouble, this notion is really no more than that of space as a field in which movement is possible and events take place. The atomic theory answered questions which had long troubled the Greeks and provided a working hypothesis for more discovery and more capacious theories of the nature of reality.

The second great achievement of Greek science was through medicine to biology. Early in the fifth century Alcmaeon of Croton saw that if a doctor is to understand the human body, he must study the bodies of animals and know how they work from the inside, and how enterprising this early biology was can be seen from the story that when a one-horned ram was brought, as an ominous portent, to Pericles, Anaxagoras had the skull cut in two and showed that the brain had not filled its proper position but had been shrunk to a point at the place in the cavity where the horn began.[29] It was from experiments like this that in the next century Aristotle advanced to his prodigious studies in biology and his own enormous number of dissections. From the desire to cure sickness by finding out its causes Greek scientists advanced to the study of the physical frame of men, and therefore of animals, insects, and fishes. What began as a purely useful technique broadened into a true science, and continued to be relatively lively and creative until the second century AD. If the atomic theory illustrates the Greek gift for arguing from an abstract theory to a whole view of the universe, medicine shows the opposite process by which the accumulated knowledge of the surgery and the sick-room becomes a whole body of coherent information on the workings of something visible and tangible. If the one grew from the desire to find principles behind phenomena, the other grew from a vivid sense of the living scene and a lively curiosity about everything in it.

The spirit of inquiry which found its culmination in these great achievements was also applied to the study of man as a social being with a generous sense of what this means. It is not perhaps wrong to maintain that this was in the first place a result of medicine. When the Greeks saw that health was largely dependent on physical conditions, they attempted other researches which are the beginnings of anthropology, sociology, geography, and history. They knew that human physique is relatively stable, and tried to account for national variations by attributing them to climate or diet, as when a Hippocratic author explains the greater mildness and gentleness of Asiatics by the tamer conditions in which they live, and the endurance, industry, and high spirits of Europeans by their hard struggle for existence.[30] Such questions belonged to *historiê* or inquiry, and the word, which was commonly associated with the study of man, is the ancestor of our own 'history'. From the start Greek historians followed certain fundamental principles. The first was that legends cannot be trusted, and Hecataeus of Miletus (*c.* 550–489 BC) may indeed be regarded as the founder of historical studies when he states his purpose: 'What I write here is the account of what I considered to be true. For the stories of the Greeks are numerous and, in my opinion, ridiculous.'[31] Legends of course had neither the authority nor the impregnability of Holy Writ, and a man was perfectly free to criticize them, but to criticize them on this scale was indeed revolutionary. Hecataeus perhaps went too far, for there is, as we now know, a kernel of truth in some ancient Greek legends, but he was justified by at least one aspect of antiquarian knowledge in his day. The Greeks liked to establish connexions with the past and did so by genealogies, but such genealogies were often created for political or personal reasons and their variety alone invited suspicion. Hecataeus wished to reform them and make them more sane and credible. This led to a second principle of Greek history. It saw man in his physical environment and attached great importance to geography. Hecataeus was at least as much a geographer as he was a historian, and though the information at his disposal was limited and often incorrect, he made a full use of it and did his best to construct a picture of the inhabited world as best he could. Anaximander had already constructed a map of it, and Hecataeus improved on this, not merely from information received from others but from his own travels.[32] No doubt such a map was sketchy, inaccurate, and full of improbabilities, but it was in itself a remarkable step forward. Thirdly, Hecataeus, like his successors, chose prose and not verse for his work. This may seem an obvious and natural decision, but in fact it marked a great break in tradition. Hitherto poetry had been the normal method of remembering the past, and had been used not only by Homer for the heroic age but by later poets for stories of the Ionian migration, the wars against Lydia, and other relatively recent subjects. In choosing prose as his medium Hecataeus emphasized his break with the old view

of the past as something inspired by the Muse and varied to
taste by each poet, and substituted for it his own scientific
ideal of something that could be found only by inquiry and
called for qualities of detachment, hard work, and ability
to sift evidence.

Though Herodotus does not agree with all that Hecataeus
says, and may at times seem ungrateful to him, he continued
his work on a grand scale in the true spirit of scientific investigation. It is true that Herodotus was also deeply touched
by epic and tragedy and applied some of their methods to his
telling of stories, but that was because he believed that this
is how things happen, and there is no good reason to think
that he was seriously wrong. Like Hecataeus, he learned
much from his own extensive travels, and his observation of
Egyptian customs and legends gave him a remarkable independence and breadth of outlook. Almost anything that
concerned men interested him, and his history is a rich
treasure of information on all manner of details relevant to
the way in which men live. If on the one hand it made him
sceptical of certain Greek claims, it also enabled him to understand his own people as only a man can who has external
standards of comparison by which to judge them. For him
'barbarians' presented many points of interest, and he was
not content to accept them as aberrations or monstrosities,
but maintained that it is the heat of the sun which blackens
faces[33] and hardens skulls.[34] He even made his own efforts
to establish rules by which physical types and divisions can
be classified, as when in discussing the Argippaei he distinguishes them from their neighbours the Scythians, by
pointing out that though they wear Scythian dress, they are
bald, snub-nosed, and bearded, speak a distinct language,
and, unlike the Scythians, live off tree fruit.[35] He established
his observations on a system of *physis*, nature, and *nomos*,
custom. The first means that each region has its own kind of
physical growth, the second that modes of behaviour differ
according to the demands of their surroundings. By this he
explained the differences which the Greeks noticed, not without contempt, between themselves and the Egyptians,[36] and
even thought it 'natural' for certain Indians to eat dead parents; for, as Pindar said, 'custom is king of all'. Yet he knew
that even customs are not immutable, and that change of
physical conditions may change them also.

His experience confirmed Herodotus in a natural openness
of mind. Though he rejects some stories because they offend
his sense of probability, and is often cautious about accepting
others, it is characteristic of him that he gives in detail some

stories about which he is himself sceptical. A signal example of this is the circumnavigation of Africa by Phoenicians sent by the Pharaoh Necho. The details which he gives, notably that at a certain point the sun 'rose on their right hand,' confirm the truth of the story.[37] Once he felt that he knew his way with a topic, he was not afraid to indulge in speculations which would have been thought intolerable in almost any century of the Christian era before the nineteenth. Of these the most remarkable is his sense of the length of historic and prehistoric time. He was bound by no dogma about the date of creation, and when he saw the alluvial deposits of the Nile in the Egyptian Delta, he compared them with five similar cases in the Aegean and ended by suggesting that, if the Nile were to reverse its course and flow into the Red Sea, it would take ten or twenty thousand years to fill it with soil.[38] He believed indeed that 'everything could happen in the length of time',[39] and it was this ability and willingness to welcome new facts and to see their importance that made him a true scientist.

In the next generation Thucydides (*c.* 460–*c.* 400 BC) wrote his history of the Peloponnesian War. In many ways the antithesis of Herodotus, he is also his heir and successor. In him the new science of history has matured by becoming more specialized, and he concentrates on what we call political history. If this means that he lacks the wide curiosity and the generous information of Herodotus, it also means that he works in a more critical temper and pays more attention to establishing the truth of even the smallest details. He examined eyewitnesses about recent events and applied to earlier periods a sharp, critical mind. Of the first he said:

'I have made it a principle not to write down the first story that came my way, and not even to be guided by my own general impressions; either I was present myself at the events which I have described or else I heard of them from eye-witnesses whose reports I have checked with as much thoroughness as possible. Not that the truth was easy to discover: different eye-witnesses give different accounts of the same events, speaking out of partiality for one side or the other or else from imperfect memories.'[40]

and of the second:

'We may claim instead to have used only the plainest evidence and to have reached conclusions which are reasonably accurate, considering that we have been dealing with ancient history.'[41]

Thucydides regarded as his first duty the careful assessment of evidence and the establishment of facts. When he had done that, he was prepared to advance, in his own austere and detached way, to suggest theories.

Like Herodotus, but in a different way, Thucydides owes something to medical science. He sets about the history of the Peloponnesian War in an almost clinical spirit, which first analyses Athens in its health and then the different flaws which corrupted its character and led to its downfall. He does this largely by indirect means, by showing the ideas which dominated the minds of the chief statesmen and politicians of the time and telling to what results these led in action. But though it is indirect, his method is that of science, at least of political science in a strict sense. He does not claim that his work will enable men to forecast the future, but he knows that a study of it will help them to understand events better, and at times he advances an abstract analysis, like that of class-war, which he certainly claims to be true of most conditions in which it arises. His concern is strictly with human actions, and he allows no part for supernatural forces, whether gods or cycles of fortune or destiny or other influences. Though he does not commit himself much about religion, he can hardly have believed in it, and he was certainly contemptuous of its more superstitious forms. He shows his scientific training in the paramount importance which he gives to intelligence. For him this is the first quality needed in a statesman, and he judges the different leaders of Athens by the degree in which they possess it. For him the barbarities demanded by Cleon or practised by the Athenians on Melos are errors of judgment, and all the more dangerous for that reason. He had indeed his own personal preferences, and he was well aware that religion and morality may be necessary to the well-being of a state, but he saw that in themselves they were not enough. Indeed, it is hard not to suspect a grave irony when he passes judgment on Nicias, who threw away the only hope of escape for the Athenian army from Syracuse by delaying in order to avert the menace of an eclipse: 'A man who, of all the Hellenes in my time, least deserved to come to so miserable an end, since the whole of his life had been devoted to the study and the practice of virtue.'[42] Yet this outlook is itself inspired by deep convictions. The moral integrity of Thucydides is as great as his intellectual, and his love of the best things in Athens gives a special depth to his dispassionate curiosity. His respect for truth was equalled by his respect for certain moral qualities, especially those which take a civic or social form, and he is a supreme example of the ability of the Greeks to maintain high standards of conduct without demanding any supernatural sanction for them. In him, as in the pioneers of medicine, the visible world has pride of place and calls for its appropriate methods of study, but this attachment to it in no way detracts from his sense of the importance of what he studied or of the grave issues which he analyses with so unflinching an impartiality.

Though Greek science and philosophy began as the allies of religion, there came a point at which the alliance was not easy to maintain. It began to be clear that scientific explanations of phenomena might conflict with religious, and some skill was needed to avoid a crisis. The early physicians faced the issue in a calm enough spirit, as when a Hippocratic author discusses the nature of epilepsy, known as 'the sacred disease':

'This disease called sacred comes from the same causes as others, from the things that come to and go from the body, from cold, sun, and the variable restlessness of the winds. Such things are divine. So that there is no need to put the disease in a special class and to consider it more divine than others; they are all divine and all human. Each has a nature and a power of its own; none is hopeless or incapable of treatment.'[43]

Though we may legitimately suspect a nice irony, there is no reason to think that such words would not command acceptance. The gods were indeed thought to be everywhere, and their work manifest in everything; so a disease might well be both divine and human. Somewhat more complicated is the case of Herodotus, who undeniably saw the gods actively at work in the minds and passions of men, but had also a keen interest in scientific inquiry and accepted scientific explanations for inanimate nature. If religion and science were at variance, he too was capable of dodging the issue. When he mentions a Thessalian legend that the ravine through which the river Peneus flows to the sea was made by Posidon, he says: 'Their tale is plausible; and anyone who thinks that Posidon shakes the earth and that clefts produced by earthquakes are the works of that god would on seeing this mountain-ravine ascribe it to Posidon. For it appeared to me to be the result of an earthquake.'[44] By this neat manœuvre neither religion **nor** science is offended. It was possible to accept both, **with c**ertain unexpressed reservations but with no overt declaration of hostilities.

This became more difficult when science and philosophy turned their attention to the gods and gave their different explanations of them. The more thorough a theory was, the more difficult it might be to fit the gods into it. Democritus, who in fact eliminated them from the government of the universe, compromised by making them a kind of psychic phenomena, who can somehow bring good or bad fortune.[45] Prodicus went further, and suggested that those things in nature which sustain life are looked upon as gods and honoured accordingly.[46] This too undermines faith, since it reduces the gods to no more than physical forces and greatly restricts their activity. A third view, even more destructive, was that of Critias (*c.* 460–403), who made a character in a play say that the gods are an invention of some great teacher who wished to frighten men into keeping the laws and did so by saying that thunder and lightning are the work of gods:

> With such dread terrors he encompassed them;
> And neatly with a word he gave the gods
> A habitation which well fitted them,
> And so extinguished lawlessness with laws.[47]

When such views were held, it is not surprising that Protagoras should sum up his own position: 'When it comes to the gods, I am unable to discover whether they exist or not, or even what they are like in form. For there are many things that stand in the way of this knowledge—the obscurity of the problem and the brevity of man's life.'[48] Though philosophy began in a religious and even devout spirit, its very consistency and truth to its assumptions often forced it into either agnosticism or scepticism, and ordinary people began to feel that it was a danger to society.

Yet though many Greeks may have regarded these new developments with alarm, it is to the credit of their political tolerance that they took no strong measures against them. Indeed, the attack on the irreligious implications of natural science did not begin until the Peloponnesian War had begun to undermine self-confidence and to give a new boost to superstition. Even so we may suspect that political motives lay behind it. When his enemies wished to attack Pericles, one of their moves was to attack Anaxagoras, who not only declared that the moon was made of earth and the sun an incandescent rock bigger than the Peloponnese but discovered the true causes of solar and lunar eclipses.[49] A dubious seer, called Diopithes, carried a decree authorizing the indictment of 'those who disbelieve in divine things or teach theories about what goes on in the sky'.[50] Anaxagoras was tried and convicted, but fortunately escaped to Lampsacus, where he lived in peace and honour. Nor was this the only case of such persecution. Diagoras, Protagoras, and possibly Euripides were tried on similar charges, but the most notorious trial came after the end of the war, when in 399 BC Socrates was tried and executed. The accusation was skilfully framed and claimed that he 'does not recognize the gods recognized by the state but introduces new divinities'.[51] Behind this lay political passion, since Socrates had been a friend of Critias, who as one of the Thirty had governed Athens with merciless brutality after its defeat in 404 BC. But the actual accusation appealed to a common prejudice that 'there is a certain Socrates, a wise man, who has studied what goes on in the sky and investigated everything under the earth'.[52] Unfortunately there was, or had been, an element of truth in this. In his early life Socrates had been interested in natural phenomena, and as such had been pilloried in 423 BC by Aristophanes in the *Clouds,* in which the pupils of Socrates are taught that Zeus does not exist and his rule has passed to Dinos, or Vortex,[53] and that rain, thunder, and lightning are not sent by the sky-god but come from unseemly disturbances in the clouds.[54] The first half of the accusation against Socrates would certainly find support in a popular travesty of his views. The second half was no less important, and referred to the 'divine sign', which Socrates claimed as an important influence in his life and which was attached to no special god. The skilful combination of two charges, neither absolutely unfounded, was, in the angry atmosphere of the time, enough to get Socrates condemned to death. No doubt he did not make things easier for himself by his defence against accusations which he could not take seriously, but it is a strange irony that he, a sincerely religious man, should be martyred for a science which he had ceased to value.

The conflict between science and religion was matched by another conflict, no less serious, between science and philosophy. The old combination, which had in the past done so much for both, broke down on the fundamental question of the nature and possibility of knowledge. While science based its system on the senses and was content with what they had to give, philosophy felt that they could not be

trusted and provided no sure basis for knowledge. On the one
hand a medical author denies the validity of abstract argument:

> 'Conclusions which are merely verbal cannot bear fruit;
> only those do which are based on demonstrated fact.
> For affirmation and talk are deceptive and treacherous.
> Wherefore one must hold fast to fact in generalisations
> also, and occupy oneself with facts persistently if one is
> to acquire that ready and infallible habit which we call
> the art of medicine.'[55]

On the other hand, philosophy had always maintained that
the reality, which is the object of thought, can be discovered only by the mind. Many views were held on the nature
of this reality, but philosophy could hardly exist if its possibility were denied, and it was clear that the gifts of the
senses or 'facts' are not enough. The issue so presented was
seen by Gorgias (c. 483–376 BC), who argued that the objects of sensation and the objects of knowledge are alike unreal, because both are concerned with not-being as well as
with being, and it is impossible to distinguish between them.
He concludes that there is nothing; that, even if there is
anything, we cannot know it; and that, even if we could
know it, we could not communicate it to anyone else.[56]
There is some paradox in this, and the notion of not-being
is open to obvious objections, but it called for an answer,
since it suggested that if the methods of philosophy were
pushed to their limit, they made philosophy itself impossible.
Protagoras tried to put forward a cure, when he taught that
'Man is the measure of all things' and that things *are* what
they *seem*.[57] Logically such a theory could lead only to sol-
ipsism and an infinite series of isolated, private universes,
whose inmates are incommunicably severed from one another.
By the end of the fifth century, the happy relations between philosophy and science had reached a crisis, and it
looked as if they could not be restored.

It fell to Plato in the fourth century to make a heroic attempt to heal these wounds. The majestic fabric of his philosophy, constructed stage by stage through a long life,
aimed at proving the possibility of knowledge and at finding
a place for the observations of the senses. He saw that, just
as in mathematics certain conclusions follow from certain
premissess, so in philosophy an argument may be developed
with equal cogency from certain accepted assumptions. He
distinguished, as others had before him, between Being and

Becoming, but against the scientists he assumed that the first is real and the only proper object of knowledge, while the second, which depends on it, is mere appearance and the object of uncertain opinion. Reality for him consists of ideal Forms, which are at once logical universals, capable of being understood, and ideal particulars, capable of inspiring an almost mystical devotion. To establish his Forms he appealed, indirectly perhaps but no less certainly, to religion, and argued that we know them through recollection from a former existence. This might in fact mean no more than that our knowledge of them is innate, but in any case it is not derived from the senses. Though this impressive system removed doubts about the possibility of knowledge, it dealt a cruel blow to science. For it meant that observation and experiment gave place to *a priori* reasoning. Plato himself was so possessed by the notion that the universe is rational that he thought it possible to dictate its structure from his own conception of the way in which the Creator ought to have made it. In his search for certainty he failed to allow that on many matters we can hope for no more than a reasonable opinion and that this may be more valuable than any dogmatic assertion.

Yet Greek mathematics, philosophy, and science survived both the agony of the Peloponnesian War and Plato's counter-reformation, and continued to thrive for some four or five centuries. It is indeed a tribute to the firmness with which their foundations were laid and to the appeal which their questions still had for men. Yet in this there was an uneasy struggle between the old experimental methods and the *a priori* methods canonized by Plato, and in this struggle the honours went on the whole to the *a priori* school. Though the claims of experiment were upheld by biology and its sturdy ally, medicine, until at least the time of Galen (AD 129–199), in other fields of inquiry abstract thinking came to be thought more honourable than empirical science. Though Archimedes built engines for the defence of Syracuse and made astonishing discoveries in applied mathematics, he thought nothing of this part of his work and refused to commit it to writing.[58] Greek mathematics, which had begun with practical leanings, became more and more abstract as it perfected its skill and its beauty. Philosophy indeed kept up its connexion with the world of action, and in Epicurus made the atomic theory a basis for conduct, but it gave little encouragement to scientific investigation, and in the end materialism made place for a world of transcendental abstractions. At the last even medicine gave way and preferred *a priori* speculation to examination of the human body. This indeed lies outside our scope, but it provides a comment on the history of mathematics, philosophy, and science in the classical age. Their strength was in their concern with the visible world, in which they sought to find permanent principles, and they can hardly be blamed if they asked questions so important and so difficult that in the end their successors paid more attention to these principles than to the phenomena which they were invoked to explain.

# CHAPTER X

# EPILOGUE

IN THE SEVENTH AND SIXTH CENTURIES Greek civilization owed much to the variety and the independence of rival city-states, each of which wished to make its own distinctive and distinguished contribution to what Pindar calls 'the delightful things of Hellas'.[1] If there was a fundamental pattern of achievement, it presented a varied surface and was all the richer for local idiosyncrasies. This cultural balance was matched, and indeed maintained, by a balance of political power in which no single state was strong enough to dominate the rest or seriously to interfere with its neighbours' way of life. In the fifth century the situation changed dramatically. After the defeat of Persia, the Greek states fell into two main divisions, the one led by Sparta and the other by Athens. While Sparta stood for the old aristocratic life on the land, with its dislike of political innovations and intellectual adventures, Athens stood for the new democratic ideal based on trade and manufacturers and welcomed innovations as means of exercising its ebullient vitality. Fear, suspicion, and jealousy inspired each side for the other, and broke out at intervals into war. In this uneasy situation Sparta retired into its ancient traditions and, setting austerity and devotion to country before everything else, lost much of its earlier grace and charm; Athens, inspired by many ambitions and confident of its ability to realize them, encouraged new developments in the arts and sciences and absorbed into itself the many different strands of Greek civilization. No other Greek state in the middle years of the fifth century can be compared with her for the range, strength, and originality of her achievement, and indeed at this time she presents the culmination of the many forces which had made the Greeks unique among peoples and given a special character to their outlook and their habits. What this meant to the Athenians themselves may be seen from a song which Euripides wrote in 431 BC, just before the outbreak of the Peloponnesian War:

199

From old the sons of Erechtheus know felicity;
The children of blessed gods,
Born from a land holy and undespoiled,
They pasture on glorious Wisdom,
Ever walking gracefully through the brightest of skies,
Where once, men tell, the Holy Nine,
The Pierian Muses,
Created golden-haired Harmony.

On the fair-flowing waters of Cephisus
They say that Aphrodite fills her pitcher
And breathes over the land
The sweet gentle air of winds,
And ever she crowns her hair
With a fragrant wreath of roses;
She sends her Loves to be throned at Wisdom's side,
And with her to work all manner of excellence.[2]

Athens believed that the gods had been unprecedentedly generous to her in their most glorious gifts and that she embodied all that was most worth having in the civilization of Greece. She was indeed the 'Hellas of Hellas', as Thucydides[3] calls her in his epitaph on Euripides.

This sense of unique powers easily became a sense of mission, and many Athenians would agree with Pericles that 'our city is an education to Greece'.[4] Some of this education was indeed imparted by peaceful means, by an inspiring example and generous help. Yet not everyone responded to these advances with willing readiness, and if Athenian civilization was not accepted voluntarily, it was sometimes imposed by brutal compulsion. The Athenian Empire brought many benefits to its members, but its policy, which was a result of self-confidence and belief in democratic ideals, could only breed distrust, fear, and hatred among those to whom such ideals were abhorrent. The expansion of Athenian power and wealth led in the end to the long Peloponnesian War between Athens and Sparta, each of whom was supported by a formidable array of allies. When Thucydides began to write the history of this war, he believed that it was 'more worth writing about than any of those which had taken place in the past'.[5] He was right; for it was indeed the fatal convulsion of the old Greece. At the end of it not only was Athens defeated, but both sides were so exhausted that something irreplaceable perished from the world. For the Athenians final defeat was a disaster which they had never thought possible. In 459–454 BC their expedition to Egypt had failed catastrophically, but this had not prevented them from continuing an active, aggressive policy in Greece. But the collapse of 404 BC was different. The skill and luck, which had guided and guarded Athens, now failed her, and she had no protection against her enemies. When in 413 BC the Athenian army was annihilated at Syracuse, Euripides had written an epitaph for the fallen: 'These men won eight victories over the Syracusans when the favour of the gods was equal for both sides.'[6] Now the favour of the gods was indeed unequal, and a recognition of it brought guilty fear for brutalities committed in the past. When in the summer of 405 BC Athens lost her fleet at Aegospotami, there was no more hope of resistance. The news was brought by the galley *Paralus*, and Xenophon tells how, as one man told the news to another, a sound of wailing went up the long walls from the Piraeus to Athens: 'That night no one slept. They wept not only for the dead, but far more for themselves, thinking that they would suffer what they had done to the people of Melos, who were Spartan colonists, when they reduced them by siege, to the people of Histiaea and Scione and Torone and Aegina and many more of the Greeks.'[7] The inconceivable had happened, and the Athenians felt that they were alike abandoned by the gods and hated by men clamouring for vengeance and able to exact it.

At a first glance the decline of Athens after 404 BC would seem to be countered by new and vigorous developments which suggest no diminution of power or effort. It is true that poetry, which had been the soul of Athenian greatness, sank either into rude sensationalism or unadventurous charm. But sculpture was to find in Scopas and Praxiteles masters who gave a new freshness to the treatment of the human body and conveyed an impression of living flesh as their predecessors never had. Oratory became almost a fine art and produced masterpieces which were studied for centuries for their language and construction and rhythms. Mathematics continued its majestic progress, when Eudoxus (408–365 BC) discovered the general theory of proportion, and his pupil Menaechmus discovered conic sections. But the great triumph of the age was the development of philosophy. Plato and Aristotle absorbed all that had been done for philosophy and science, subjected it to a searching criticism, and organized their own systems on a prodigious scale. Plato handled philosophy with a fullness and a coherence beyond any precedent, and even today we can but marvel at the unsurpassed power with which he formulates question after question of fundamental importance and presents his discussions in a language miraculously lucid, consistent, and lively.

Of all the many answers which men have given to questions about the nature of reality and knowledge, his have lasted longest and won the largest assent. Aristotle attempted something different. In his encyclopaedic attempt to systematize the whole of knowledge as it existed in his day and to enrich it with his own remarkable discoveries, he not only made valuable contributions to metaphysics and logic but turned the medical studies of the previous century into a true science of biology and wrote on ethics one of the very few books which we neglect at our peril. Through this double achievement the fourth century has a place of high honour in the history of human thought, but neither in Athens nor elsewhere in Greece did these new triumphs fully compensate for what had been lost.

Behind this impressive façade it is impossible not to discern a diminution of vitality and confidence, a tendency to question much that had before been taken for granted, and a refusal to attempt tasks which did not offer immediate results. The expense of spirit which had been the glory of the fifth century gave place to a sense of shame, to a guilty rejection of much that had been sought and honoured. Though both tragedy and comedy survived, neither bore any resemblance to its old self. Tragedy, which had gloried in being a national art and spoken for the whole people, became almost a private pastime concerned with the cultivation of delicate mannerisms for a limited, aesthetic end. In comedy, even Aristophanes, who had so late as 405 BC lavished all his old exuberance and fancy on the *Frogs*, tried in the *Ecclesiazusae* in 391 BC to make up for his lack of inspiration by a cold, synthetic obscenity, which bears no relation to his old gay bawdry. More seriously, the philosophers, who were deeply concerned with the lessons of history, agreed that the Periclean age was a disastrous failure. When Plato wishes to allot blame for the decay of Athens, he mentions not the corrupt demagogues who succeeded Pericles, but Themistocles, Cimon, and Pericles himself, and his complaint is: 'They have filled the city with harbours and dockyards and walls and tributes instead of with righteousness and temperance.'[8] It is a sweeping rejection of the past, of the world into which Plato himself was born and in which his family played a distinguished part. In his boyhood he had seen the fall of Athens, and the bitter memory of it haunted him all his days. He could come to peace with himself only by condemning those who had attempted too much and failed in the end, and by devising schemes of government in which their policies and performance could not be repeated. Nor is Aristotle more generous. For him the growth of democracy in Athens under Ephialtes and Pericles was the assumption of tyrannical powers by the populace, and its leaders were worthless demagogues.[9] Both he and Plato denied the greatness of Periclean Athens and rejected its fundamental assumption, that its citizens could be trusted to take even the most important decisions because they were free and responsible men.

The cracks and flaws in Greek civilization became more manifest after the death of Alexander in 323 BC. The Hellenistic age, which followed, won indeed its extraordinary successes in bringing Greek habits to barbarian peoples, nor was it unproductive in art and science. But it suffered to a greater degree than the fourth century from a failure of confidence, from the absence of a fixed centre to which it could give its trust. The old religion sank either into the formal conduct of rites or into a rationalism which deprived the gods of mystery and almost of divinity. New superstitions swept the world, and in the welter of them the Greeks lost their sense of the special relation of man with the gods. At the one extreme, Hellenistic monarchs arrogated to themselves the titles and the honours of godhead. Though there is a splendid effrontery in the insistence of Antiochus Epiphanes, 'the god manifest', (c. 215–163 BC) on identifying Jehovah with the Olympian Zeus, and himself with both, and on having a cult, 'the Abomination of Desolation', in the court of the temple at Jerusalem,[10] and though there is a truly heroic magnificence in the last hours of Cleopatra, when she clothed herself in her royal robes and put to her breast the asp, minister of the Sun-god Re, that she might be joined with him, her father, in death,[11] yet even these proud examples cannot hide that the worship of kings and queens as gods was a denial of the whole Greek conception of man. At the other extreme was the popular tendency to save effort by ascribing everything to the gods, notably through astrology. The notion that a man's life, from the cradle to the grave, is determined by the constellations under which he is born came from the East and was fundamentally opposed to the Greek belief in free human beings. But in their conviction of failure the Greeks welcomed it, feeling that, if all is predestined, there is no point in battle against the stars. It was easier to study them and anticipate what was going to happen; then one would be prepared for it and able to accept it. In their different ways both king-worship and astrology killed the old religion and ushered in a twilight of the gods.

The long decline of the Hellenistic world illustrates by contrast the distinction of the great age which preceded it. From the eighth century to almost the end of the fifth the Greeks developed their civilization with an unrivalled rapidity and variety of accomplishment. The results are so impressive that we are liable to neglect some indications that the structure was not always built on firm foundations. The very speed of growth made it difficult to assimilate some changes into established use and wont. In religion the predominance of the Olympian gods never eliminated cults and beliefs which belonged to older and more earthy creeds. In politics the passage from monarchy to aristocracy still left openings for ambitious adventurers to seize the powers, if not the titles, of kings, and the passage from aristocracy to democracy left in even the most democratic states social groups which would stick at nothing to regain lost privileges. The extension of frontiers by conquest or colonization usually left among the victims a burning resentment which turned to violence at the first favourable opportunity. Moreover, the civilization of which the Greeks dreamed, with its love of leisure and its demand for wealth to support it, called for richer resources than their austere land could provide. In many undertakings they were hampered by poverty, and most populations lived so close to starvation that a small interference with their economy might well mean ruin. Athens fell in the end to Sparta because she relied on supplies of corn from the Black Sea, and when these were cut off by the destruction of the Athenian navy, there was no choice but surrender. This also meant that once war ceased to be a seasonal pastime and was prolonged, like the Peloponnesian War, for many years, it left both sides exhausted and impoverished almost beyond recovery. Nor was Greece in the least secure in its Mediterranean setting. Its population was never comparable to that of the huge monarchies of Asia, and it was fortunate that in the eighth and seventh centuries these were too busy attacking one another to think of invading Greece. When Persia began to move under Darius and Xerxes, it took all the efforts of a united Greece to hold its own, and even then the Persian menace remained a reality which it was unwise to forget. Greek civilization was indeed perilously poised. If it was to survive and flourish, it had to maintain both its own equilibrium and its immunity from foreign attack.

On this none-too-stable foundation the Greeks built their way of life, and in its main characteristics we can discern a similar system of balances, which, while it lasts, is rich in lively results, but is too easily shaken, and, when it is broken, brings down too much with it in its fall. The variety in unity which gave shape to Greek politics encouraged local effort and individuality, but collapsed when one or other power gained an ascendancy over its neighbours and cramped their initiative. The cult of individual honour, which did much for the service of the State and inspired heroic devotion and self-sacrifice, could, if it were soured by wounded pride, turn against the state and work incalculable harm. The gods, who had a dual position as sources of power and as champions of morality, might be invoked to support either against the other, and in so doing lost much of their authority and dignity. The notion of goodness, whether in the good man or the good life, with its happy inclusion of all manner of things which men love and honour, might in times of depression or defeat shrink to a mere part of itself, to the notion of virtue as Diogenes (*c.* 400–*c.* 325 BC) saw it, in which only goodness matters, and tradition, religion, civil and domestic loyalties, wealth and honour are alike dismissed in favour of a return to primitive nature. The fine arts, in which reason and the emotions worked together for a single, satisfying end, might be forced to limit the scope of one or the other and end in either a narrow aridity or a prodigal disorder. Natural science, which was not originally or fundamentally opposed to religion and displayed at times something close to a religious spirit, might, when religion claimed too much for itself, turn against it and start a counter-offensive in which it refused to admit the existence of anything beyond the visible scene. Even philosophy, which throve so long as it assumed that a world of Being and a world of Becoming exist in some kind of relation to one another, reached a dead end, when it insisted that only one or the other can command belief. It is to the undying credit of the Greeks, and the main source of their influence and their renown, that for some three centuries they maintained these precarious balances and built upon them the lofty structure of their achievement. Every change involved a risk, but so long as the Greeks kept their confidence in themselves, the risks were surmounted, and civilization consolidated its new positions with style and assurance.

At the centre of this scheme of balances, closely interwoven with it and implied in most of its ramifications, lay something which held it together and gave meaning to it. This was the conception of man's nature and place in the sum of things. In no matter were the Greeks more courageous or more rational than in their assessment of humanity, its limitations, its possibilities, and its worth. They differed fundamentally from their contemporaries in Asia, who thought that the great mass of men were of no importance in comparison with the god-kings for whose service they existed, and from their contemporaries in Egypt, who believed that life in this world was but a trivial preliminary to the peculiar permanence of life in the grave. The Greeks both recognized that men are worthy of respect in themselves, and were content that they should win this in the only life of which we have any knowledge. But they saw at the same time that the significance of human behaviour depends on powers which lie outside it, that man is not alone in the universe and cannot be dissociated from powers above and beneath him. If he resembles the gods on the one hand and the beasts on the other, it is for him to take note of this and to turn it to his own profit. Though he has his own nature, which is neither that of a god nor of a beast, yet it cannot thrive entirely on its own resources and must look beyond itself to see what it should seek and what it should avoid. This consciousness of dimensions outside the human sphere was deeply ingrained in the Greeks. Though they had no single myth about the creation of man, most myths agree that he was made from the earth, and that this was the work of the gods. This symbolized his intermediate position, but his ability to rise upward is symbolized in the myth of Prometheus, who teaches men the arts of life and delivers them from their first confusion and ignorance in which they lived 'like shapes of dreams'.[12] The Greeks were conscious of the humble nature of human origins, but saw in them a summons to unrealized potentialities. They felt the need of something external to brace them to effort and make them worthy of themselves.

This desire for another dimension, for something beyond the recognized sphere of humanity, is denied by Protagoras' doctrine that 'man is the measure of all things'. In arguing that man can know nothing but himself and that he shapes everything to his own ideas and sensations, Protagoras implicitly abolished the sense of a 'beyond' which gave to Greek thought a driving impulse and sense of direction. Before Protagoras undermined the ancient confidence, it was commonly accepted that man, so far from being the centre of the universe and being encompassed by an infinite Unknowable, was in fact part of a larger, more embracing scheme. In this belief the Greeks found both comfort and inspiration, comfort because they felt that they were not lost and alone in an impenetrable darkness, and inspiration because, in their desire to grasp this 'beyond', they released unsuspected forces in themselves. The natural and first place to find it was in the gods. Whatever they may have meant to the religious experience of individuals, they played a large part in common thought by suggesting that there are powers outside man, greater indeed than he is and not fully intelligible, but still intelligible enough for him to wish in some ways to resemble them, to make the most of their help and guidance, to pay attention to their concern for his doings, and to approach them in such ways as his limited faculties and opportunities allow. This conviction is to be seen at its clearest in poetry and sculpture. Just as Aeschylus and Sophocles demonstrate through their dramatic events that the actions of men have a special significance because they are related to a celestial world, so the sculptures of Olympia and the Parthenon show how strength and joy reach their highest point when the gods inspire them. To the ordinary man this would mean that, though he was only human, he could, by knowing about the gods and relying upon their support, succeed in all manner of things which he would not otherwise have the competence or the courage to face. Through this other dimension the sense of obstruction which dogs humanity was reduced, if not broken, by the revelation of many ways to extend the scope of action or of personality. Though the Greeks knew that they could not climb the brazen sky, they were conscious of its presence and of the contrast and the challenge which it offered to them.

The gods provoked man to rival them so far as he could, and made him aware of possibilities beyond his common round or his usual self. In probing the mysteries around them, the Greeks found new calls to thought and action, and most new branches of speculation suggested possibilities outside their particular sphere. To some men science gave the extension of vision which others got from religion, and was no less productive of rich results. Inquiries into the *physis,* or nature of things, led to an increasingly more generous notion of human powers and of their capacity to shape nature to suit their own ends. In fact, the very idea of nature, obscure indeed and hard to grasp but always powerful and present, could evoke its own kind of religion and the inspiration which comes with it. The study of the human body in medicine led beyond the healing of the sick to ideas of man as a creature living in a physical environment, which he may not be able to control but can at least exploit for his own improvement. In mathematics the belief in numbers implies a transcendental order, which not only gives a special

delight to those who study it, but makes them feel that they
have found something solid and permanent behind the
shifting appearances of things. The lessons of geometry can
be translated into the work of men's hands in architecture
or the patterns of sculpture and painting, and the man who
does this passes beyond the usual realm of the senses to a
different, more commanding, and more detached level of experience. So too in philosophy, when Anaxagoras advanced
his theory of Mind as a primal, efficient cause, he opened
the way to wider speculations: 'Mind has power over all
things, both greater and smaller, that have life; Mind has
power over the whole revolution, so that it began to revolve
in the beginning. And it began to revolve first from a small
beginning; but the new revolution now extends over a larger
space, and will extend over a larger still.'[13] If an expanding power of this kind lay behind phenomena, it was a legitimate conclusion that it worked also in men and forced them
to new achievements. It did not matter very much where the
Greeks found this something outside themselves, so long as
they found it, and in their greatest days they relied upon
it to extend their aims and their capacities.

We might think that in the fourth century this external
dimension was by no means forgotten. Plato's Forms are his
equivalent to it, and his God, however remote and in-
definite, is undeniably divine; Aristotle's conception of the
contemplative life is all the more impressive because he
ascribes it to God and says of man that 'we must, so far as
we can, make ourselves immortal';[14] the mathematicians had
a notion of form as fine and as precise as any held in the
fifth century. A Greek of this time might be expected to
feel that beyond his specifically human domain lay others
which belonged to a more embracing system not entirely outside his reach. But this is not quite what happened. The
impressive intellectual achievements of the age were on
the whole conducted in a rarefied, detached atmosphere of
pure thought. Though the mathematicians never lost their interest in astronomy and made dazzling excursions into
mechanics, they tended to treat their inquiries as part of a
self-contained system which bore little relation to common
life or the needs of action. By making God devote eternity to
pure thought, Aristotle cut Him off from the ordinary world
of men, and even if he made Him a model which some
might try to follow, this was restricted to a select few and
brought no comfort to many others who might have benefited
from an ideal shaped more closely to their requirements. Even
though Plato makes the visible world depend on the ideal

Forms, he does not show how it does so, and it means much less to him than the Forms. In different ways the great thinkers helped to break up the universe in which the Greeks had enjoyed the illumination of a lower order of things by a higher and had felt that there was always a hope of transcending their conventional limitations in some unforeseen direction. When this higher order was isolated in itself or reserved for a few select initiates, it lost much of its old inspiring influence. It emphasized that the ordinary man must rely on his own experience and not look beyond it. Instead of reinforcing and extending the whole round of human activities, the new speculations confined them to a man-centred world and destroyed the consciousness of a superior dimension which had given a special splendour to the Greek vision of existence.

The assumptions which gave such an impetus to thought and action were well fitted to the Greek notion of personality and of the way in which it behaves. The Greeks assumed that it is natural for the intelligence and the emotions to work together. They had no distrust of the emotions as such, and, though they knew that they may bring a man to disaster, the same could be said of his reason, and indeed much of their tragic vision is centred on the fatal misjudgments and misapprehensions of men. If a man allowed his intelligence to follow his emotions and at the same time not be deluded by them into too precipitate action, he behaved as a healthy being should. Just as a man who acted from his emotions alone might be condemned for intemperance or incontinence, so a man who acted purely on calculation was somehow inhuman and liable both to harm others and to frustrate his own purposes. The truest wisdom lay in a properly balanced personality, in which neither side triumphed at the expense of the other. What this meant can be seen from the place given to *erôs*, which means in the first place passionate love, but extends its meaning far beyond physical desire to many forms of intellectual and spiritual passion. For Parmenides it is the child of Necessity and the force which makes men live and thrive;[15] for Democritus it is the desire for beautiful things;[16] for Euripides it is the inspiring spirit of the arts;[17] for Pericles it is what devoted citizens feel for their city;[18] for Socrates it is the pursuit of noble ends in thought and action. These different forms of *erôs* agree in making it a power which drives a man to throw his full personality into what he does, which sustains him in powerful exertions and impels him to unusual efforts, which sets his intelligence fully and actively to work and gives him that unity of being, that harmony of his whole nature, which is the spring of creative endeavour. It not only removes many doubts and hesitations but by concentrating all a man's faculties on a single point sharpens his vision of it and enriches his understanding. If the complete force of a man's nature works as a single power, he is a full man, and no Greek of the great days would have denied that this was the right and natural way to behave.

This sounds simple enough, and would indeed be so, if in the fourth and later centuries philosophers had not tried to dismember the self, or at least to subordinate active parts of it to some central principle other than an over-riding harmony. When Plato classed all the emotions, except proper pride, as appetites and said that they were naturally hostile to the reason and should be subordinated to it, he robbed the reason of its main source of strength and prepared the way to that hardening and stiffening of it which became characteristic of the exclusively philosophical life. When Stoicism, led by its founder Zeno (335–263 BC), argued that nothing matters but virtue and that it is to be found in following the purposes of the Cosmos, he eliminated the emotions, even pity, because they disturb the rational calm which should be the end of life. Stoicism might produce its martyrs to duty, but it hardly produced full human beings. Equally, when Epicurus (341–270 BC) said that all that matters is the pursuit of happiness, and that this is to be found in simplicity, affection, and withdrawal from public affairs, he might indeed encourage a tranquil saintliness in private life, but he excluded those emotions which find their fulfilment in social or creative endeavour. If we wish to see what these new systems of psychology and ethics meant, we have only to compare a typical Platonist or Stoic or Epicurean not only with Homer's uninhibited and yet balanced heroes but with any typical figure of the fifth century. What we miss is the full, instinctive reaction to events, the lack of any obstruction from a theory of what a man ought to be, the lively play of all his faculties together over a wide field of activity. So long as they believed in the unity of being and maintained it against attempts to distort or disfigure the self, the Greeks faced their issues with undivided powers and had all the impetus which comes from an unrestricted use of energies. It was this which gave fullness and depth to their arts, in which emotions and intelligence are inseparably and completely at work, and it was this also which enabled them in many spheres of active life to impose on their most passionate convictions a rational order which made them at once persuasive and practicable.

Greek civilization was ultimately made possible by a belief in the special worth of man. The Greeks did not see him as a corrupt and fallen being. Though they had legends, perhaps of oriental origin, of a Golden Age in the far past, which had perished through some mysterious process of decay, they did not think that men of later times must bear the guilt for its disappearance. If they believed in sin—and it is hard to describe otherwise what they felt about offences against the gods—they did not think that human nature was from the beginning corrupted by it, nor did they place hopes in any prospect of redemption. They saw that man was indeed an unprecedented creature, worthy of awe and wonder in the scale of his inventions and his enterprises. Sophocles speaks for them when he makes a chorus sing:

> There are many strange wonders, but nothing
> More wonderful than man.[19]

Once indeed they had thought that some peculiarly gifted men were literally the sons of gods, whose divine qualities they inherited, and that others were at least the peers of gods. Even in the fifth century some aristocratic families claimed descent from heroes like Aeacus, and therefore from Zeus, and Pindar regards it as a sign of their divine blood that they win victories in the athletic games.[20] But this was a special, aristocratic notion, almost irrelevant to ordinary views of man's dignity and possibilities. What mattered was the belief that he deserves respect for something unique in him and has unanswerable claims to find his own destiny.

This notion received a wider application in the teleological conception that, since man has a certain nature, this nature finds its fulfilment in certain ends. In other words, just as everything serves some purpose or other, so man serves a purpose in the scheme of things and realizes his full nature in it. This is to develop his *aretê*, or inborn capacities, so far as he possibly can. How he can best do this was a legitimate matter for discussion and found various answers from Homer to Aristotle. But in all of these views it is assumed as beyond dispute that man has such an end and that it is fine and noble. By reaching it he becomes, in the wide Greek sense of the word, 'good'. In the fifth century such a notion has inevitably a social reference, and *aretê* was found in the full development of the individual inside the social frame. Sophocles again makes the right point when he says that man has turned his special gifts to a good purpose and developed his specifically human nature:

> Speech too, and wind-swift thought,
> He has taught himself,
> And the spirit that governs cities.[21]

This sense of human worth and its potentialities underlies much of Greek speculation. Because of it the Greeks believed in liberty, since only the free can fully realize their natures; and they were quite logical in doubting whether a slave can have *aretê* in any real sense, since he is not free to be himself as he would wish to be.[22] Nor in their best days was this notion of *aretê* at all narrow; it included most things that men seek and admire. It followed that man was indeed worthy of encouragement and that society existed to help him to reach the limit of his gifts. The gods need no such help, and beasts are below it, but man is a social animal who, through his dealings with other men, rises above the condition of animals and comes in some way near to that of the gods. Just because he strives and struggles, he has a special claim to respect and must be allowed to complete his own nature. Though such ideas did not become very explicit until Aristotle built his ethical system on them, they are present in Greek thought from early times and form the foundation of its most important assumptions and conclusions.

The special worth of man depends on his ambiguous position before the gods. On the one hand he derives much of his powers from them. In words which Plato attributes to Protagoras: 'As man had a share of the divine, he was first of all the only creature to believe in gods because of his kinship with godhead.'[23] The Greeks could not but think that the qualities displayed by man in his upward struggle pointed to something beyond his limited human nature. They explained this by his kinship and association with the gods and by the readiness of the gods to inspire and help him. Qualities, which we assume to be strictly human, were thought to be partly divine, and if they were found in more than usual measure, the man who had them was called *theios*, which meant originally 'divine' and never less than 'like the gods'. This was not vanity or complacency, but a real attempt to appreciate what is most remarkable in human nature by ascribing it to a superior origin. So far the Greeks went with some confidence. But at this point they stopped; for they knew that man cannot be fully and finally like the gods because he is doomed to death. Sophocles, after enumerating man's conquests over nature and ability to meet almost any emergency, points the paradox:

> Without resource
> No to-morrow finds him. From Death alone
> He shall not win deliverance,
> Though from mortal sicknesses
> He has planned many ways of flight.[24]

If this was so, it was clear that the special and characteristic glory of man differs from that of the gods; that through his very resemblance to them he is forced to find his own fulfilment, which cannot, in the nature of things, be the same as theirs. Though at times they allow him to share their blessings, in the end he must fight alone. So, despite their belief in the divine elements in man, the Greeks gave him his own *aretê*, which is to do his utmost with his human nature, and in this they detracted in no way from his glory, but felt that at his best he deserves honour almost comparable with that of the gods but independent of it, different from it, and reserved for him alone. He is neither a beast nor a god, and that is why he is strange and wonderful.

The gods live for ever and pursue their unceasing activities in time, but man comes soon and suddenly to an end, and very few Greeks would have believed that it is possible for him after death to share as an equal in the bliss of the gods. Most would have thought that, if there is an after-life at all, it is unlikely to be a prolongation or a fuller version of life in this world. They found the completion of men's efforts elsewhere than in hopes of reward, or even of renewed activity. This was that, whereas the gods are, literally, everlasting, a man who had done something really worth doing passes outside time into a timeless condition, in which his *aretê* is fixed and permanent. The Greeks did not explain this very clearly or trouble about its implications, but it lies behind their statues, their epitaphs, their funeral *lêkythoi*, their gravestones, above all their songs which recall a man as he was at his triumphant best and enshrine him in the memory of later generations against the enmity of time. The man so remembered was the true man, the essential self, who by his exertions had found his full range and passed outside the changing pattern of his development into his ultimate reality. Celebration in visible memorials or in song gave an appropriate crown to a man's career, but they were

worth nothing if he had not won them by his deserts.
What mattered was that he should fulfil his human *aretê*
and attain his own kind of perfection in being truly himself.
This is his special, his unique privilege, and it is indeed worth
having; for it depends on the full use of faculties which can
easily be allowed to lie idle and are brought into action only
by some powerful conviction or passionate impulse towards
a distant and often unattainable goal.

In the dawn of Greek history Achilles knows that he is
fated to die young, but, unlike the Babylonian hero, Gilgam-
esh, who to the last struggles to escape from death, he accepts
his doom. Though he has the blood of a goddess in him, and
though he surpasses all other men in his prodigious powers,
he has no ambition to be a god. He acquiesces in his human
state, which presents its own challenge and offers its own
glory. He embodies the heroic outlook of the Greeks in that
he uses his superb qualities to realize the fullness of his
manhood. Though he is fully conscious of his gifts, he accepts with proud resignation the doom that awaits him:

See what a man I am also, both strong and comely to look on.
Great was the father that bred me, a goddess the mother
  who bore me;
But over me stand death and fate's overmastering power.
To me a dawn shall come, or a noontide hour, or an eve-
  ning,
When some man shall deprive me of life in the heat of the
  battle,
Shooting at me with a spear or an arrow sped from a
  bow-string.[25]

In the flaming sunset of Greek history, Alexander saw himself as a second Achilles and carried his conquests to lands
of which no historical Achilles can ever have heard. In his
irresistible march from victory to victory, he showed no
embarrassment when he was hailed by an Egyptian oracle
as the son of Zeus Ammon; and later, when he had tasted
to the full of unprecedented power, he asked the Greek cities
to honour him as a god. Like Achilles, he died young, having
done far more than any other man could have done and leaving behind him a renown which was for centuries to haunt
the imaginations of Europe and Asia. Yet in claiming, with
whatever private reservations, to be a god, Alexander rejected his Greek heritage. A late legend, which is not
likely to be more than a legend, tells that, when at Babylon

in his last sickness he knew that he was dying, he crawled
out at midnight on all fours to drown himself in the
Euphrates, hoping that his body would be lost and that
men would believe that he was in truth immortal. His attempt failed. His wife brought him back to die in his bed, and
all knew that he was only a man.[26] The story is a myth
which points a moral. The unique splendour of the Greeks
is that, with all their sense of the divine qualities in man and
of his closeness to the gods, they knew that he was not and
could not be a god, and they were content and proud that
he should find his own magnificence and be ready to live
and die for it.

# NOTES

## CHAPTER 1: THE UNITY OF THE GREEKS

1. *Critias* IIIb.
2. *Iliad* I 528, XVII 209. So too Posidon is called 'blue-haired' at *Il.* XIII.
3. Thucydides I 4.
4. *Republic* VI 507.
5. *Prometheus Vinctus* 89–90.
6. *Antigone* 334–7.
7. Herodotus VIII 144.2.
8. Aeschylus, *Agamemnon* 1050; fr. 150; Ion of Chios fr. 76; cf. Hdt. II 57.1.
9. IV 109.1; IV 194; III 38.4.
10. Aristotle, *Politics* 1255a 28; *Nicomachean Ethics* 1145a 31.

## CHAPTER 2: THE HEROIC OUTLOOK

1. Iamblichus, *Vita Pythagorae* 58; Cicero, *Tusculanae Disputationes* V 9.
2. Fr. 29 D–K.
3. *Rep.* IV 441a; but cf. *Laws* IX 863b.
4. *Nic. Eth.* 1123a 20 ff.
5. Thuc. II 40.1 (R. Warner).
6. *Il.* XI 783.
7. Fr. 8.10 ff. Diehl.
8. P. Friedländer, *Epigrammata* No. 25.
9. Fr. 16 Diehl.
10. Thuc. II 42.4 (R. Warner).
11. Anacreon fr. 100.1–2 Diehl.
12. 'Simonides' fr. 80 Diehl.
13. Simonides fr. 82 Diehl.
14. Thuc. II 42.2 (R. Warner).
15. Aesch., *Septem Contra Thebas* 232; Sophocles, *Ajax* 293, Euripides, *Heraclidae* 476–7; Aristot., *Pol.* 1260a 30; Democritus fr. 274 D–K.
16. *Memorabilia* II 4.1.
17. *Nic. Eth.* 1159a 27, 1155b 31.
18. *Il.* IX 663–8.
19. Aristot., fr. 611 Rose.
20. *Inscriptiones Graecae* XII 3. 536 ff.
21. J. D. Beazley, *Some Attic Vases in the Cyprus Museum.* pp. 6 ff.
22. *Olympian* I 40 ff.
23. Thuc. VI 54.2.
24. Plutarch, *Lycurgus* 17.
25. Plut., *Pelopidas* 18.
26. *Rep.* III 403b.
27. *Laws* VIII 835d–842a.
28. *Nic. Eth.* 1148b 29.
29. Iamblich., *Vit. Pyth.* 232.
30. Diogenes Laertius I 75.
31. 1247–8.
32. Hdt. VII 104.1.
33. Thuc. VI 92.4 (R. Warner).
34. Alcman fr. 1.16–18 Diehl; Pindar, *Pythian* X 27; *Nemean* III 21.
35. Frs. 3.5–10; 4.5–8; 7–10 Diehl.
36. Pind., *Pyth.* VIII 8–18.
37. Thuc. II 64.5 (R. Warner).
38. *Il.* IX 406–9.
39. *Odyssey* XI 218–22.
40. *Od.* XXIV 5 ff.
41. *Od.* XI 488–91.
42. Fr. 2 Diehl.
43. Thuc. II 43.3 (R. Warner).
44. P. Friedländer, *Epigrammata* No. 71.
45. Fr. 85.

## CHAPTER 3: THE GODS

1. II 53.2.
2. *Nem.* VI 1–7.
3. *Pol.* 1254b, 34.
4. *Il.* I 37–42.
5. Plato, *Laches* 198e.
6. *Il.* I 63; *Od.* XIX 560 ff.
7. *Il.* 194 ff.
8. Plut., *Theseus* 35; *Themisto-cles* 15.
9. *Ol.* VI 57 ff.
10. Fr. 1.5 ff. L–P.
11. Thuc. II 17.2.
12. Hdt. I 32.1.
13. *Iphigeneia in Aulis* 1089–97.
14. Fr. 175 D–K.
15. Fr. 182 D–K.
16. *Trachiniae* 1276–8.
17. *Il.* XXIV 28–30.
18. *Il.* XXIV 527–33.
19. Soph., *Oedipus Coloneus* 1389 ff.
20. *Laws* XI 931c.
21. *Phaedrus* 114b; *Gorgias* 526b; *Rep.* X 614c.
22. Fr. 2.25–32 Diehl.
23. *Eumenides* 996–1002 (G.
Thomson).
24. Thuc. V. 104 (R. Warner).
25. *Rhetoric* 1391b 2.
26. *Magna Moralia* 1208b 30.
27. Fr. 13 Diehl.
28. Fr. 19 Diehl.
29. Fr. 82 D–K.
30. *Laws* X 899d–905a.
31. *Nic. Eth.* 1158a 35; *De Cae-lo* 279a 18.
32. *Pyth.* II 49–51.
33. Cic., *De Deorum Natura*, I 22.
34. Iamblich., *Vit. Pyth.* 28.
35. Fr. 4.20 Diehl.
36. I 91.
37. *P.V.* 515–18.
38. Fr. 10 Diehl.
39. *Ol.* I 52 ff.; IX 29 ff.
40. Thuc. V 105.1 (R. Warner).
41. *O.C.* 1224 ff. (W. B. Yeats).
42. Theognis 425 ff.; Eur. fr. 452; Bacchylides V 160–2; Alexis fr. 141. 14–15.
43. *Pyth.* VIII 95–7.

## CHAPTER 4: CITY AND INDIVIDUAL

1. *Pol.* 1252b 29.
2. Thuc. II 37.2.
3. Ibid. I 84.3.
4. Fr. 44 D–K.
5. Hdt. VII 104.4.
6. *Il.* 238; XVI 387.
7. *Works and Days* 220–1.
8. Fr. 114 D–K.
9. *Il.* XVI 384–92.
10. Plat., *Protagoras* 322c–d.
11. *Ant.* 365–7.
12. Plat., *Crito* 50b, 51b.
13. *Ant.* 450–60.
14. *Pol.* 1269a 11-22.
15. Xenophon, *Mem.* I 2.42.
16. Thuc. II 37.3.
17. Lysias VI 10.
18. Hdt. III 81.3.
19. Fr. 16. 1–4 L–P.
20. 197–200.
21. Xen., *Cynegeticus* 5.33.
22. Idem, *De re equestri* II 9.
23. Homeric Hymn XXX 9–16 (H. T. Wade-Gery).
24. *Isthmian* II 41–2.
25. *Ol.* XIII 6–8.
26. Thuc. I 70.8–9 (R. Warner).
27. Ibid. II 41.5 (R. Warner).
28. Fr. 5 Blass.
29. *Ol.* I 3–4.
30. *Pyth.* I 94–6.
31. 1179–1182.
32. Diog. Laert. I 81.
33. Hdt. III 80.5.
34. Thuc. VI 54.5.
35. *Rep.* IX 573a ff.
36. *Pol.* 1113b 1 ff.
37. Fr. 332 L–P.
38. 'Theognis' 349–50.
39. Aristot., *Pol.* 1310a 9.
40. Fragmenta Chorica Adespo-ta 5 Diehl.
41. *Eum.* 977–87 (G. Thom-son).
42. Thuc. III 82 (R. Warner).
43. *Works and Days* 182–191 (T. F. Higham).
44. Thuc. I 138.6.

## CHAPTER 5: THE GOOD MAN AND THE GOOD LIFE

1. *Nic. Eth.* 1096a 23.
2. *Il.* II 408; VI 478; III 237.
3. *Il.* III 179; II 732; XVI 165.
4. *Sept.* 52–3 (E. R. Bevan).
5. Thuc. II 40.1 (R. Warner).
6. Plat., *Rep.* I 331e.
7. Thuc. II 40.3 (R. Warner).
8. Fr. 99 Bowra.
9. Fr. 4.24–6 Diehl.
10. Thuc. I 138.3; II 65.6.
11. Fr. 181 D–K.
12. Plat., *Lach.* 198d ff.
13. *Rep.* IV 442c.
14. Fr. 112 D–K.
15. *Ag.* 763–71.
16. Aristot., *Pol.* 1253a 4.
17. Hdt. I 170.3.
18. Fr. 3 Diehl.
19. Athenaeus XIII 603e.
20. Diog. Laert. VIII 64.
21. Fr. 119 D–K.
22. Scolia Attica 7 Diehl.
23. Fr. 236 Pearson.
24. P. Maas, *Epidaurische Hymnen* pp. 148 ff.
25. Thuc. II 51.4 (R. Warner).
26. *Nem.* VII 1–4.
27. Pausanias II 13.3.
28. *Anthologia Palatina* VI 271; Diodorus V 73; Paus. V 34.6; Athen. IV 139a.
29. Paus. VI 23.8.
30. Hesiod, *Theogony* 341; Aesch., *Supplices* 686;
    *Anth. Pal.* VI 278.
31. Fr. 1.51–4 Diehl.
32. Fr. 130. 32–5 L–P.
33. Bacch. IX 27–32.
34. Hdt. V 47.
35. *Isthm.* V 14.
36. Fr. 2 Diehl.
37. Fr. 284 Nauck.
38. Plat., *Rep.* I 330a.
39. Theogn. 173–8.
40. *Isthm.* II 10.
41. *Nic. Eth.* 1122a 35.
42. Fr. 209 Bowra.
43. *Isthm.* V 1–3.
44. *Ol.* XI 13.
45. Ibid. VI 1 ff.
46. Frs. 392 and 94. 18–20 L–P.
47. Fr. 3 Diehl; Athen. XII 526a.
48. Hdt. VI 11–14.
49. Athen. XII 518c ff.
50. Fr. 148 L–P.
51. Hom. Hymn II 194–206 (T. F. Higham).
52. Soph., *Trach.* 144–50.
53. 1069–70.
54. Fr. 2.5 ff. Diehl.
55. Eur., *Heracl.* 637–40.
56. Soph., fr. 949 Pearson.
57. Idem, *O.C.*, 7–8.
58. Plat., *Rep.* I 329c.
59. *Paroemiographi Graeci* I 346.
60. Soph., fr. 950 Pearson.

## CHAPTER 6: MYTH AND SYMBOL

1. *Hippolytus* 1423–7.
2. *Theogony* 535 ff.
3. Hes., *Theogony* 154 ff.
4. *Il.* XIV 347–9.
5. *Od.* XII 129–30.
6. Hes., fr. 160 Rzach.
7. *Il.* I 68 ff.
8. Hes., *Scutum* 216 ff.; Apollodorus, *Bibliotheca* II. 4.2.
9. Hdt. IV 13.1; Max. Tyr. 38.3.
10. Diog. Laert. I 109.
11. Pliny, *Historia Naturalis* VII 52.
12. *Pyth.* X 30–4.
13. *Nem.* III 43–63.
14. *Nem.* X 55–90.
15. *Ol.* VII *passim*.
16. Fr. 1.11–14 D–K.
17. Xen., *Mem.* II 1.21–34.
18. Aesch., fr. 161 Nauck.
19. Virgil, *Georgic IV* 454–503; Ovid, *Metamorphoses* X 1–7; Conon, *Narrationes* 45.2.

### CHAPTER 7: IMAGINATION AND REALITY

1. *Theogony* 32.
2. *Apology* 22b; *Phaedr.* 244a–245c.
3. *Theogony* 30 ff.
4. *Pyth.* IV 3; *Nem.* III 1.
5. *Lysis* 216c.
6. 'Theognis' 17.
7. *Il.* VI 357–8.
8. *Poetics* 1445b 15.
9. *Theogony* 27–8.
10. *Pyth.* III 28 ff.
11. *Nem.* VII 22–4.
12. *Ol.* I 33–4.
13. *Poet.* 1451b 3.
14. Soph., *Trach.* 766 ff.
15. Eur., *Her.* 932 ff.
16. Eur., *Hipp.* 1214 ff.
17. *Il.* XIX 407 ff.
18. Ibid. VIII 186 ff.
19. *Od.* XVII 291 ff.
20. Ibid. X 113.
21. Hdt. I 8.
22. *Nic. Eth.* 1123a 22.
23. Eur., *Hipp.* 732–51.
24. Fr. 956 Pearson.
25. Soph., *Oedipus Tyrannus* 1071–2.
26. Ibid. 738.
27. Eur., *Hipp.* 1441.
28. *Ag.* 495.
29. *Ol.* VI 82.
30. *Persae* 101–4.
31. *Il.* I 157.

### CHAPTER 8: THE PLASTIC VISION

1. Plut., *De Gloria Atheniensium* 3.
2. 'Hippocrates', *de Victu* 11.
3. Xen., *Mem.* III 10.2.
4. Aristot., *Poet.* 1448a 5.
5. Ibid. 1461b 12.
6. Ibid. 1450a 27.
7. *Ennead* I vi. 1.
8. Galen, *De Temperatura* I 9.
9. *Timaeus* 31c ff.
10. *Il.* XVIII 372 ff.
11. Diodorus Siculus LV 76.
12. Fr. 195 D–K.
13. *Ag.* 416–19.
14. Plat., *Phaedr.* 275d.
15. Xen., *Mem.* III 10.4.
16. *Poet.* 1448b 11 ff.
17. Diog. Laert. I 89.
18. Fr. 48 Diehl.

### CHAPTER 9: THE PLACE OF REASON

1. Proclus on Euclid I p. 65.7–11.
2. Diog. Laert. I 27.
3. Proclus on Euclid I p. 157.10.
4. Aristot., *Metaphysics* 985b 23.
5. 'Hipp.' *Epidemics* III 16.
6. Aristot., *De Anima* II 5.
7. Stobaeus, *Eclogae* I 1.29b.
8. Simplicius, *In Physica* 24.13.
9. Fr. 94 D–K.
10. Fr. 41 D–K.
11. Fr. 1.35–64 Diehl.
12. Fr. 1 D–K.
13. Fr. 197.
14. *Ajax* 646 ff.; Diogenes of Apollonia, fr. 3.
15. Frs. 40–2 D–K.
16. Fr. 1.1–2 D–K.
17. *Ol.* I 30–4.
18. Fr. 18 D–K.
19. Fr. 118 D–K.
20. Fr. 112 D–K.
21. Aelian, *Varia Historia* VIII 24.
22. *Placita Philosophorum* I 3.34; Pseudo-Plutarch, *Stromateis* fr. 3.
23. Fr. 30 D–K.
24. Fr. 21 D–K.
25. Fr. 180 D–K.
26. 'Hipp.', *Precepts* 6.
27. Fr. 910 N.
28. Archimedes, *Sand-reckoner.* 11.

29. Plut., *Pericles* 6.
30. *Air, Waters, Places* 16.
31. Fr. 1 Jacoby.
32. 1 T 12a Jacoby.
33. VII 70.
34. III 12.
35. IV 23.
36. III 48.
37. IV 42–3.
38. II 11.
39. V 9.
40. I 22.2 (R. Warner).
41. I 21.1 (R. Warner).
42. VII 86.5 (R. Warner).
43. *Sacred Disease* I.
44. VII 139.4.

45. Fr. 166 D–K.
46. Fr. 5 D–K.
47. Fr. 25 D–K.
48. Fr. 4 D–K.
49. Diog. Laert. II 8; Hippocrates I 8.6.
50. Plut., *Per.* 32; Diod. XII 38.
51. Xen., *Mem.* I 1.1.
52. Plat., *Apol.* 18b.
53. *Clouds* 878, 1471.
54. Ibid. 376 ff.
55. 'Hipp.', *Precepts* 2.
56. Fr. 3 D–K.
57. Fr. 1 D–K.
58. Plut., *Marcellus* 17.

## CHAPTER 10: EPILOGUE

1. *Pyth.* X 19.
2. *Medea* 824–45.
3. *Anth. Pal.* VII 45. It is also ascribed to Timotheus.
4. Thuc. II 41.1.
5. I 1.1.
6. Plut., *Nicias* 17.
7. Xen., *Hellenica* II 2.3.
8. *Gorg.* 519a.
9. *Pol.* 1274a⁷ ff.
10. I Maccabees 1.54.
11. Plut., *Antonius* 86.
12. Aesch., *P.V.* 447 ff.
13. Fr. 12 D–K.

14. *Nic. Eth.* 1177b 33.
15. Fr. 13 D–K.
16. Fr. 78 D–K.
17. *Med.* 544–5.
18. Thuc. II 43.1.
19. *Ant.* 332–3.
20. *Nem.* III 64–5.
21. *Ant.* 354–6.
22. Aristot., *Pol.* 1259b 18.
23. *Protag.* 322a.
24. *Ant.* 361–4.
25. *Il.* XXI 108–13.
26. *Historia Alexandri Magni*, ed. W. Kroll III 32.4–7.

# INDEX

Achilles, 33, 35, 38, 39, 43, 46, 50, 65, 98, 146, 214.

Aeschylus (525–456 BC), 25, 51, 70, 73, 78, 93, 98, 101, 102, 125, 147.

Age, old, 113 ff.

Alcaeus (fl. 590 BC), 83, 92, 106.

Alcibiades (c. 450–404 BC), 45.

Alcmaeon of Croton (fl. 500 BC), 181, 188.

Alcman (fl. 640 BC), 106.

Alexander (356–323 BC), 21, 31, 33, 77, 203, 214.

Anaxagoras (c. 500–c. 428 BC), 188, 194, 208.

Anaximander (born 610 BC), 163, 180, 183.

Anaximenes (fl. 546 BC), 183.

Animals, 147, 162.

Anthropology, Greek views of, 25, 188.

Antiochus Epiphanes (c. 215–163 BC), 203.

Apollo, 56, 63, 71.

Archilochus (fl. 648 BC), 37, 83.

*Aretê*, 211, 212, 213, 214.

Archimedes (c. 287–212 BC), 186, 197.

Architecture, 164 ff. 169.

Ariphron (fl. c. 400 BC), 104.

Aristarchus of Samos (c. 310–230 BC), 186.

Aristophanes (c. 450–c. 385 BC), 36, 88, 141, 195, 202.

Aristotle (384–322 BC), 40, 58, 67, 77, 81, 89, 91, 97, 139, 146, 188, 203, 208.

Artemis, 56, 59, 63, 68.

Athene, 56, 58, 68, 87.

Atlantis, 132.

Atomic theory, 187.

Barbarians, 26, 78.

Bacchylides (fl. 5th cent. BC), 107.

Beautiful, the, 137.

Centaurs, 129, 163.

City-state, 21 ff., 77 ff.

Class-war, 92 ff.

Cleopatra (69–30 BC), 203.

Climate, 16.

Coinage, 89.

Constitution, political, 82 ff.

Courage, 98, 99, 100.

Comedy, Attic, 140 ff.

Death, 49 ff., 76, 213.

Death, life after, 51, 213.

Delphi, 60 ff., 156.

Delphic charioteer, 172.

Democracy, 84 ff.

Democritus (c. 460–c. 370 BC), 183, 187.

Empedocles (c. 493–c. 433 BC), 103, 184.

Epimenides (6th cent. BC), 55.

*Erôs*, 209.

Euripides (c. 485–c. 406 BC), 15, 44, 88, 107, 116, 127, 145, 150, 185, 199.

221